CRISIS, STABILIZATION, AND ECONOMIC REFORM

Crisis, Stabilization, and Economic Reform

Therapy by Consensus

MICHAEL BRUNO

CLARENDON PRESS · OXFORD
1993

Oxford University Press, Walton Street, Oxford OX2 6DP

Oxford New York Toronto
Delhi Bombay Calcutta Madras Karachi
Kuala Lumpur Singapore Hong Kong Tokyo
Nairobi Dar es Salaam Cape Town
Melbourne Auckland Madrid
and associated companies in
Berlin Ibadan

Oxford is a trade mark of Oxford University Press

Published in the United States
by Oxford University Press Inc., New York

British Library Cataloguing in Publication Data
Data available

Library of Congress Cataloging in Publication Data
Bruno, Michael.
Crisis, stabilization, and economic reform: therapy by consensus | Michael Bruno.
"Clarendon lectures."
Includes bibliographical references and index.
1. Inflation (Finance)—Israel.   2. Economic stabilization—Israel.
3. Israel—Economic policy.   4. Israel—Economic conditions.
5. Inflation (Finance).   6. Economic stabilization.
7. Economic policy.   8. Economic history—1971–1990.   I. Title.
HG1210.B78   1993   338.9—dc20   93–16300
ISBN 0–19–828663–5

Set by Hope Services (Abingdon) Ltd
Printed in Great Britain
on acid-free paper by
Bookcraft (Bath) Ltd
Midsomer Norton, Avon

*Dedicated to the memory of my father
and mother, who inspired both reason
and soul*

Preface and Acknowledgements

THIS book studies the anatomy of severe economic crises as well as comprehensive programmes designed to effect their cure. My interest in this area has been both academic and practical, the latter from the point of view of a policy adviser and more recently also as a policy maker. Along with many colleagues, I share a sustained scientific interest in studying the puzzles and normative economics of countries, like my own, that once enjoyed an enviable growth record and reasonable price stability, but went into protracted high inflation and low growth crisis in the 1970s and/or in the 1980s. I was also fortunate enough to have the opportunity to put some of my ideas (and those of others) to the test, primarily in my own country and, more marginally and indirectly, through mutual discussions with policy makers, in several other countries.

Each of these two types of involvement might have justified a separate research product, not least because of the different degree of detachment and objectivity with which they can be pursued by the same author. Given the timing and my preoccupations, however, such separation was not feasible. This book therefore attempts to combine a detailed first-hand account and analysis of a quasi-laboratory experiment in one country with a somewhat more detached comparative study of this and related crises, stabilization efforts, and reform episodes in Latin America. A brief assignment by the International Monetary Fund in early 1992 also enabled me to incorporate a preliminary comparative evaluation of the new (and quite different) reform environment of Eastern Europe.

An earlier version of this study originated with a set of three invited Clarendon Lectures which I gave at Oxford University in 1988. The pressure of my duties as Governor of the Bank of Israel prevented me from writing up my lecture notes in promised book form at that time. This may have proved a blessing in disguise. Post-stabilization developments in the Israeli economy, the successful similar 1988 stabilization programme of Mexico, as well as the reform process in other Latin American economies have, since delivery of the 1988 lectures, unfolded in many interesting, often unexpected, and divergent ways. Moreover, since the dramatic political opening-up of Eastern Europe in 1989 there have been the added preliminary lessons of an attempt to apply shock therapies and far-reaching reforms in a much more complex environment. The result is a considerably looser connection between the original lectures and the present book than would normally be warranted.

As experience accumulates one gets a better feel for the practical and theoretical intricacies of the adjustment and structural reform process in a greater variety of middle-income countries. Detailed case-studies are necessary building-blocks, but they remain isolated unless an attempt is made to look for common elements without which no scientific edifice can be constructed. On the other hand, premature generalizations in an area such as this can also lead one astray. Somehow one must try to strike a balance, which is what this book attempts to do.

There is also a related methodological issue—the inevitable need to take an eclectic approach to the theory of economic reform. *Ad hoc* implementation of an idea or a programme of action has often preceded systematic *ex post* theorizing about why it might or might not work in a particular context (the application of wage–price controls is only one example). This may also explain why, at this stage of our knowledge, it is unlikely that one discipline or theoretical approach can give a full answer to the varied questions that arise in such context. The case-histories and respective policy episodes analysed here involve interesting angles that come under the heading of economic history, open-economy macro-economics and growth, public finance and monetary theory, and last, but not least, political economy and political science. Their respective tools are relevant to the analysis and, at the same time, there is something to be learned in these fields of study from the case-histories that are our subject of enquiry.

While part of the theoretical literature cited in this book can at times become quite technical, I have tried to keep the discussion as non-technical and intuitive as possible. With the exception of parts of Chapter 3 (on the inflationary process), mathematics and formal econometrics are entirely avoided, in the hope that this will make the book accessible to a wider audience with no more than very basic training in economics.

This book would not have come into existence without the generous support of institutions and the collaboration and help of many individuals over the years.

The National Bureau of Economic Research in Cambridge, Mass., headed by Martin Feldstein with Geoffrey Carliner, generously continued my past enrolment as Research Associate even while I was in public office. This, plus the remnants of an NSF grant, enabled me to 'escape' for very brief summer stays during 1987–90, thus keeping one foot in research and writing. My stay as Visiting Professor at the Department of Economics at MIT, in the academic year 1991/2, for which I thank Rudi Dornbusch and Peter Temin, as well as the facilities of NBER, provided a very congenial means of taking a year's break, to write up this book and discuss its contents, after completing my five-year tenure at the Bank of Israel and before returning to my teaching duties at Hebrew University. No less heartfelt thanks go to WIDER in Helsinki, to its Director Lal Jayawardena, as well as to the McDonnell Foundation for providing the financial support during part of 1991/2. Likewise, I am very grateful to the Research Department of the International Monetary Fund for enabling me to stay as Visiting Scholar during part of that year. Finally, I thank Balliol College in Oxford for generously hosting me during the 1988 lecture series.

Attempts to solve economic puzzles and the design of economic policies were the result of numerous discussions, debates, joint papers with and among many individuals, not all of whom can be mentioned in the preface to a book. Among those to whom I owe most I would like to single out Stanley Fischer, who has been much more than my co-author in two papers that were central to my thinking on high inflation and its stabilization. Stan has played an important role both in the analysis of the inflationary process and its cure and, together with Herbert Stein (as US advisers), in facilitating the actual implementation of Israel's stabilization programme at a crucial stage. He has since then been a constant source of personal support and advice and, finally, has carefully read a draft of this book and given many very valuable comments.

I have shared with several Israeli colleagues the excitement of being involved in the fascinating Israeli stabilization experience. To Emanuel Sharon, Director of the Ministry of Finance at a crucial planning and policy implementation period, I owe my own involvement in the planning team in 1984–5 as well as a very fruitful policy collaboration after my appointment to the Bank Governorship. Numerous discussions with, and the sharp insights of, Nissan Liviatan, my colleague at the Hebrew University, both in the planning stages and during the interesting post-stabilization developments, have been a permanent source of help and pleasure.

It is with deep sorrow that I have to mention Eytan Berglas, of Tel Aviv University, as one who is no longer with us. His sudden and untimely death in August 1992 has deprived the Israeli economics profession of one of its most erudite and exemplary members. He was an invaluable member of the planning team in 1984–5 and a very helpful colleague and collaborator in subsequent years, when he became Chairman of Bank Ha-Po'alim. Even though we did not always agree, I am grateful to him for many helpful discussions and interchanges, over the years, on various macro-policy and banking issues.

With my colleagues at the Bank of Israel, especially at the Research Department, I have shared views and helpful insights on processes over many years and long before I returned to the Bank in 1986. The longest and deepest association has been with Mordechai Fraenkel, Director of Research and thereafter my senior colleague at the Bank. Many of my ideas were first thrashed out with him. David Klein and Avi Ben-Bassat, at present the two Senior Directors of the Bank, contributed significantly to the design of the money and capital market reforms in Israel. The help of Leora Meridor, present Director of Research, in the course of the writing up of this book, as well as that of Rafi Melnick, Sylvia Piterman and Meir Sokoler, at various stages, is also gratefully acknowledged.

Interchanges with several fellow economists-cum-policy-makers in Latin American and East European economies have been an important source of inspiration. Among these let me single out Pedro Aspe and Miguel Mancera in Mexico, Domingo Cavallo, José Luis Machinea, Guido Di Tella, and Juan Carlos de Pablo in Argentina, Mitja Gaspari in Yugoslavia, Leszek Balcerowicz in

Poland, and Vaclav Klaus in Czechoslovakia. I am grateful to Massimo Russo, Director of the European Department I at the IMF, for enabling me to get a close view of East European reform, the subject of Chapter 7. I am indebted to him, to his deputy Michael Deppler, and to many other members of his department, as well as to their counterparts in Eastern Europe, for many helpful insights from their first-hand experience. This study was carried out under the auspices of the Research Department of the IMF during 1991–2.

I received many helpful comments on earlier drafts of various chapters of this book from Alberto Alesina, Leszek Balcerowicz, Eli Berman, Olivier Blanchard, José de Gregorio, Mordechai Fraenkel, Elhanan Helpman, Leo Leiderman, Nissan Liviatan, Rafi Melnick, Leora Meridor, Emanuel Sharon, Carlos Vegh, and Eran Yashiv. I am very grateful to all of them.

Margret Eisenstaedt of the Maurice Falk Institute for Economic Research in Israel has, as always, been a most erudite editor and graphic designer, patiently processing the sporadic flow of drafts from a distant author. Her voluntary help and general advice along the way have been prized assets. Rochelle Furman and David Roseth at NBER and Hyla Berkowitz in Jerusalem faithfully helped with the typing. Last but not least, Oxford University Press and especially its Economics Editor Andrew Schuller deserve my utmost thanks for their patience in waiting for a promised book that, for a while, looked as if it would never make it.

M.B.

Contents

List of Figures

List of Tables

Abbreviations

BOI	Bank of Israel
CBS	Central Bureau of Statistics
COLA	cost-of-living allowance
CPI	consumer price index
EMS	European Monetary System
IBRD	International Bank for Reconstruction and Development
IFS	IMF, *International Financial Statistics*
IMF	International Monetary Fund
JEDG	(American–Israeli) Joint Economic Development Government Committee
MANX	manufacturing exporters
MIC	middle-income country
MIT	Massachusetts Institute of Technology
MK	member of Knesset
NFB	non-financial business
NIC	newly industrialized country
NIS	New Israeli Shekel
OECD	Organization for Economic Co-operation and Development
PATAM	(Israeli) foreign-exchange linked bank accounts
PIT	personal income tax
SNA	Standardized National Accounting system
SOE	state-owned enterprise
VAT	value added tax
WDR	IBRD, *World Development Report*
WDT	World Bank, *World Debt Tables*
WEO	IMF, *World Economic Outlook*

1

High Inflation, Growth Crisis, and Reform: Historical Perspective and Brief Overview

1.1 Recent Comparative International Experience

In the past two decades, and especially since the early 1980s, several countries, both in Latin America and elsewhere, have gone through rather extreme inflationary experiences, along with a substantial growth slow-down. This has taken place largely as a result of internal economic and political crises reflecting a failed response to external shocks, and mounting debt. While these crises can be attributed to common internal roots, notably large budget deficits, the nature of the inflationary process as well as other structural characteristics of the crisis have varied across countries and over time.

Broad international comparisons suggest that low growth and relatively high inflation have in recent decades often gone together. A recent study by Levine and Renelt (1990) has shown that during the period 1960–89 the relatively fast growers (fifty-six countries above the mean growth rate, among 109 countries) have on average had an inflation rate of 12 per cent per annum, while the relatively slow growers (the remaining fifty-three countries below the mean) have on average had inflation rates of 31 per cent. The slow growers have on average also been afflicted by greater foreign exchange problems. Likewise, the most severely indebted countries in recent history, by World Bank definitions,[1] have had, during the 1980s, very high inflation and relatively low growth, as Table 1.1 shows.

[1] There are twenty middle-income countries (out of fifty-eight countries in the category) that have encountered the most severe debt-servicing difficulties in terms of at least three of the following ratios: debt to GNP (over 50%), debt to exports (above 275%), accrued debt service to exports (over 30%), and accrued interest to exports (20%). See *WDR* (1991), p. xi.

TABLE 1.1   *Growth and inflation of the heavily-indebted countries,
1980–1989 (compared with 1965–1980)* (%)

	Annual rate of inflation of GDP deflator 1980–9[a]	Annual GDP growth[a]	Total external debt as percentage of GNP at end of 1989[b]
Severely indebted countries	141(29)	1.9(6.1)	54(38)
MICs	73(21)	2.9(6.2)	46(36)
OECD	8(4)	3.0(3.8)	—

[a] Number in brackets refers to 1965–80.
[b] Number in brackets refers to 1980.

There are isolated cases of countries and periods of high inflation in which growth none the less continued—Brazil in the
1970s is an obvious example. But during the most marked high
inflation outburst, 1980–5, the highest inflation countries (including Brazil) were very slow growers (with negative per capita
growth) and have in most cases also substantially increased their
external debt ratios.

Table 1.2 ranks the thirteen middle-income countries[2] with
average annual inflation rates of at least 30 per cent during
1980–5. They have almost all shown more negative per capita
growth rates than, and increased their debt/GNP ratios above the
average for, the MIC group. The table also indicates that for
most of the countries in question the first half of the 1980s
marked a sharp departure from their past inflation record. While
several of the countries had had above-average inflation rates in
the past, in ten of the thirteen countries the historical inflation
rates had been below the 30 per cent level. Moreover, eight of
the ten countries for which data are available had had positive
average per capita growth rates during the preceding fifteen years
and in more than half of the countries (notably Israel, Brazil,
Mexico, Yugoslavia, Turkey, and Ecuador) past growth rates had
exceeded the OECD average. It is to the combined phenomenon
of a high inflation and low growth crisis that we turn our attention in this book.

[2] Of these, Turkey, Yugoslavia, and Israel are not included in Table 1.1. On
the other hand, Chile (whose inflation, previously high, had subsided by 1980) is
not included here, but will come in later on.

TABLE 1.2 *Inflation growth and debt in inflationary middle-income economies, 1980–1985 (and 1965–1980)*

	Average annual rate of inflation of GDP deflator (%)[a]	Average annual rate of growth of GDP per capita (%)[a]	Increase in total debt percentage ratio to GNP[b]
1. Bolivia	569 (16)	−7.3 (2.0)	45 (93)
2. Argentina	343 (78)	−3.0 (1.7)	36 (48)
3. Israel	196 (25)	−0.1 (3.8)	22 (81)
4. Brazil	148 (31)	−1.0 (6.3)	18 (31)
5. Peru	99 (21)	−3.9 (1.2)	38 (51)
6. Mexico	62 (13)	−1.8 (3.2)	25 (30)
7. Uruguay	45 (58)	−4.6 (2.0)	64 (17)
8. Yugoslavia	45 (15)	0.1 (5.2)	19 (26)
9. Turkey	37 (21)	2.0 (3.5)	17 (34)
10. Costa Rica	36 (11)	−2.2 (3.4)	67 (60)
11. Poland	35 (. .)	−0.4 (. .)	33 (16)
12. Nicaragua	34 (9)	−3.2 (−0.5)	80 (105)
13. Ecuador	30 (11)	−1.4 (5.1)	19 (54)
Mean[c] of 50 middle-income economies	57 (21)[d]	−0.6 (4.0)[d]	18 (28)
Mean[c] OECD	8 (6)[d]	1.7 (3.2)[d]	. .

[a] Numbers in brackets refer to 1965–80 average.
[b] Numbers in brackets refer to debt percentage as of 1980.
[c] 'Mean' refers to 'All Countries' in *WDT*.
[d] Mean is weighted by size of country (*WDR*).

Sources: Cols. 1 and 2: *WDR* (1987); col. 3: *WDT* (1987–8).

1.2 Explosive Hyperinflations of the 1920s

Before we go into the more recent experiences it is of some interest to recall some of the historical antecedents of very high and even extreme inflation rates. The most natural candidates are the European hyperinflations between the two World Wars. Historical investigation of extreme economic phenomena is interesting for its own sake, but is particularly important for the light it may shed on the validity or irrelevance of an economic theory when stretched to the limit, for which the German hyperinflation of 1923 has provided the classic example. There has been a flood of books and papers in the economic literature, written by some of the most illustrious authors,[3] and even though the event took

[3] A selective list of references includes Keynes (1923), Graham (1930), and Bresciani–Turroni (1937). An interesting personal account was given by Schacht (1927).

place some seventy years ago, researchers keep writing about it and finding new aspects to highlight. Two of the most important questions are the relevance of this extreme phenomenon to other types of inflationary experience, and the issue of the social costs and benefits of both hyperinflation and its stabilization.

According to a definition introduced by Cagan (1956), a hyperinflation sets in when the monthly rate of price increase exceeds 50 per cent. For its most important attributes a broader definition of hyperinflation as being over 25 per cent a month will also hold. Table 1.3 lists the four most famous cases in terms of several relevant statistics.[4] Fig. 1.1 charts the price-level index, using a logarithmic scale,[5] over the four-year period 1921–5. All the inflations peaked at a monthly rate of 100 per cent or more (with Germany at close to 30,000 per cent!) before their shock cure brought inflation down all at once, by means of an orthodox set of measures involving sharp fiscal and monetary reform.

Many aspects of these very extreme monetary experiences have been studied over the years, and we will come back to some of these in the course of our discussion, but there is one aspect that must command our immediate attention. The quick end that was put to these processes—virtually overnight—looks, on the face of it, like a very appealing policy solution. Using the language of rational expectations, once the government signals a credible shift of policy (via sharp institutional reforms, such as a credible fiscal balance and the creation of an independent central bank), private-sector expectations and inflationary behaviour can apparently be dramatically changed. This is the main policy lesson of Sargent's (1982) well-known paper, which, he felt, was equally applicable to the much more moderate, garden-variety inflation in the USA after the second oil shock.[6]

---

[4] Strictly speaking, Cagan defines the end of hyperinflation as the month before it falls below 50% with the additional condition that it stays there for at least a year. Since this would also include individual intervening months in which inflation falls below the threshold, this would imply a somewhat longer period than indicated in Table 1.3, but for our purpose a simple strict count of months above the threshold is equally indicative.

[5] The advantage of using a logarithmic scale is not only because of the explosive nature of the numbers. Any vertically equidistant pair of numbers will represent the same rate of price change. The monthly rate of inflation is thus measured by the slope of the curves at each point.

[6] I have elsewhere compared this analogy to that of attempting to learn the hydraulics of the slow-moving Mississippi River from observing the free fall of

TABLE 1.3 *Hyperinflations of the 1920s (1920–1924)*

	Average monthly rate (%)	Peak monthly rate (%) (date in brackets)	No. of months with inflation > 50% (> 25% in brackets)	No. of years with inflation > 100%
Germany	949	29,525 (Oct. 1923)	11 (20)	4
Poland	33	275 (Oct. 1923)	9 (16)	3
Austria	17	129 (Aug. 1922)	4 (10)	3
Hungary	17	98 (July 1923)	5 (9)	3

Sources: Cagan (1956) and Sargent (1982).

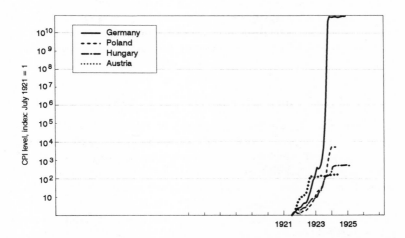

FIG. 1.1   Four hyperinflations of the 1920s

While very attractive, the perception of such a 'cold turkey' solution by itself can also be misleading. First of all, it may give the impression of having been virtually costless, namely with no obvious real disruption or large-scale unemployment, which was indeed Sargent's claim. That contention was subsequently questioned in the context of Germany and some other hyperinflations

water in the Niagara Falls. With suitable adjustment, the Sargent (1982) analysis is, however, very pertinent to high inflation processes.

of the 1920s. In several of the cases there followed, albeit sometimes at a considerable time-lag, some serious disruptions in the
real economy, including very high, even if only short-lived,
periods of unemployment, a fact that was not so obvious from
the earlier research.[7]

But there is another, at present more relevant, aspect in which
that episode may be misleading. In view of the more recent high
inflationary experiences discussed here, all hyperinflations appear
to have been very intense and very brief explosive processes, with
high (more than three-digit annual) inflation lasting no more
than three or four years. Strictly speaking, the German hyperinflation (using the narrow definition of months with more than
50 per cent inflation) lasted only eleven months (in the other
three economies, much less than that). Even if we consider as a
reference point a monthly rate of over 25 per cent, the length of
the period for the extreme case of Germany is no more than
twenty months (see Table 1.3, third column).

1.3 Chronic High Inflation in Recent History

Consider now the period since World War II. The four countries
that had the biggest price increase during the thirty-five years
from 1950 until 1985 were Argentina, Bolivia, Brazil, and Israel.
They are included in Table 1.4 and Fig. 1.2 among a group of
eight high inflation countries of recent history.[8] Of these four,

---

[7] The point was made most forcefully, for the case of Germany, by Peter
Garber (1982). For some of the other countries see Wicker (1986). There is similar evidence on some hyperinflations that came in the wake of World War II.
These will not be discussed separately here (see Yeager 1981; Dornbusch,
Sturzenegger, and Wolf 1990). There is some question, however, as to the extent
to which the real cost incurred in these cases was directly associated with the stabilization process itself. For an alternative point of view see Vegh (1992), who
concludes that of nine hyperinflations (four after World War I, four after World
War II, and Bolivia in 1985) in five there seem to have been no costs related to
the monetary stabilization *per se*.

[8] This list is not exhaustive (e.g. Peru and several other Central American
economies that appear in Table 1.2 are not included here). Seven of the countries
(excluding Poland) were chosen (together with Turkey, which is not included
here) for a 1990 conference in which policy makers from the various countries
compared economic experiences (see Bruno *et al.* 1991). The list of countries was
made up with the aim of having two countries in each of four categories, respectively: successful orthodox stabilizations (Chile and Bolivia), successful (Israel and

Bolivia turns out to have had a classical 1920s-type hyper-inflation. During the period starting in 1970, before inflation peaked at 182 per cent a month in February 1985, there were only four years, just preceding the explosion, in which inflation passed the annual three-digit mark. Comparing the slope of Bolivia's profile in Figure 2.2 with that of the 1920s quartet of countries in Figure 1.1 (the two figures are drawn to a similar scale) the two processes do indeed look alike. In terms of Table 1.3 Bolivia falls between the column entries of Poland, Austria, and Hungary in the 1920s.

In the other three countries (Argentina, Brazil, and Israel) inflation, by contrast, was of a very different species. It was a chronic, more prolonged, high and accelerating, yet quasi-stable, inflationary process. It is interesting to note that the inflation profiles of two countries as vastly different in size and structure as Brazil and Israel, for example, were very similar throughout most of the 1970s and early 1980s (compare the two respective curves in Fig. 1.2).[9] Along with the quasi-stability of this process of high chronic inflation, it was usually much more prolonged. It could last up to five or even eight years and show monthly rates of inflation of between 5 and 25 per cent, or annual rates of three digits for a substantial length of time.

Table 1.4 presents high inflation data for Chile before 1979, for Argentina, Brazil, and Israel before 1985, and for Mexico before 1988, as well as a similar chronic inflation process, at lower rates, for Yugoslavia and Poland (up to 1990). Although the root of high chronic inflation, like hyperinflation, turns out to lie in the existence of a large public-sector deficit, the quasi-stability of the dynamic process will be shown to come from an inherent inertia strongly linked with a high degree of indexation or accommodation of the key nominal magnitudes (wages, the exchange rate,

Mexico) and failed (Argentina and Brazil) heterodox programmes, and two more recent members of the high inflation club (here Poland more appropriately joins Yugoslavia and replaces Turkey for that purpose).

[9] So-called eye-econometrics can, of course, go only part of the way but the general appearances are telling none the less. We note the series of 'flats' in the two curves, representing a step-wise increase in the inflation rate, a subject to which we shall return in Ch. 3. We also note that already in the 1970s Argentina produced higher inflation rates, bordering at times on hyperinflation (as in 1975–6, see Fig. 1.2). After their respective failures to stabilize, Argentina and Brazil both entered hyperinflation and their two profiles, in turn, became very much alike.

TABLE 1.4　*High inflation, hyperinflation, and stabilization, 1970–1991*

Country (year of major stabilization programme in brackets)	Average monthly rate (%)[a]			Peak monthly rate (%) (date in brackets)	No. of months with rate > 50% (> 25%) in brackets	No. of years with annual rate > 100%	
	1970–9	1980–5	1986–91			1970–9	1980–91
	(1)	(2)	(3)	(4)	(5)	(6)	(7)
Chile (1975)	7.6	1.7	1.5	88 (Oct. 1973)	1 (1)	4	—
Bolivia (1985)	1.4	18.5	1.7	182 (Feb. 1985)	9 (16)	—	5
Argentina (1985)	6.8	11.9	18.9	197 (July 1989)	6 (19)	5	12
Brazil (1986)	2.4	7.9	22.4	84 (Feb. 1990)	4 (19)	—	10
Israel (1985)	2.6	9.1	1.4	28 (July 1985)	— (1)	—	6
Mexico (1988)	1.2	3.9	4.7[b]	15 (Jan. 1988)	— (—)	—	3
Yugoslavia (1990)	1.4	3.4	14.6	60 (Dec. 1989)	3 (8)	—	5
Poland[c] (1990)	0.3	2.3	9.0	77 (Jan. 1990)	2 (5)	—	3

[a] Monthly averages refer to periods from Jan. of the first year to Dec. of the last year.
[b] From Apr. 1988 to June 1992 the average monthly rate was 1.6%.
[c] Based on annual data up to 1987 and monthly data for 1988–90.
Source: IFS.

and the monetary aggregates) to the lagged movements of the price level. It reflects the way an inflation-prone system attempts to protect itself from the evils of inflation, applying a sedative that helps to give it a longer lease on life but thereby also delaying its more fundamental cure.

Graphical representations and numbers must, of course, reflect other underlying quantitative and qualitative differences. The first characteristic of *hyperinflations* which emerges from all historical accounts is a virtual breakdown of the monetary and financial systems. With monthly rates of inflation reaching three, four, and five digits[10] domestic currency loses its *raison d'être* even in terms of the basic transactions motive—people move to gold, foreign exchange, or commodities except where use of domestic means of payment is mandatory by law (for payment of taxes, use of public utilities, etc.). With it go the well-known descriptions of

[10] In one recorded historical case it even reached eight digits. In Greece, the monthly rate for Dec. 1944 reached 85 million %! (see Cagan 1956: table 1, p. 26). More generally, the explosive character of hyperinflation can be gauged just by looking at a histogram in terms of numbers of *digits* of monthly inflation.

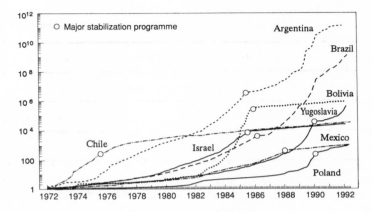

Sources: See tables 1.3 and 1.4.

Fig. 1.2 Eight high inflations, 1972–1992

truckloads of newly printed notes being carried from the printing presses to the central bank and to the banks, virtually blocking the streets of Berlin. The historical extreme of the German 1923 explosion, from the vantage-point of the end of this century, can best be gauged from the mere fact that it took Argentina, the most inflationary economy in the world, twenty years to accomplish the 100 billion times increase in price level that Germany of the 1920s reached in only two years. Given the tenfold increase in the time-span (and correspondingly lower intensity) it cannot represent an identical phenomenon.[11]

The second characteristic, which applies to all intensive inflationary experiences but in the case of hyperinflation reaches extreme proportions, is the shortening of nominal contracts, down from months to weeks, days, and sometimes even hours.[12] A third characteristic that singles out hyperinflations is the

---

[11] For some time there appears to have been confusion over terminology, when the two historical episodes were first compared. The title of an excellent early survey by Dornbusch and Fischer (1986), who undoubtedly followed common usage, was 'Stopping Hyperinflations Past and Present', where the 'present' ones were all the cases mentioned above. I myself was drawn into a similar confusion.

[12] There is a famous anecdote that used to be told in Israel at the height of three-digit inflation, but actually dates back to Germany of the 1920s. It relates to the advantage of a taxi ride over bus transportation from the point of view of the passenger—in a taxi you pay at the *end* of the trip, so your money does not depreciate in the meantime.

extreme form of budgetary deficit finance. In Germany, for example, the ratio of deficit to public spending was 65 per cent in 1920/1 and reached 98.7 per cent by November 1923, the bulk of it financed by the printing press, with tax revenues being virtually wiped out. As we shall see, this was definitely not the case in any of the high chronic inflations, although the fiscal lag has been of considerable importance.

Consider first the deficit and tax-revenue ratios for Bolivia (see Morales 1988 and Sachs 1987), which lie close to the previous hyperinflations. Its deficit/GDP ratio was 8 per cent in 1981, reached 27 per cent in 1984, the year before stabilization, and came down again to 9 per cent in 1985. The tax-revenue/GDP ratios for the same years were 9–10 per cent (1981), 2.6 per cent (1984), and 1.3 per cent (1985). Tax erosion of that magnitude never occurred in any of the other three high-inflation countries mentioned. Argentina and Brazil had a tax/GDP burden of about 30 per cent right through the 1980s, and Israel was running a ratio of around 40–50 per cent (with the lower bound occurring only once, before the height of the crisis). A similar comparison holds for the ratio of seigniorage revenue to GDP (namely the ratio of the increment in M1 to GDP): Argentina's ratio up to 1985 was stable, at about 5–7 per cent, Brazil's at 2–3 per cent, and Israel's at 2 per cent throughout most of the period; at the same time, Bolivia's seigniorage revenue ratio rose from 1.6 per cent in 1981 to 16 per cent in 1984.[13]

Moderate versions of chronic inflation, exhibiting some of the characteristics of indexation and monetary accommodation, were already apparent in Latin America in the 1950s. An early reference to the qualitative difference between hyperinflation and what at the time was termed chronic inflation appears in an important study by Felipe Pazos (1972), based on an analysis of inflationary experience in Latin America during the immediate post-war period up to the end of the 1960s (1949–70). During that period a number of countries showed two-digit inflation rates over prolonged periods of time, with very rare single-year peaks of over 100 per cent. The four major examples at that time were Argentina, Brazil, Chile, and Uruguay, with annual rates of

---

[13] This is only a statement about the nature of hyperinflation. Seigniorage is of importance for the understanding of the inflationary process even when it is relatively small. See Ch. 3.

20–30 per cent for a period of ten to fifteen years and occasional annual peaks of 70 per cent and 90 per cent (reminiscent of Brazil and Israel in the 1970s and of Turkey, for example, in the more recent past). There are only two cases of inflation exceeding 100 per cent—Argentina with 114 per cent and Uruguay with 125 per cent in 1959.[14]

Pazos points out the difference between the chronic inflation processes he was observing at the time and the historical hyper-inflations:

1. The explosive nature of seigniorage revenue, as well as the lack of correlation between the size of government deficits and rate of inflation in the 'chronic' case (we shall return to this important characteristic in Chapter 3).
2. The difference in terms of length of contract. Pazos discusses the staggering of wage and price decisions under chronic inflation, COLA arrangements that link today's inflation to past inflation in what has come to be termed 'inflationary inertia'. These are institutional arrangements that attempt to immunize the system against the costs of inflation and thus prolong the disease and postpone its cure, a characteristic that could not be found in the explosive hyperinflations.
3. Pazos also discusses the role of exchange-rate adjustments to balance-of-payments crises, a point that will feature prominently in our subsequent discussion.
4. Finally, in the chronic inflations of the 1950s and 1960s grad-ualist stabilization and disinflation policies were followed, unlike the 'shock' treatments of the 1920s.

This last point is precisely where the high-inflation experience of the 1970s and 1980s differs from the chronic inflationary processes of the preceding two decades.

1.4 Emergence of the 'Heterodox' Approach to Stabilization

The inflations of the 1970s and 1980s brought in a new ele-ment—far higher average and peak rates of inflation in processes which otherwise resembled earlier 'chronic' experiences much

---

[14] For a study of the earlier Latin American experience in reference to the more recent episodes see Kiguel and Liviatan (1991).

more than those of the 1920s hyperinflations. As long as inflation stayed below a monthly rate of 5–6 per cent (roughly corresponding to an annual rate of no more than two digits) its cure could be gradual, as in the case of the garden-variety, more conventional type of inflation known to the industrial world, of annual rates never exceeding 25–30 per cent. It was the large external shocks of the 1970s and 1980s, the oil and commodity price hikes, and the debt crises, that brought about the new species of galloping, yet for a time quasi-stable, rates of inflation in the three-digit annual range.

For both economic and political reasons a gradual cure for the latter type of high inflation is in general unlikely to be feasible, mainly because the real disruptions caused by an asynchronized disinflation of prices, wages, money, and/or the exchange rate become prohibitive as inflation climbs to three digits.[15] Chile's economic and political crisis of the early 1970s, which led to a prolonged military dictatorship, is the only case since 1970 in which a high inflation process, bordering on hyperinflation, has gradually evolved into relative price stability (note the lack of clear 'kinks' in Chile's inflation profile in Fig. 1.2 after 1974). The economic and social costs of the Chilean stabilization were indeed very high, strengthening the case for shock therapy in the subsequent case-histories (see Chapter 6).

The effects of shock therapy in a case of high chronic inflation, however, tend to be much more complicated than for hyperinflation because there is a persistence of inflation that has to be broken in addition to the introduction of a sharp fiscal and monetary reform. Given inflationary inertia, the orthodox cure is necessary but not sufficient. The correction of fundamentals does not by itself remove inflationary inertia, as the Mexican example of the mid-1980s (in addition to that of Chile in the 1970s) has

---

[15] A simple numerical example will illustrate the point. Suppose an attempt is made to reduce inflation gradually from a monthly rate of 10% by slowing down the monthly rate of devaluation to 7%. If price and wage disinflation is sluggish due to inertia, each month of delay will cause a real appreciation of 3%, which will very quickly accumulate to a large loss of competitiveness. In the extreme case of no change in inflation, the cumulative real appreciation over a year would reach 43%(!), which cannot be sustainable and must lead to expectations of policy reversal and thus to an exchange-rate collapse. Similar arguments apply to asynchronized movement of prices and wages or money. Analogous *relative* deviations of nominal growth at 10% inflation *per annum* are quite common and need not cause any problem in the short run.

shown. Supplementary direct intervention in the nominal pro(
such as a temporary freeze on wages, prices, and the excha
rate, can substantially reduce the initial cost of disinflation, a₅ it
helps to avoid—or at least moderate—the fluctuations that would
otherwise occur in *relative* prices.

The two-pronged approach to stabilization, applied to
Argentina, Brazil, and Israel in 1985–6 and later to Mexico
(1988), came to be known as the *heterodox* programme. Two of
these countries, Argentina and Brazil, went into hyperinflation in
1987, while in the two other countries, Israel and Mexico, the
'shock' approach to stabilization was successful, and the structural adjustment process has been much more gradual. What the
recent example of Argentina and Brazil has shown is that if the
high-inflation process is not terminated in time, it is likely to
revert to a 'classic' hyperinflation.[16]

This discussion leads one to a four-stage typology of inflationary processes, with the numbering of the stage, or type, roughly
corresponding to the number of digits of annual inflation. These
stages can be sequenced by the existence or absence of some key
institutional or behavioural attributes. Failure to stabilize a stage
I (garden-variety) inflation (single digit, or with spurts that at
most reach an order of 20 per cent, say) plus systematic indexing
(and/or monetary accommodation) may lead to chronic inflation
(stage II, with inflation anywhere between 20 and 100 per cent).
In the presence of large price shocks this may, in turn, lead to
high chronic inflation (stage III, going up to 1,000 per cent or
thereabouts) such as occurred in the 1970s with oil, commodity
prices, and devaluation shocks, and is likely to happen in a com-
mand-economy as prices are decontrolled, fiscal deficits are not
eliminated, and indexation mechanisms are introduced. Failure to
stabilize a stage III economy will eventually move the system into
hyperinflation (stage IV), as in Argentina and Brazil. Countries
can, of course, move directly from stage I (or II) to stage IV without going through stage II (or III). This has been true for most
classic hyperinflations and was also the case in the recent hyperinflations of Eastern Europe—in Yugoslavia and Poland in 1989,
and in Russia in early 1992. In all these cases liberalization of a

---

[16] All of these countries' recent examples of developments in the aftermath of
sharp disinflation are included in Bruno *et al.* (1991).

repressed price system, without correction of fundamentals, led to hyperinflation almost at once.[17]

1.5 Structural Crisis and Reform as Protracted Processes: An Overview of the Issues

The different characterizations of inflationary processes raise some interesting theoretical questions bearing on the foundations of macro-economic and monetary theory, which can be put to the test in terms of relevance at its polar extremes. In the absence of the ability to conduct critical empirical experiments, as is common in the physical sciences, such extrema provide a close substitute. To what extent can the nominal system be divorced from the real economy? For given disequilibrium in the real economy is there an equilibrium rate of inflation (or more than one such equilibrium)? What, if anything, makes it stable? What is a 'nominal' anchor of a system? Next, broadening the scope to political-economy issues—why are stabilizations delayed and what is the optimal timing of a sharp stabilization? These are some of the questions that come up in the face of the varying extreme monetary phenomena observed in the course of the last two decades.

So far we have concentrated on the different characterizations of high inflation. The latter, however, is only the outer, nominal (i.e. monetary) manifestation of a deep underlying disease in the *real* economy, almost like the high fever of an ailing body. Stabilization *per se* is at times no more than a successful dramatic reduction in the body temperature or the initial crisis surgery in preparation for the real surgery or healing process, which may be protracted and painful. The economic and political roots of the crisis and the adjustment and structural reform process are more institution-specific and more varied across countries than is the inflationary process once it erupts. It would

---

[17] From a political-economy point of view it may be easier to cure a hyperinflation than a high chronic inflation. This raises the interesting policy question as to when it is optimal to conduct the sharp stabilization cure. As one of my Israeli colleagues put it—has the situation deteriorated badly enough to be good for us policy advisers? Obviously, there are cases when the state of the economy needs to worsen before it can be cured. This idea can be grounded within a modern political-economy approach (see Drazen and Grilli 1990, and further discussion in Ch. 8).

thus be a mistake to conclude, from the fact that stabilizations look remarkably alike among the hyperinflation episodes or within the high chronic inflation category, that equally simple generalizations necessarily apply either to the underlying fundamental roots of the crisis or to the structural reform strategies required.

As we shall see, there will be enough material suggesting common factors as well as identifiable differences across countries to merit some subsequent attempt at greater generalization. However, to get at it requires, in the first stage, a deeper investigation of individual country experiences over longer time-periods rather than a superficial view across larger country samples. This is all the more so since the number of successful and sustainable reforms among the crisis countries mentioned is thus far limited to only three or four countries.

In this introductory stage we confine ourselves to a subsample of six of the Western economies appearing in the earlier tables and reconsider their aggregate growth and inflation performance over thirty years, 1960 to 1991 (see Table 1.5). Starting our comparison from 1960 enables the choice of a thirteen-year reference period, 1960–73, which was part of the 'Golden Age' of post-World War II rapid growth.[18] The second period, 1973–80, is delimited by the two major oil shocks, while the third period, 1980–5, marks the debt crisis, with the 1985 signpost as the year of major stabilization programmes in three of the countries (Israel, Bolivia, and Argentina) closely followed by a fourth country, Brazil, in 1986. Mexico embarked on its fiscal reform within that period, although its comprehensive stabilization came later, in 1988. The data in Table 1.5 are also displayed in graphic form (see Fig. 1.3) with the four subperiods marked from *A* to *D*. For scale convenience they are grouped into two separate sets of graphs as between the high- and hyperinflation countries (which also happens to fit the ordering in Table 1.5).

All six countries showed substantial positive growth in the Golden Age, before the first oil shock, although both Chile's and Argentina's growth was relatively low compared to the reference group of MICs.[19] Two of the countries, Israel and Brazil, had

---

[18] One could start in the early 1950s, but to get a broad reference benchmark period in most cases this does not make much difference.
[19] Using the World Bank definition as it appears in the *WDR*.

TABLE 1.5 *Per capita growth and inflation in six countries, 1960–1991 (annual %)*

	1960–73		1973–80		1980–5		1985–91[a]	
	Growth	Inflation	Growth	Inflation	Growth	Inflation	Growth	Inflation
Chile	1.8	50[b]	1.1	138	-2.1	22	4.4	20
Israel	5.6	7	0.1	55	-0.1	173	1.8	18
Mexico	3.4	4	3.7	21	-1.8	62	-0.8 (1.7)	61 (25)
Bolivia	3.2	7	0.9	21	-7.3	569	-0.8 (0.3)	42 (19)
Argentina	2.3	26	0.1	157	-3.0	343	-0.2 (1.5)	299 (92)
Brazil	7.1	37	4.0	44	-1.0	148	-0.1	624
MICs	3.2	7	3.1	20	-0.6	57	1.3	95[c]
OECD	3.6	5	2.0	11	1.8	7	1.6	4

[a] Numbers in brackets refer to the subperiod 1989–91, except for Argentina, where growth refers to 1990–1 and inflation to the year between the last quarters of 1990 and 1991.
[b] 1963–73.
[c] 1985–9.

Sources: Growth (per capita) 1960–80 from Summers and Heston (1991); 1980–90: *WDR* and *IFS* (OECD: per employee). Inflation (CPI): *WDR* and *IFS*.

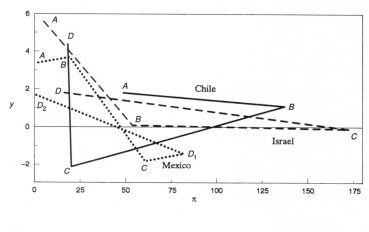

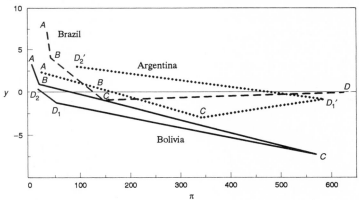

Notes: *A*: 1960–73; *B*: 1973–80; *C*: 1980–5; *D*: 1985–91; (*D₁*: 1985–9; *D₂*: 1989–81; *D′₁*: 1985–90; *D′₂*: 1990–1)

FIG. 1.3   Growth and the rate of inflation by subperiod, 1960–1991

ranked among the world's fastest growers in the post-war period. Chile was the first country to get into a high-inflation crisis in the 1970s, even before the first oil shock set in; Israel was a close second, with the sharpest drop in growth in 1973. Argentina's growth dropped to zero in period *B* and, as shown earlier, it had the highest inflation rate (with Chile coming close). Mexico (bolstered by oil revenues and external borrowing) and Brazil (by borrowing) 'sailed through' the two oil shocks with relatively high growth (compared to the OECD and MIC averages shown) and moderate inflation.

When world interest rates shot up at the beginning of period C all these countries sank into deep waters on all three counts— negative growth, high inflation, and mounting external debt.[20] Bolivia, as already mentioned, is an outlier in that its extreme inflation (and highly negative growth) during period C turned out to have been a relatively brief episode, and does not belong in the present discussion.[21]

The ordering of countries in Table 1.5 roughly corresponds to the order of return to growth in 1985–90, or degree of success in the reform process, after the protracted twelve-year crisis period 1973–85. Only the first three countries have shown positive per capita growth, at least (for Mexico) since 1988. Bolivia may be approaching positive growth. All four countries, we saw, have shown inflation rates in the 20 per cent range (Mexico, again, only since 1988). Argentina precedes Brazil in our list on account of the most recent, apparently much more successful, recovery of 1990–1.[22] We note that the ordering of the countries roughly corresponds to their ordering in terms of both growth and inflation differentials between periods D and A.

As we shall see, the length of the crisis and some of its economic and political characteristics invoke the quasi-stability image of vicious circles around a low-level equilibrium 'trap'. For the same reasons exit from the 'trap' requires a large concerted push towards a higher-level, that is, 'superior', equilibrium (and the build-up of virtuous circles around it). In both crisis and

---

[20] The debt/GNP ratio increase during the period 1980–5 (and the initial 1980 ratio) appears in Table 1.2. Chile's comparable numbers, which do not appear in Table 1.2, are 99 for the ratio increase during 1980–5 from a 1980 initial level of 46 (namely by the end of 1985 its debt ratio reached 145%).

[21] Bolivia also differs from all other Latin American countries in the group in its level of development, one of whose measures is a per capita GDP of less than $1,400 in 1988, compared to a level of 4,000–5,000 for all four other countries (see Summers and Heston 1991).

[22] This part of the ordering could also be justified formally in terms of the difference between 1985–90 and 1960–73 growth rates, which for Brazil remains the most glaring gap. We again note that from a high inflation, which was similar to Israel's in periods B and C, Brazil overtook Argentina in a hyperinflation of similar characteristics in period D.

reform the political environment plays an important role. We thus supplement the basic data set by quoting some indices of democracy and political freedom in the various countries, for three points in time, in Table 1.6. This is based on the work of two political scientists, Bollen (1990) and Gastil (1990), measured on a scale of 0 to 1.[23]

TABLE 1.6 *Indices of political rights and civil liberties*

	Bollen	Gastil	
	(1960)	1976	1985
Chile	1.00	0.17	0.25
Israel	0.95	0.75	0.83
Mexico	0.80	0.50	0.50
Bolivia	0.60	0.33	0.75
Argentina	0.63	0.25	0.83
Brazil	0.91	0.42	0.75
OECD			
USA	0.95	1.00	1.00
France	0.90	1.00	0.92
Finland	0.97	0.83	0.83
Spain	0.11	0.50	0.92
MICs			
Hong Kong	0.00	0.42	0.42
Korea	0.52	0.25	0.42

Sources: Bollen (1980, 1990); Gastil (1990); Helliwell (1992).

Israel has the highest index in the group, of the order of European democracies, while Chile had the lowest index throughout most of its crisis and structural reform period. Chile had been an established democracy until 1973 and after fifteen years of military rule returned to full-fledged democracy only in the most recent past (no comparable numerical measure for the latter period exists as yet). We also note the sharp political transformation that

[23] The sources as well as the scale transformation come from Helliwell (1992). As Helliwell shows, Bollen's measures are on average biased upwards compared to Gastil's. For our purposes the measures for 1976 and 1985, coming from the same source, are more relevant.

had taken place in Argentina and Brazil by 1985, which classifies them as 'transitional democracies'[24] and may go part of the way towards explaining the more recent political and economic co-ordination failures in these countries (see Chapter 6). Is Mexico's recent more successful structural reform at least in part associated with the more autocratic features of single-party rule? Both Mexico and the earlier example of Spain, like some of the fast growers of South East Asia, are cases in which economic reform preceded political reform. This particular aspect of the sequencing of reforms is of interest in the context of the most recent developments of Eastern and Central Europe. Unlike Yugoslavia (which by now is no longer a unified economy), Hungary (and to some extent Poland) opted for *perestroika* before *glasnost* (see Chapter 7).

In the next four chapters of this book we limit our observations to the only economy in the above sample which is not in Latin America, namely Israel. Quite apart from letting comparative advantage dictate an author's choice of which country to investigate in greater depth, it is my belief that the Israeli case is of substantial general interest. Of the countries in question it combines, for a case-study, the advantages of a particularly sharp, as well as prolonged, worsening of economic performance in the face of common external shocks, proven success in a stabilization strategy that was followed in a number of other cases, as well as the maintenance of its democratic political system throughout the whole period. It is an example of 'therapy by consensus'. In this as well as some other respects it can serve as an example for the macro-economic problems that may be faced by some of the Eastern and Central European economies with the advent of political emancipation.

Chapter 2 analyses the developments in Israel's real economy and the internal political environment, both of which explain the origins of the crisis and its persistence, while Chapter 3 turns to the dynamics of high inflation under accommodation to price shocks. Chapter 4 takes up in detail the political economy of failed partial attempts to stabilize as well as the reasons for delays in the implementation of a heterodox programme which had been proposed in various versions since the beginning of 1981. Inherent

---

[24] The terminology appears in Kaufman and Stallings (1991).

risk aversion and short-term planning horizons of politicians as well as inconclusive professional debates amongst economists each played their respective delaying roles in the process, culminating in the economic and political impasse that led to the design and final implementation of the shock-stabilization programme in 1985. Chapter 5 completes our study of the Israeli case by analysing the gradual (and costly) fight to establish credibility of both the fiscal and nominal anchors in the aftermath of sharp stabilization as well as the ongoing structural reform process.

In Chapter 6 we return to the Latin American part of the scene. Apart from the difference in political environment and some other inherent structural differences, in comparison with Israel, such as the lesser role of defence and foreign aid and a larger role of primary exports, Latin America has had a much more protected trade regime. Israel had already substantially opened up its economy to free trade in the 1960s,[25] while the Latin American economies were characterized by extensive trade restrictions and import-substitution bias has been a marked feature of their development strategy. Substantial trade liberalization at the onset of a major reform has thus become an important ingredient of the structural adjustment process, starting with Chile in 1974 and continuing with Mexico in 1988 (and more recently Argentina). In most other respects, notably the political economy of budget deficits and of stabilization delays, the dynamics of high inflation, the failed partial attempts at stabilization, and financial fragility, Israel's and some of the Latin American countries' experiences are remarkably similar. Chapter 6 discusses the lessons from Chile's costly orthodox stabilization and successful, though slow, process of structural reform. It further considers the reasons for the failures, until recently, in the case of Argentina and Brazil (with a brief digression on Bolivia) and also discusses the 1990–1 turnaround in Argentina. The chapter ends with a comparison of the successful Mexican reform with that of Israel. There was considerable similarity in programmes, but enough differences in underlying

---

[25] There has been a certain protective set-back, by reintroduction of non-tariff barriers in the 1970s. The ongoing structural reform thus also includes a renewed pre-committed trade liberalization process for the 1990s (see Ch. 5). However, the remaining scope of opening-up at the stabilization stage was small in comparison to a typical Latin American economy.

institutions and market structure to make this comparison a particularly relevant one.

In Chapter 7 we consider the most recent stabilization and reform experience in six Eastern European countries, starting with the earlier Yugoslav and Polish shock programmes of 1990 and followed by Czechoslovakia, Bulgaria, and Romania in 1991. Hungary, which had a much longer and earlier reform experience, also carried out a successful and more conventional stabilization programme in 1991. The analysis of the dramatic developments in Eastern Europe concentrates on the underlying similarities of the macro-economics of stabilization across countries and regions, and attempts to isolate the particular problems that are common to Eastern and Central Europe but substantially different from the earlier experience elsewhere. The overriding problem is that of successfully integrating macro-economic stabilization with the fundamental reform of the micro-economy (i.e. creation of a market economy) right from the start. The context of the ex-communist economies, even more than elsewhere, raises vexing issues of sequencing of economic reforms and the choice of 'big bang' versus gradualist reform strategies. While it is much too early to judge the potential success of the far-reaching reforms already undertaken in Eastern Europe, the protracted crisis and reform experience in the previous set of economies can at least set warning signals for macro-policy during the transition and, to some extent, also for some institutional aspects of the micro-economy.

Some of the more general policy lessons from the combined experience of Israel, Latin America, and Eastern Europe to date, and an attempt at analytical synthesis of the framework for discussion of the inflation and growth crisis as well as the adjustment and reform, are taken up in the concluding chapter.

2

The Gathering Storm: Israel's Structural Crisis in the 1970s

The Israeli economy, like Israeli society, has always provided a fascinating area of research. Although the state was born in 1948 its economic structure had been laid down at least twenty-five years earlier.[1] Within just a few decades a thriving, modern, and diversified economy grew up based on foundations that existed by the end of World War I. From the early 1920s the Yishuv, the country's Jewish population, rose from only 80,000 to 600,000 in 1948 (a 7.5-fold increase) while the gross national product grew twenty-five times over the same period. In the first twenty years after independence, 1948 to 1972, the country's population quadrupled while its GNP increased tenfold. Thus, in the space of fifty years the population grew thirty times, while its economic activity increased by a factor of 250, truly astonishing figures. In the course of half a century per capita GNP rose from just 15 per cent of the US per capita GNP in 1922 to over one-half of the corresponding US figure for 1973, or three-quarters of the average per capita GNP prevailing in Western Europe, a feat surpassed at that time only by Japan.[2]

[1] The year 1922 can be taken as a reasonable starting-point for quantitative measurement. It was the first year for which we have properly defined economic indicators, compiled and analysed by the late Robert Szereszewski, who fell in the Six Day War. The study appeared posthumously (Szereszewski 1968).

[2] It is interesting to point out that during the period 1948–73 Israel's total GNP on average grew faster than Japan's, a statement that remains correct (because of Japan's post-1973 growth slow-down) even for the average of the whole period 1948–91. In per capita terms, however, the comparison with Japan is very different. According to the Summers and Heston (1991) estimates during the period 1960–73, Israel's per capita GDP relative to the USA grew from 0.39 in 1960 to reach 0.57 in 1973. During the same period Japan's ratio grew from 0.27 (in 1960) to reach the same ratio as Israel's, 0.57, in 1973. At the end of the period covered by the data (1988) Israel's ratio stood at only 0.51 ($9,400, compared to $18,300 for the USA), while Japan's continued to grow to 0.67 ($12,200 in absolute terms). Once we include the post-1973 period, Hong Kong and Singapore, of course, surpass even Japan. The corresponding GDP per capita

Being a small economy, by any measure,[3] and relatively poor in natural resources (except for its initial endowment of human capital), Israel was a very open economy right from the start (with an import-to-GNP ratio of the order of one-half), it had an early start on substantial import liberalization in the 1960s, and based its development strategy on industrial export-led growth with a large—and growing—high-tech. component. While beset with severe defence problems, culminating in three major wars (1948, 1967, and 1973), it had also enjoyed relatively abundant supplies of foreign aid, which helped bridge over the period in which fast-growing exports could increasingly catch up with a larger share of Israel's import requirements, the ratio rising from approximately one-tenth in 1948 to two-thirds by 1972.

The year 1973 marked the end of the Golden Age of growth and the economy entered a very deep and protracted crisis. Economic growth almost came to a halt, the balance-of-payments deficit rose to alarming proportions, and, worst of all, Israel began to experience a high inflation process of an extreme nature. The Yom Kippur War of October 1973 ushered in a decade and more of economic stagnation. This period, sometimes known in Israel as 'the lost decade', was a time of deep economic and social crisis in every sense of the word, affecting not only the country's economic structure but also its norms of socio-economic behaviour.

Was this crisis primarily the result of international developments or did its origins lie closer to home? This question has been the subject of considerable research, much of it included in a series of research papers put out by the Falk Institute for Economic Research at the height of the crisis, in 1982–4.[4] While these studies were quite extensive, and their conclusions basically held through the subsequent reform period, it is none the less interesting to take a fresh look at the diagnosis of the crisis from the vantage-point of a period of recovery.

---

figures (relative to the USA) at these three points in time, respectively, for Hong Kong (Singapore) were 0.23 (0.21), 0.39 (0.33), and 0.72 (0.57).

[3] Its area is only 22,000 square km. and its population by the end of 1991 was still less than 5 million (neither figure includes the administered territories of the West Bank and the Gaza Strip, together amounting to an approximate additional one-third). Israel's GNP in 1991 was about $45 billion.

[4] Ben-Porath (1986).

2.1. *Growth and Productivity: A Historical Perspective*

We start by examining the development and composition of business-sector GDP—the contributions of factors of production, capital, and labour, and the unexplained residual, 'total productivity', which captures the effects of changes in factor quality and utilization, as well as any other elements that might help explain why output should have grown faster than factor input. For this purpose, we will use the analytical framework which was first applied by Gaathon (1971) to the Israeli economy.[5]

Fig. 2.1 shows the average business-sector GDP growth rate since 1950 by subperiods (the figures appear in Table 2.1). Two periods, 1950–60 and 1961–72, are characterized by a very fast rate of GDP growth. This was the result of a significant labour force contribution deriving from successive waves of immigration,

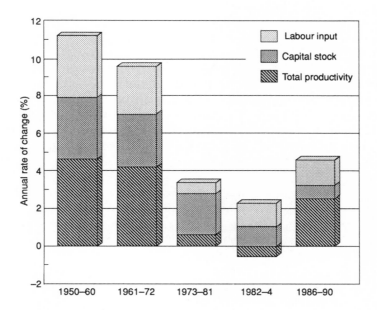

Source: Table 2.1.

FIG. 2.1 Product, factor inputs, and productivity in the business sector, 1950–1990

[5] See also Metzer (1986) and Syrquin (1986).

TABLE 2.1 *Business-sector GDP, factor input, and productivity in Israel, 1950–1990 (annual percentage growth)*

	1950–60	1961–72	1973–81	1982–4	1986–90
GDP	11.2	9.7	3.4	1.9	4.8
Labour input[a]	3.3	2.7	0.6	1.3	1.4
Capital input[a]	3.2	2.8	2.2	1.1	0.7
Total productivity	4.7	4.2	0.6	–0.5	2.6

[a] Factor input calculated by weighting the rate of growth of each factor by its share in business-sector GDP (approximately 75% for labour and 25% for capital, with variable weights). Total productivity is calculated as a residual: GDP growth rate less weighted growth rate of factor inputs.
Sources: 1950–81: Syrquin (1986) and Metzer (1986), based on Gaathon's method (1971). 1982–4, 1986–90: BOI, *Annual Reports* (1987, 1990).

as well as substantial capital investment which accompanied the growth process and made it possible. Some 30 per cent of GDP growth can be attributed to each of the labour and capital inputs. Overall productivity accounts for the 40 per cent unexplained residual. The twenty-five years prior to the birth of the state had, by and large, been characterized by the same growth pattern (see Syrquin 1986).

Fig. 2.1 highlights the dramatic fall in the growth rate after 1973, from some 10 per cent to an average of 3–4 per cent until 1981, and 1.9 per cent in the years 1982–4. This drop is even more dramatic when the subperiod 1961–7 (which includes the recession of 1965–7) is taken out of the second rectangle. Between the Six Day War and the Yom Kippur War business-sector GDP grew at an average annual rate of 12 per cent(!) before declining to just a quarter of this growth after 1973.

The diagram also reveals several other notable features. First, there was a very significant decline in the contribution of labour to GDP growth after 1973. The growth rate of business-sector employment dropped from approximately 4 per cent a year to only 1 per cent. This is only partly explained by the decline in immigration after 1973. No less influential in reducing business-sector employment was the increasingly large entry of new members of the labour force into the public service sector. By the very nature of their employment these workers make no direct contribution to business-sector GDP.

Secondly, there was a sharp drop in the residual productivity element, whose contribution fell from 4 per cent in the years of rapid growth to only 0.6 per cent in 1973–81, falling even further (to the point of *negative* productivity growth) in 1982–4. This is all the more remarkable when considering the surprising fact that the capital stock continued to grow rapidly even after 1973 (see the middle segment of the rectangles in Fig. 2.1). The relatively unperturbed growth in capital stock can be attributed to the unprecedented government subsidization of investment, whereby half of investment finance constituted a government transfer to the business sector.[6] At least part of these investments was made in activities that would otherwise not be profitable and thus led to the accumulation of substantial unutilized capital stock, financed at significantly negative real interest rates. The eventual need to replace such credit by more realistically (and, right after the 1985 stabilization, by excessively) priced market credit resulted in severe financial complications later on (see Chapter 5). The continued growth in measured capital stock at the same time as productivity was progressively declining implies a substantial waste of resources and illustrates only too well the argument that massive subsidization of investment does not necessarily lead to viable economic growth.

2.2 *International Comparison of Growth and Inflation*

1973 was a watershed year world-wide, not only in Israel. The oil and commodity price shocks seriously hit most of the industrial world and also many Third World countries, causing a substantial growth slow-down, rising unemployment, and accelerating inflation. To get a proper perspective on the Israeli case it makes sense to compare (as has already partly been done in Table 1.5) the two dimensions of the crisis for Israel with the average performance record of both the industrial and the middle-income countries. A more stringent test would be to compare Israel with a narrower class of middle-income countries to which Israel has always belonged, that of the manufacturing exporters among the MICs (termed the MANX, below). This is done in Fig. 2.2 for

---

[6] Most of it came in the form of an implicit inflation subsidy associated with the availability of huge nominal (i.e. unindexed) loans at a time of accelerating inflation—the estimate is from Litvin and Meridor (1983).

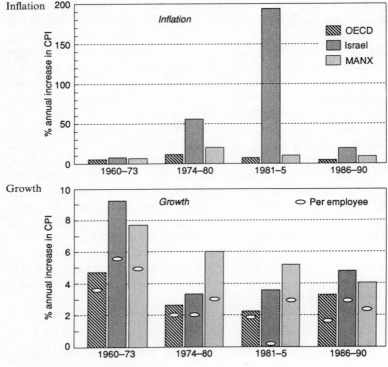

Sources: IFS and WDR.

Fig. 2.2   Inflation and growth: International comparison, 1960–1990

GDP (and GDP per employee) growth and for the mean (or median) inflation rate.[7]

[7] The left-hand rectangle of each grouping in Fig. 2.2 represents all the OECD economies, while the right-hand one represents the group of semi-industrialized economies defined by the IMF as manufacturing exporters (manufacturers having accounted for more than 50% of the country's exports in 1984–6). For the years 1960–80 we averaged twelve countries for which data exist in the Summers and Heston (1991) study: Brazil, China, Hong Kong, India, Israel, Korea, Portugal, Singapore, Taiwan, Thailand, Turkey, and Yugoslavia. For 1981–5 and 1986–90 the data refer to the aggregate defined by the IMF in the *WEO* Apr. 1989 and Oct. 1991, respectively, as manufacturing exporters. The latter include the above twelve, with the exception of Portugal, and also include Tunisia and the Eastern European economies that were or became members of the IMF: Hungary, Romania, Poland, and, more recently, Czechoslovakia and Bulgaria. For inflation during 1981–90 the median, rather than the weighted mean was taken (Brazil, Israel, and Yugoslavia would otherwise tilt the number in the direction of the one appearing in Table 1.5).

The figure again highlights the fact that during the rapid growth years (1960–73) the Israeli economy developed faster than the two reference groups, in terms of both GDP and GDP per employee, while its inflation rate was only slightly higher than that prevailing in the industrialized world. Next, the comparison shows that the industrial countries were hit by the recession and the inflation of the 1970s but to a considerably smaller extent than Israel (the MANX suffered from inflation, but not from impeded growth). This difference became acute in the early 1980s when GDP per employee fell and inflation rose sharply in Israel while receding elsewhere.[8] The period after 1985, in which Israel, on average, did better than the two reference groups, will be discussed in Chapter 5.

A more detailed analysis of the performance of the industrial economies indicates that while they all suffered from continued unemployment and inflation (stagflation) resulting from the oil and other raw material price shocks, they managed to recuperate, with varying degrees of success, through appropriate adjustment policies.[9] The most successful country in this respect was Japan, which had and still has very high fuel and raw material import requirements. By conducting proper fiscal and wage policies Japan not only succeeded in extricating itself within a few years from the severe recession of 1974–5, it also managed to revolutionize its industrial production processes, ensured that failing industries were closed down, and generally turned the situation to its benefit. Smaller European countries such as Austria and Finland provide other positive examples.

Israel's failure to extricate itself from the slump (more on inflation will be said in the next chapter), let alone its embroilment in an even worse crisis, must be attributed to the lack of a suitable macro-economic policy response rather than to purely external factors. Israel's situation was admittedly aggravated by the Yom Kippur War and the resulting heavy defence burden but, as we

[8] In this context it is important to emphasize again that the reference number measures the median. The mean inflation for the MANX during the two periods 1980–5 and 1985–90, respectively, was 35 and 58.

[9] For an analysis of the effect of the world-wide effects of the price shocks see Bruno and Sachs (1985). Another study of mine (see in Ben-Porath 1986: Ch. 14) provides a detailed analysis of the effects of the external shocks on the Israeli economy as well as of the failure of the macro-economic policy to respond by a suitable fiscal and structural adjustment policy.

shall see, this alone cannot explain either the depth or the duration of the crisis.

The failure to adjust manifested itself in two areas. One was the underlying failure (mainly of government, but also in the business and household sectors) to balance incomes and outlays—a constant attempt to live beyond one's means. The second element, which is not totally unrelated to the first, was an excessive increase of real wages over productivity, leading to a sharp fall in the rate of return to capital in the business sector. We here concentrate mainly on the government budget and on the size of the public sector and its ramifications.

2.3 The Government Budget: From Growth to Redistribution

The Israeli economy has sometimes been caricatured as one of the most extreme cases of more or less fully government-controlled economies in the western hemisphere. While this may have had an element of truth in the 1950s and 1960s government-led development phase, even then only small parts of the economy could have been described as subject to the rules of a command economy, such as is usually associated with pre-1989 Eastern Europe. The bulk of the economy, even the largely collectivized agriculture, was essentially market-oriented even though most of the land was publicly owned and investment was controlled and financed by the government. There continued into the 1970s, however, substantial and widespread government control in some key areas such as the financial, foreign-exchange, and capital markets, while the labour market has always been under the heavy influence of the trade union federation (Histadruth).

During the years of crisis, after 1973, some of these controls, particularly in the financial and capital markets, took a deeper hold. In large part this has been the result of the need to provide steady (and relatively cheap) finance for the persistently large government budget deficit. Table 2.2 presents the main data on public-sector income and expenditure as a percentage of gross national product by subperiod in the three decades from 1960 to 1990.[10] It is interesting to note the substantial rise in the size of

[10] The public sector is here defined to include central and local government, the Bank of Israel, as well as the Jewish Agency. The latter takes care of the funding

the overall public-sector deficit already during the growth period. From a state of near balance in the first half of the 1960s (as in the 1950s), the economy went into a deficit equivalent to 12.6 per cent of GNP in the Golden Age between the Six Day and the Yom Kippur Wars (1967–72). During this period there was a rise in civilian public service expenditure as well as in direct government investments and subsidies and, in particular, in defence expenditures. At the time the economy did not require any significant increase in tax rates as rapid growth made easy borrowing possible both at home and abroad. The government was also able to borrow substantial amounts from the Bank of Israel (an option that was removed only much later, with the post-1985 legislation). While an economy grows, the demand for real balances and real bonds grows with it, so that up to a certain point the enlarged deficit may have no inflationary effect. As we shall see, this habit proved fatal when growth collapsed.

The first seeds of future troubles were thus sown as far back as the boom period between the two wars. It was a highly expansionary phase dominated by a 'we can do anything' psychological attitude that came in the wake of the great (and deceptively quick) victory in the 1967 war. It seemed possible to increase every component of government spending and 'wave every flag' at the same time: that of defence, economic development, and, in particular, to respond to the new needs of social welfare. The latter became the focus of the economic-policy debate towards the late 1960s and early 1970s when the War of Attrition on the Suez Canal ended and an Israeli version of a 'Black Panther' movement became prominent.[11] At that time there was no real balance-of-payments constraint and the only gradually emerging sign of

of some important public services such as part of immigrant absorption expenditure. The definition of public-sector accounts used here differs from the standardized system (SNA) now being applied in BOI publications in that the non-profit service sector is here not part of the public sector, but is a beneficiary of its transfers. While a case could be made for its explicit inclusion, the new data exist only for the period after 1981. I am indebted to Leora Meridor for the 1986–90 update of her 1985 estimates.

[11]The flag-waving analogy is taken from the public controversy surrounding the approach of the then Defence Minister Moshe Dayan, who coined the phrase by claiming that 'we cannot wave all the flags at once'. What he implied is that top priority still had to be given to the new defence expenditure requirements, even when set against the pressing social issues.

.2   Public-sector expenditures and revenues, 1960–1990 (% of

	1960–6	1967–72	1973–84	1985–90
1. Total public sector expenditures	**36.8**	**55.3**	**76.0**	**61.1**
Public civilian consumption	11.8	11.3	11.6	10.6
Social transfers	5.4	9.1	16.0	18.0
Public-sector investments	4.9	5.4	4.1	2.4
Subsidies (*plus* indirect subsidies on credit)	3.4	5.6	12.9	4.4
Real interest payments	1.6	2.9	5.7	9.8
Defence expenditures	9.7	21.1	25.7	15.9
2. Total revenues	**35.6**	**42.7**	**58.8**	**60.1**
Taxes and income from property	32.6	38.6	47.7	47.5
Unilateral transfers from abroad	3.0	4.1	11.0	12.6
3. Total deficit	**1.3**	**12.6**	**17.3**	**1.0**

Source: BOI calculations for 1960–83; see Meridor (1985), updated.

impending trouble was a certain domestic imbalance showing primarily in the labour market.

At this time an extensive new social security transfer system was introduced, comprising mainly child allowances and other welfare allocations as well as expanded health and education programmes. The prevailing attitude among relevant circles (supported by many economists, myself included) was that with a thriving economy (remember that business-sector GDP was growing at an annual rate of 12 per cent on average, with greatly increased exports and no real threat to the balance of payments), the time was ripe for redistribution in favour of the underprivileged. The impetus given to social expenditure should, of course, have come to a halt at the time the crisis broke out. But given the inertia in social policy commitments there was no will (or political force) to bring it about. The social group that was affected, mainly Jews of North African origin, felt left out of the political system. The gradually weakening position of the ruling Labour Party in the 1960s and 1970s, which was correlated with the increase in the voting power of the oriental parts of the population (who on the whole tended to vote for Likud), made it particularly vulnerable to such legitimate social demands.

Table 2.2 shows that the growth in social expenditure derived from an increase in transfers from 5 per cent of GNP in 1960–6 to 9 per cent in 1967–72, to 16 per cent in the post-1973 era, and even higher after 1985. There was an even more pronounced upward shift in the various types of subsidies, notably those implied by the cheap finance of investment, the significance of which we have already discussed. With the concurrent growth in interest payments on internal and external debt (see below) and the further growth in defence expenditures (which were now financed by increased US military aid) government spending reached an all-time high of 76 per cent of GNP(!), on average, during more than a decade, 1973–84.

At the same time gross tax revenues grew by a substantial 9 percentage points to reach 48 per cent of GNP. (Net taxation, after subtracting transfers from tax receipts, increased at a much lower rate; however, it is *gross* taxation that affects growth incentives negatively.) Despite increased foreign aid, the overall public-sector deficit rose to an unprecedented 17.3 per cent of GNP during the crisis period. This average figure applied, with only minor fluctuations, to the entire twelve-year period. While sporadic attempts were made to curtail the budget (notably in 1976, by the last Labour Finance Minister Rabinovitz, and in 1979, by Yigael Horowitz, a Likud Minister who served briefly before he was forced to resign) the excessive public-expenditure levels, accompanied as they were by very low growth, reflect myopic behaviour on the part of successive over-indulgent governments that opted for short-term expediency over long-term reform.

It is also important to point out the nature of government involvement in the income redistribution process. In the course of the crisis period, rather than support individuals' own human and tangible capital formation, government intervention increasingly took the form of direct commodity subsidization, extension of welfare and child allowances, and other forms of patronizing support that are not conducive to self-reliance. It did come as a political and social response to demands to increase the share of the national pie among the underprivileged, but no effort was made to condition such support by incentives to work harder and produce more.[12] Thus the form of public support, quite apart

[12] An alternative to the children's allowance scheme consistent with the self-reliance principle would be to replace transfers to the parents of large families by direct financial aid to the 'children' as they graduate from army service, conditioning the use of such aid to investment in either housing, physical investment in plant and equipment, or investment in the individual's own higher education. I had occasion to propose this alternative scheme in 1975 (during a brief spell as economic policy adviser to Finance Minister Rabinovitz). But by the time this

from its high wage tax finance, may in itself have contributed to
the contraction in the growth rate.

Democratic governments, of course, in some sense always
reflect the will of the people. Since private consumption continued to grow unabated at very high annual rates of 3 per cent per
capita during 1973–82, compared to 3.6 per cent in the preceding
Golden Age 1965–72 (while GNP per capita was growing at only
1 per cent annually, down from 5.6 per cent in the preceding
period!) what was there to complain about? Illusions about fake
prosperity can be maintained by populist governments for quite
some time.

Returning to the public-sector accounts, what the figures show
is that with the upsurge of the 1970s crisis the government failed
to adjust its order of priorities to the changing circumstances,
both external (raw material price shocks and the ensuing world
recession) and internal (heavily increased defence expenditure and
a reduced growth rate in population and the labour force). The
only part of the budget to be reduced after 1973, a cut which
eventually caused considerable long-term damage, was direct government investment in infrastructure (see Table 2.2). In political
economy terms, this part of the budget is easiest to slash since
there is no immediate political constituency that gets hurt, only
the welfare of future voters.

2.4 Ballooning Internal and External Debt

The harmful implications of the large deficit and the very size of
the public sector have manifested themselves in a number of
areas, especially in a rapid increase in the external and internal
debt. The growth in the external debt was associated with persistent balance-of-payments problems and the need for price-level
adjustments—devaluations and subsidy cuts—which, given the
well-lubricated and accommodative wage–price–money supply
mechanism, led to sustained shifts in the inflation rate (see next
chapter). The growth in the internal debt contributed to the
crowding-out of the private sector from the capital market, and
discouraged private finance of investment and growth, partly

was proposed the vested political and social interest in maintaining the existing
allowance scheme was already too entrenched to allow for any reform.

'compensated' by the distortive public subsidies to investment. At the same time the increased internal debt and debt-management policy[13] limited the degrees of freedom of monetary policy, a subject to which we shall return when discussing the loss of control over inflation.

Fig. 2.3 summarizes the external and internal debt profile that resulted from the cumulative public-sector deficit. External debt increased from a mere 20 per cent of GNP before 1967 to between 40 and 50 per cent at the onset of the crisis period. At that time the profitability of capital still justified its continued finance by foreign borrowing. The same argument no longer applied, however, to the doubling of the external-debt-to-GNP ratio in the following decade. Looking at the profile of the internal debt, its rise is even more striking than that of the external debt: from 10 per cent of GNP in 1965 and 40 per cent in 1973, it increased to almost 140 per cent at the height of the crisis, by which time the combined external and internal debt amounted to more than double the GNP level. Most of the private savings of economic agents, both households and businesses, was thus primarily mobilized (through various coercive mechanisms—more on this below) to finance a massive accumulation of government bonds rather than direct capital formation.

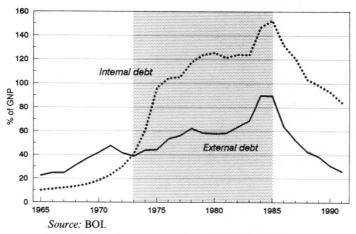

Source: BOI.

FIG. 2.3 Israel's internal and external debt, 1965–1991

[13] For quite a few years the government was also intervening in the market to keep the price of its bonds high and the real interest cost of new bonds low.

Real public debt accumulation of such proportions is unprecedented among reasonably well-ordered economies. It is true that during World War II Britain, for example, accumulated an internal debt that was equivalent to over double the level of GNP. The British debt, however, was set in nominal terms and could thus be eroded by the inflation that came in the wake of the war. This is in contrast to the Israeli internal debt, all of which was index-linked and thus inflation-proof.

2.5 Implications for the Structure of Employment

Apart from the protracted government deficit which affected the scale and cost of the debt, the sheer size of government expenditure was a significant factor in the growth slow-down. On the one hand, it required a high level of taxation which tended to hamper savings, investment, and the willingness to supply labour. On the other hand, it mobilized physical resources, primarily in employment, at the expense of the ones available to the private sector.

The implications for the labour market are represented in Fig. 2.4. The lower curve shows the unemployment rate as a percentage of the labour force from 1960 onwards. Apart from the tem-

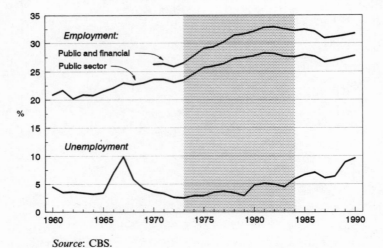

Source: CBS.

Fig. 2.4 · Israeli employment and unemployment, 1960–1990

porary sharp rise at the time of the 1966–7 recession, the unemployment rate in Israel during the crisis has been consistently lower than that in Europe. This was particularly true in the 1970s, when Israel's unemployment rate was around 3–4 per cent of the labour force compared to 8–11 per cent in Western Europe. Only in the early 1980s did Israeli unemployment start to rise to around 5–6 per cent.

The relatively low level of unemployment does not, of course, reflect a higher rate of employment in the business sector. The growth rate there fell dramatically after 1973, just as it did in Europe. The reason can clearly be found in the concurrent substantial rise in public-sector employment, from 20–2 per cent of total work-force in the early 1970s to 28–30 per cent by the end of that decade, as can be seen from the middle curve in Fig. 2.4. The upper curve[14] in the figure combines the percentages of employees in the public sector and in the financial sector. The latter sector increased very significantly as a direct by-product of high inflation, but declined thereafter.[15] The gap between the upper curve and a 100 per cent line (not shown in the figure) represents the percentage of employees in the NFB sector which, as stated, fell substantially and only began to rise again after 1983–4, when public-sector employment stopped rising.

The striking changes in the distribution of employment away from normal private production for the market are even more glaring when incremental shares of the various sectors in total employment are calculated. Between 1958 and 1972, which were years of high growth, the NFB sector absorbed 73 per cent of the increase in the overall number of employees in the economy, with the public and financial sector taking up the remaining 27 per

---

[14] The percentages of employees in the two upper curves of Fig. 2.5 were calculated on the basis of total employment in the economy and not the total labour force, as is the case with the rate of unemployment. This discrepancy, however, only marginally affects any comparisons between relative employment and unemployment figures.

[15] These should be taken as minimum indicators of employment in public and financial services. During the period in question there were additional employees in the business sector who were involved mainly in the supply of 'public services' (such as internal defence) or 'financial services' (instead of physical production) but were not counted as such in the statistics. Another important qualification has to do with the categorization of the relative contribution of that part of the business sector involved in production for defence purposes (see Berglas 1986, and Halperin 1987).

cent. These percentages were almost completely reversed between 1973 and 1981, when the share of that sector in incremental employment fell to only 37 per cent while 63 per cent swelled the ranks of the public and financial sectors.[16] This was reversed again after the 1985 reform.

2.6 Savings, Investments, and Rates of Return

In conclusion, we have seen that every aspect of public-sector policy—with regard to its transfer policy and high taxation, the misallocation of labour force, distorted subsidization of private investment (while reducing government's own investment in infrastructure)—all of these were working in the direction of hampering sound economic growth. Moreover, government's own lack of restraint had a direct behavioural impact on the response of economic units in the private sector. We have already mentioned the household sector. We defer a more detailed discussion of the distortive effects on the business sector to a later stage because these came into the open only after stabilization. Suffice it to say at the present stage that an excessive increase in real wages throughout the period 1975–85 showed up in a rising share of labour in national income and a substantial drop in the profit share and in the rate of return to capital (see Fig. 2.5). At the same time there was a substantial increase in long-term real interest rates.[17] Both of these factors should, *ceteris paribus*, have depressed private investments.

As Table 2.3 shows, the investment share in GNP dropped only slightly in the crisis years. As discussed earlier, this was one of the distortive outcomes of the subsidized interest-rate policy at a time of accelerating inflation. If this anomaly is not enough, there was another strange attribute to the savings–investment balance in the economy. Along with rising private living standards, individuals could also afford to keep reasonably high private savings rates out of their rising real disposable (transfer-inclusive) incomes. Savings were almost exclusively in the form of mount-

---

[16] The figures for the twelve-year period from 1973 to 1984 were 48 and 52%, respectively.

[17] Between 1975 and 1985 real rates of return on government indexed bonds rose from around 1–2% to 6–7%, most of the increase taking place in the first half of the 1980s (Fig. 5.3).

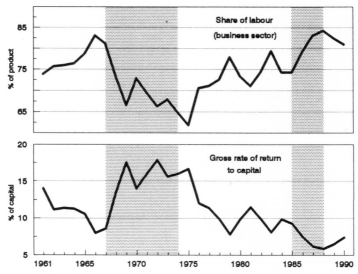

Source: BOI.

FIG. 2.5 Share of labour in product and rate of return to capital, 1961–1990

TABLE 2.3 *Savings, gross domestic investment, and the current account, 1960–1990[a] (% of GNP at current prices according to the official exchange rate)*

	1960–72	1974–9	1980–4	1985–90
1. Total savings	22.6	20.3	18.0	17.0
Private	(20.6)	(28.0)	(23.9)	(15.8)
Public	(2.0)	(–7.7)	(–5.9)	(1.3)
2. Gross investments	27.6	27.2	22.2	16.0
3. Net current account (1)–(2)[b]	–5.0	–6.9	–4.2	1.0

[a] There is a break in the series in 1980, after which the public/private breakdown conforms to the 1988 SNA. The two series were spliced in 1980.
[b] Advance payments for defence imports have been calculated as actual imports and are included in defence imports.
Source: Research Department, BOI.

ing indexed government debt. The seeming paradox of increasing private incomes and an almost stagnant GDP, remember, can be made up by transfers from the government sector and from abroad. But, given substantial public-sector dissaving, total savings in the economy did not, of course, match up to the level of aggregate investments. The difference between the two is the other side of the very large current-account deficit and the mounting external debt. In short, here is an economy in which the government provides the means by which the household sector is seemingly enriched by holding on to more and more financial assets whose future value, at some point, must become doubtful (as in fact it did after 1983—see the next chapter). At the same time the productive potential of the economy, in the true sense of the word, gets impoverished while the behaviour of the business sector becomes more and more distorted.

2.7 The Self-Reinforcing Nature of the Structural Crisis: A Partial Summary

Before turning to the high inflation implications of the crisis, this may be a suitable juncture at which to summarize a number of salient features of the crisis in the real economy, as they come out of the Israeli experience, all of which suggest that the drop in the growth rate tended to be a self-reinforcing process. Later this will enable us to draw some comparisons and show similarities with the Latin American experience. Here are a few of these points:

1. Israel's high growth period until the early 1970s created expectations of a 'large potential pie' from which all demands could be satisfied. In particular, there were pent-up social demands based on genuine concerns over unbalanced distribution of the pie during the preceding growth period.
2. A weakening of internal political and social consensus takes place, accelerated by the existence of strong unsatisfied social groups outside the political centre (in some of the Latin American economies this clearly took a much more extreme form[18]).
3. An unexpected real shock suddenly shrinks the potential pie (oil prices in 1973, 1979; real interest rates, mainly in the Latin American context, in 1981).
4. The period already begins with, or rapidly develops, a large public-sector deficit in which social transfers and subsidies

---

[18] See Dornbusch and Edwards (1991).

(usually not growth-inducing) loom large. Expenditure c
if any, tend to concentrate on infrastructure investmᴄᵢᵢ.,
which usually has no obvious political constituency and
whose growth costs will be borne only in the future.

5. The existence of foreign-exchange resources or borrowing
   possibilities forms an escape valve, enabling continuing sat-
   isfaction of conflicting demands and higher real wages
   which, in turn, reduce competitiveness and increase the
   external imbalance.

6. Distortions in relative price structures induce distorted
   employment and investment decisions (e.g. inflated financial
   systems, misinvestments in the real economy, excessive
   investment in real estate), which delay the open unemployment and add little to (or destroy) the 'healthy' part of the
   long-run productive capital stock.

As we shall see below, all or most of these attributes also manifested themselves one way or another in the Latin American
context.[19] But so far we have looked only at the real side of the
economy. The self-reinforcing 'trap' elements of the crisis cannot
be fully understood without consideration of the inflationary
process, to which we now turn.

---

[19] Some structural differences have already been mentioned in Ch. 1 and will
be taken up again in Ch. 6.

3

3

Shocks and Accommodation: The Dichotomy and Mechanics of High Inflation

3.1 Introduction[1]

The protracted government deficit discussed in the previous chapter was the major source of inflationary pressures in the economy. Yet the relationship between the deficit and the inflationary process had to be of a kind that is different from the one analysed in conventional textbook descriptions of the link between excess demand and the price level in single- or two-digit inflation. First and foremost, as can be seen from Fig. 3.1, there was no clear time-series correlation between the size of the deficit and the rate of inflation. The ratio of the deficit to GDP remained between 10 and 20 per cent for over fifteen years while inflation kept rising in step-wise fashion.

This apparent lack of positive correlation had already been observed by Pazos (1972) in the context of the more moderate chronic inflation in Latin America in the 1950s and 1960s. More recently, in the context of Israel's high inflation, Liviatan and Piterman (1986) have argued that there may even be a negative relationship between budget cuts and the rate of inflation due to the price-level increasing measures (such as subsidy cuts and devaluations) that were usually applied in the course of contractionary fiscal policy. The implication of such a finding might be misinterpreted to imply that fiscal balance may not be a necessary condition for sustainable disinflation. One theoretical line of argument, pursued by Drazen and Helpman (1990), was to show that when budget deficits are unsustainable (namely they imply an unbounded present value of future government debt) this induces expectations of future policy change. But with uncer-

---

[1] For a detailed analysis of the high inflation process in Israel up to the end of 1983 see the chapters by Liviatan and Piterman (ch. 16), Bruno (ch. 14), and Bruno and Fischer (ch. 7) in Ben-Porath (1986). The present discussion draws on and updates my previous work, especially the joint paper with Stanley Fischer.

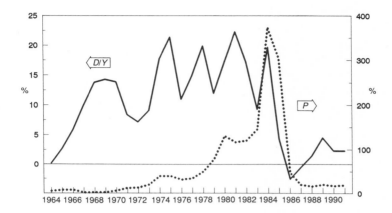

Note: Public-sector deficit as percentage of GNP.

Sources: BOI (deficit) and CBS (inflation).

FIG. 3.1   Total public-sector deficit and annual rate of CPI inflation, Israel, 1964–1991

tainty with respect to both the timing and the post-stabilization mix of policies between expenditure cuts, tax increases, or changes in money growth, fluctuations in the rate of inflation may occur in ways that may seem to be unrelated to the budget deficit, even though the deficit is the primary cause of inflation.

One simple approach to the budget as a source of the inflationary process, with which we shall start our discussion, is to consider the link of the form of finance, namely seigniorage revenue and the average rate of inflation, on the hypothetical assumption that one is observing fluctuations around steady states. This will be shown to give at least some lead on the possible long-run relationship between the monetization of deficits and the rate of inflation. We then turn to a closer historical look at the changing trade-off between inflation, real GDP growth, and the current account, leading to the detailed dynamics of the inflationary process without which the 'shocks and accommodation' nature of the process cannot be understood. Part of the reason for the progressive acceleration of inflation will indeed be found in the connection between the budget deficit and the balance-of-payments deficit, and the government response in the form of devaluations and subsidy cuts. While this does not absolve the budget deficit the 'original sin', the transformation of price-level shocks into ;celerating rates of inflation has to do with the adaptation to 'living in sin', namely the accommodative monetary process and the close linkage of the exchange rate, prices, wages, and money. It is this system which enhances rapid price increases and eventually eliminates a stable 'nominal anchor' and thus allows the inflationary process to diverge even while the budget deficit remains more or less stable, though on a high plateau. There is a related aspect of the disappearing trade-off, as inflation accelerates, between economic activity (or unemployment) and the rate of inflation, which is a manifestation of what in monetary theory is called the neo-classical dichotomy of the real and monetary systems. We start with the analysis of deficit finance.

3.2 Budget Finance, Seigniorage, and Average Inflation

Because of the quasi-stability of inflation plateaux, at least until 1981, one may approach the study of the inflationary process on the simplified 'as if' assumption that we are observing a sequence of steady states. One may then ask what are the determinants of steady state inflation as gauged from the components of government deficit finance.

In a closed economy we may write the government budget constraint as:

$$G - T = dY = \dot{H}/P + \dot{B} , \qquad (3.1)$$

where G is government expenditure, T are taxes, Y is GNP, H is base money, B are real indexed bonds, and a dot indicates change in a variable over time. For simplicity, interest payments on bonds are here included in G.

In an open economy, if d_h is the domestic deficit ratio to GNP, and d_f is the ratio to GNP of the foreign deficit in domestic prices (net of unilateral transfers including interest payments), these sum up to the government's total deficit. If $\dot{B}_f$ is the change in net government external debt (net of the change in exchange reserves) and $E\dot{B}_f/P$ is its change in constant domestic prices, we may write:

$$d_h Y = \dot{H}/P + \dot{B} + (E\dot{B}_f/P - d_f Y) . \qquad (3.2)$$

Thus equation (3.1) continues to hold for an open economy if d is reinterpreted to be the *domestic finance ratio*, that is, the domestic deficit net of the difference between foreign debt finance and net foreign expenditure.

Equation (3.2) as an accounting identity can be illustrated from the Israeli deficit finance data of Table 3.1, to whose analysis we turn below. What equation (3.2) amounts to is stating that the total (domestic and foreign) deficit (col. 5) can be analysed in terms of three sources of finance: money creation (col. 6), increases in the domestic debt (col. 7), and increases in the foreign debt (col. 8). Equivalently, one may look at the domestic finance (money plus domestic debt, namely cols. 6 and 7) as the part of the domestic deficit (col. 3) that is not financed by net sales of foreign exchange to the central bank. The latter is the foreign debt finance (col. 8), *minus* net foreign expenditure (col. 4). Redefining dY to be the *domestic finance* component of the deficit, this accounting identity amounts to the same as the right side part of equation (3.1).

To turn an accounting identity into a meaningful economic relationship some restrictive assumptions have to be made. Assume a steady state in which the ratios $H/(PY)$ and B/Y are constant. The first constancy implies that in a steady state the growth rate of high-powered money is equal to the inflation rate (π) *plus* the growth rate of output (n). Similarly, a constant B/Y implies that the growth rate of bonds is equal to the growth rate of output (n). Accordingly, in a steady state the government budget finance constraint can be written in the form

$$d = (\pi + n)h + nb , \qquad (3.3)$$

where h denotes the ratio of the stock of high-powered money to nominal GNP $[H/(PY)]$ and b is the ratio of real bonds to GNP (B/Y). If we denote by v the ratio of net wealth to GNP ($v = h + b$), then (3.3) can be rewritten in the form:

$$\pi = (d - nv)/h . \qquad (3.4)$$

Equation (3.4) provides a convenient approach to analysing the determinants of the growth rate of the monetary base and thus, in steady state, of the inflation rate. nv represents the amount of deficit that can be financed by the government through the sale of bonds and printing of money without increasing their respective

TABLE 3.1 Government deficit finance, 1960–1990 (% of GNP)

	Domestic expenditure[a] (1)	Taxes[b] (2)	Domestic deficit (1)–(2) (3)	Net foreign expenditure[c] (4)	Total deficit (3)–(4) (5)	Base money creation[d] (6)	Domestic debt finance[e] (7)	Foreign debt finance[f] (8)	Unaccounted finance (9)
1960–4	27.0	28.8	-1.8	1.2	-0.6	2.5	-3.3	0.3	
1965–7	32.0	29.6	2.4	2.8	5.2	2.2	0	2.0	
1968–73	41.0	34.4	6.6	6.6	13.2	3.2	5.4	4.6	
1974–7	56.4	42.1	14.3	3.3	17.6	2.6	4.7	10.4	
1978–80	60.7	45.5	15.2	2.0	17.2	2.0	7.3	6.9	
1981–3	61.0	46.5	14.4	-0.3	14.1	2.1	7.2	4.9	
1984	57.2	40.9	16.4	-3.6	12.7	2.9	0.2	5.3	4.4
1985	54.9	47.9	7.0	-7.6	-0.6	5.8	-6.5	-3.9	4.0
1986–90	50.8	47.5	3.3	-2.0	1.3	-0.1	0.3	-0.9	2.0

Note: Definitions of cols. 1, 4, 7 have been slightly altered between the two sources by an order of no more than 1–2 %.

[a] Includes goods and services, subsidies, transfers, and interest on the public debt.

[b] Includes all direct and indirect taxes and transfers to government.

[c] Government expenditure abroad (mainly armaments) plus interest on debt minus unilateral transfers (mainly US government).

[d] Change in money base minus BOI interest rate on bank deposits.

[e] Includes indexed bonds, and, after 1977, BOI PATAM accounts. Figures are net of repayments and of loans to the public sector (8.9% in 1968–73, 4.3% in 1974–7, and very small afterwards).

[f] Defined as a residual between col. 5 independently measured, and the sum of cols. 6–8. In 1981–3 a small residual of 1–2% is included in col. 7. In 1960–80 col. 7 estimated as a residual, for lack of independent data.

Sources: 1960–80: Meridor (1985); 1981–90: Bank of Israel. Data based on old SNA definition (the *Annual Report* in recent years has switched to the new SNA definition in which the non-profit, publicly financed institutions are considered part of the public sector).

ratios to GNP. The more rapid the growth rate of output, the greater the share of the deficit that can be financed in a non-inflationary way. The larger the government deficit (or, rather, its domestic finance component) d, the higher the inflation rate in steady state; and the larger the monetary base, the lower the inflation rate need be.

One may take this framework one stage further, by considering the demand for high-powered money as a function of expected inflation and the stability or instability of the dual inflationary equilibria that can be derived from the resulting model (see Bruno and Fischer 1990). At this stage, however, we only apply equation (3.4) as an organizing framework for looking at the data for the average inflation rates during different subperiods under the assumption that the average inflation rate represents a hypothetical steady state. Table 3.1 gives the breakdown of deficit finance by subperiod from 1960 to 1990. We note that with the shift to high budget deficits after 1968 the bulk of finance was provided by an increase in both domestic and foreign debt, a point already made in Chapter 2. However, as long as the growth rate was high, large deficits could be sustained without much growth in the debt-to-GNP ratio. After 1974 this was no longer the case.

Turning now to the application of equation (3.4) in Table 3.2, for each subperiod we may calculate the difference between the ratio of domestic government finance (d) and the part of the growth in net financial assets (money and debt) that individuals would be willing to hold given GNP growth and the average financial asset ratio (i.e. nv). The ratio of the resulting net injection to the money base should be consistent with the underlying inflation rate.[2]

The result indicates that the shift in the underlying average inflation rate from one phase to another could be related to three important successive developments: the rise in the deficit between the two wars (1968–73), the decline in the growth rate after the 1973–4 crisis, and the probable drop in the demand for money after 1977, when the foreign-exchange linked bank deposits (PATAM) were introduced (see discussion in Section 3.3). The

---

[2] For an empirical application of this framework to the analysis of the jumps in the inflation rate see Melnick and Sokoler (1984). A similar framework was first discussed by Liviatan (1983a).

TABLE 3.2 *Government injection to money base and the rate of inflation, 1965–1990(%)*

	1965–7	1968–73	1974–7	1978–80	1981–3	1984–5: II	1985–90: III
	(1)	(2)	(3)	(4)	(5)	(6)	(7)
1. Financial asset ratio $(h + b)100$	0.5	0.6	1.0	1.1	1.3	1.2	1.0
2. Percentage money base to GNP (h)	12.5	13.4	9.8	5.2	2.7	2.1	5.2
3. GNP growth (n)	3.2	10.3	2.6	3.5	2.3	2.0	3.8
4. Domestic government finance ratio (d)	2.2	8.6	7.3	9.3	8.9	4.9	2.3
5. Of which: growth factor (lines 1 × 3)	1.6	6.2	2.6	3.9	3.0	2.4	3.8
6. Net injection (lines 4 – 5)	0.6	2.4	4.7	5.4	5.9	2.5	–1.5
7. *Net injection* money base (lines 6/2)	5.0	18.0	48.0	104.0	219.0	119.0	–28.0
8. Inflation rate	5.0	11.0	40.0	97.0	141.0	385.0	18.0
9. Hypothetical money supply (h^x) (lines 6/8)	12.5	21.9	11.8	5.6	4.2	0.7	—

Notes: This table is an extension of Bruno and Fischer (1986: table 4), which only covered the period up to 1983 (cols. 1–5). All numbers are in percentages except for line 1 which is a simple ratio.

Sources: Line 1: Yariv (1982) plus update (1965–7 figure assumed same as 1970; 1968–73 is the average for 1970–3). Line 2: BOI, *Annual Reports*. Line 3: CBS. Line 4: lines 6 and 7 in Table 3.1. Line 8: CBS.

index shows an implied money-base growth rate (219) that is higher than actual inflation (141) in 1981–3 and a reverse relationship at the time of runaway inflation 1983–5. Column 7, for the post-stabilization period, indicates (with a negative net injection ratio) that the determinants of the long-term inflation were at least consistent with an elimination of the fiscal finance source of inflation after 1985.

Line 9 in Table 3.2 gives the hypothetical numbers for the supply of real base money balances (h) that would equate lines 7 and 8, that is, these numbers are derived from the ratio $(d - vn)/\pi$. Thus, in the period 1981–3, the data are consistent with a disequilibrium in the direction of excess money supply (monetary expansion) while in 1984–1985: II they are consistent with a converse excess money demand (monetary contraction) situation.[3]

[3] Real interest-rate behaviour and the monetary policy stance are consistent with this characterization (see respective BOI, *Annual Reports* for 1983–5). Had

This particular analysis should, of course, be treated with care and, strictly speaking, is mainly a consistency check. We know that the government deficit is not necessarily exogenous to the inflation rate, due to the Olivera–Tanzi effect, nor is the choice of how deficit finance would be allocated between domestic and foreign sources. Nor do we know to what extent the drop in the growth rate after 1973 was entirely exogenous to the rate of inflation. A more complete analysis would have to take these various factors into account. But the more problematic assumption that is implicit in this analysis is that we are observing a series of approximate steady states. While this may have been correct in earlier periods, it is certainly not the case for the period 1983–85: II. Both that period and the discrepancy between inflation and the measured injection ratio in the preceding plateau (1981–3), in any case, suggests that the seigniorage model by itself cannot capture the dynamics of the inflationary process.

We now turn to a more detailed discussion of the trade-offs between the real economy and the inflationary process and then to the dynamics of inflation.

3.3 From Single- to Three-Digit Inflation: The Changing Trade-off between Real GDP, Inflation, and the Current Account[4]

In the 1950s and 1960s, during the rapid growth period, Israel was running a relatively mild inflation rate of 6–7 per cent throughout (see Table 3.3 and Fig. 3.2). Price indexation of wages (a time-honoured practice introduced by the British authorities during World War II) and of savings made this inflation a relatively costless by-product of rapid growth. In the early 1970s an overheated economy, aided by the beginnings of moderate external commodity price increases, pulled inflation rates into the two-digit range. In moving from phase 4 to phase 5 of the inflation process in Table 3.3, 1973 clearly marks a water-

we averaged over the period 1981–1985: II as a whole, the average injection ratio would be 216, which fits the average inflation rate of 202 for the same five-year period.

[4] The more analytically inclined reader may prefer to glance at the underlying model in s. 3.4 before reading the present, mainly descriptive, account in which the subsequent model is implicit.

Shocks and Accommodation

TABLE 3.3 Inflation, money, growth, and wages, 1960–1990 (annual rates, based on quarterly data)

Phase	Number of quarters	CPI[a]	Money (M1)	Liquid assets (M2)	GNP growth	Real wage in manuf.
1. Normal growth (1960: I–1965: I)	20	7 (3)	17	—	9.6	3.4
2. Recession (1965: I–1967: I)	9	8 (8)	16	—	–1.5	5.2
3. Recovery (1967: II–1970: I)	11	2 (1)	9	—	14.6	2.4
4. Boom (1970: I–1973: III)	14	14 (8)	25	36	9.1	2.2
5. War and oil shock (1973: III–1977: II)	15	36 (17)	27	29	2.6	2.9
6. Traverse (1977: II–1979: IV)	10	71 (29)	37	75	3.0	1.0
7. Plateau (1979: IV–1983: III)	15	123 (15)	97	127	1.6	7.5
8. Runaway inflation (1983: III–1985: II)	7	389 (86)	289	393	5.3	4.3[b]
9. Stabilization (1985: IV–1990: IV)	20	18 (7)	56[c] (29)	32[c] (23)	4.2	5.6[b]

[a] Numbers in parentheses are standard deviations.
[b] Observations refer to business sector.
[c] Annual averages; numbers in parentheses refer to 1987–90.

shed, signalled by world-wide commodity and oil price shocks. Likewise, before the crisis, the civilian current-account deficit of 11–14 per cent of GNP during 1965–72 had been very comfortably financed by ample public and private transfers. That, too, shot up during the oil crisis of 1973–4 to above 20 per cent of GNP,[5] a subject to which we return below.

Up to 1977 the process of inflation in Israel does not appear to have been qualitatively different from that in the OECD countries. Even after jumping to 40–50 per cent after the Yom Kippur War, inflation declined slowly to an annual rate of 25 per cent by

[5] This figure does not include the substantial increase in defence expenditure on foreign goods, after the Yom Kippur War, which was separately financed and can therefore be excluded from the present discussion. If one includes defence expenditures the jump between 1972 and 1974 was from around 20% of GDP to around 35%. In current dollar prices the current-account deficit actually quadrupled from $1 to 4 billion within two years!

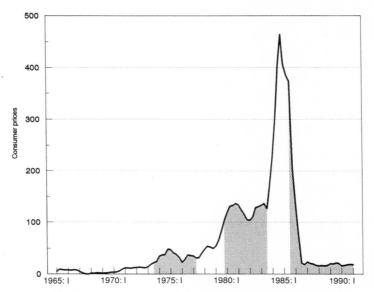

Note: Annual percentage; quarter to corresponding quarter.

FIG. 3.2 Israeli CPI inflation

the first half of 1977. However, after the financial liberalization of October 1977 the economy appeared to move into a new era, with inflation seemingly capable only of rising in step-wise fashion to new plateaux along which inflation appeared temporarily stable (note the relatively low standard deviation relative to the mean, particularly in the 'plateau' phase between 1979 and 1983).

The simultaneous developments in the real and the monetary economy and the sharp changes that took place after 1973 can be visualized by casting growth and inflation into a quasi-Phillips curve framework (Fig. 3.3*a*). As shown in Chapter 2, aggregate unemployment rates do not tell the story of real activity in the Israeli business sector because of the large increase in public sector employment. To measure relative slack we use annual deviations from 6.2 per cent, which was the mean business-sector GDP growth during 1964–81 (as a proxy for average capacity growth[6]), for the relative slack indicator on the horizontal axis.

[6] The choice of this mean rate, which is somewhat arbitrary, is based on the study for the period 1965–82 (see Bruno 1986) in which a version of Fig. 3.3*a* first

The vertical axis measures the annual rate of CPI inflation.[7] We apply a logarithmic scale for the inflation rate so as to enable the incorporation of the two-digit and three-digit inflation periods within one figure.

Fig. 3.3*a* also incorporates the comparable OECD data (see broken line) which are calibrated to the Israeli data by doubling the measure of both variables. This is based on the working assumption that Israel's 'normal' growth and inflation rates corresponded to twice the OECD averages as indeed they had been during the Golden Age up to 1973 (see Fig. 2.2).

Any analysis of the main macro-economic trade-offs in an open economy would be incomplete without a simultaneous examination of the main developments in the external account. Inflation is, at least within the low level 'garden-variety' range, a measure of the strain on internal (non-tradable) resources. Excess demand in an open economy spills over into the tradable-goods sector and, at given real exchange rates, widens the import gap. Likewise a major function of aggregate demand contraction is to reduce the demand for imports, especially in a small and highly open economy like Israel's. A convenient graphical representation of the simultaneous changes in the external accounts is to collate the first Phillips curve framework (Fig. 3.3*a*) with one in which the vertical axis is replaced by the ratio to GDP of the civilian current-account deficit (the total current-account deficit minus defence imports, which are not directly related to economic activity). This is done in Fig. 3.3*b*. We can now turn to an account of the main developments in terms of the three-way trade-off represented by the twin figures.

The period 1965–7 was a deep Keynesian recession in Israel (see phase 2 in Table 3.3): the implied Phillips curve was very flat

appeared. In a companion paper by Metzer (1986) that appeared in the same volume, the average capacity growth rate was estimated to have been 9.5% during 1960–72 and only 5.5% during 1973–82, which is somewhat less than the 6.2% rate applied here. Had we applied different capacity growth rates for the two periods the output shifts in Fig. 3.3*a* during 1965–72 would appear smaller and those after 1973 somewhat larger. There are sound reasons to believe that a systematic updating of Metzer's analysis would yield a higher rate for the period after 1985, or, at least, since 1989 (the start of large-scale immigration from the former USSR). The use of a uniform reference rate throughout the whole period has the advantage of simplicity and does not affect the qualitative results.

[7] For the years 1985–91 inflation *during* the period is used, rather than period averages.

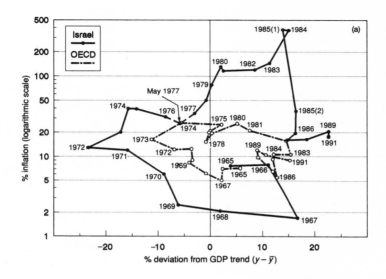

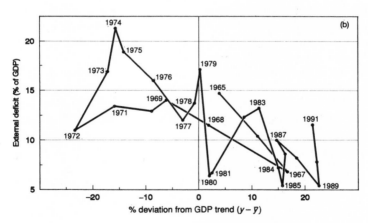

FIG 3.3*a*   Inflation and output slack, Israel and OECD, 1965–1991
FIG 3.3*b*   External deficit ratio and output slack, 1965–1991

and its slope closely resembled the one implied for OECD during
1965–9. Next came an almost horizontal line between 1967 and
1969 (phase 3)—a phenomenal output, as well as capital stock,
expansion (mean annual rate of almost 15 per cent GNP growth
during three years) with virtual price stability (2 per cent annual

inflation). There had been considerable slack in the labour market. Unemployment, discussed in Chapter 2, reached 12 per cent at the beginning of 1967, on top of which came a considerable influx of Arab labour from the post-1967 administered territories as well as renewed Jewish immigration from abroad. Likewise there had been reserves of unutilized capacity. By 1969–70 full employment was gradually being approached and, while growth continued at a rapid pace, the strain of maintaining very high rates of public expenditure (on defence, social services, and income maintenance—see Chapter 2) was beginning to tell. The movement from 1969 to 1972 in Fig. 3.3a now suggests a very much steeper Phillips curve, though still with the 'right' negative slope (cf. the curve for OECD).

Fig. 3.3b suggests analogous time phasing for the current account. During the recession (1965–7) the civilian deficit ratio fell sharply (from around 15 to 7 per cent) subsequently returning to the earlier level (13–14 per cent) by 1969–71, illustrating the short-term trade-off between growth and the current account which is dominated by the key relationship between imports—of raw materials and investment goods—and domestic demand. Also, the end of the 'euphoric' boom, 1972, was marked by a remarkable spurt in exports.

Once growth came to a halt, the subsequent period, 1973 to mid-1977 (phase 5 in Table 3.3), looks like a bloated version of the bell-shaped output–inflation trade-off of OECD (in Fig. 3.3a). The rightward slope in 1973–4 reflects the first oil- and commodity-price aggregate supply shock, which, in the case of Israel, was exacerbated by indirect tax measures and a large devaluation (in November 1974) to counter the very large increase in the current-account deficit (see the analogous shift in Fig. 3.3b).

Finance Minister Rabinovitz's 1975–7 orthodox stabilization programme, coming in the wake of the substantial devaluation in November 1974 (from 4.5 to 6 IL/$), involved a substantial cut in the government deficit (see Fig. 3.1) and a very stringent monetary policy. In terms of the commodity market (a more formal analysis appears in the next section), this implied a leftward movement of the aggregate demand schedule, which brought about a dramatic improvement in the current account and some restraint in inflation, which had already risen to 40 per cent per annum, at the cost of a substantial further slow-down in the economy (see Figs. 3.3*a* and 3.3*b*). Rabinovitz, a soft-spoken former schoolteacher, took over the job, in mid-crisis, from the fiery Pinhas Sapir, who had been a great developer of Israel's industry in the 1950s and 1960s. Rabinovitz was the last Labour Party Minister of Finance, before the May 1977 election turnaround that for the first time brought in a right-wing Likud government.

Rabinovitz also turned out to be the last successful economic reformer for many years. In his own quiet but forceful way, and with the co-operation of the Histadruth (the federation of trade unions) he passed a major inflation-proof income-tax reform that has survived all the subsequent storms. He also introduced the VAT system into the economy, reformed the COLA system, and, finally, moved the exchange-rate regime from a fixed to a crawling peg. The latter decision eventually proved fatal to the dynamics of inflation, but mainly for reasons that had to do with subsequent developments in the rest of the economy. However, by the time the Likud Party, under Menahem Begin, took over in 1977, Rabinovitz had left behind a major bad legacy of long-reigning socialist governments—a bloated public service sector and a large and persistent deficit, which was to last for another eight years, until the major 1985 reform.

The most marked feature of Fig. 3.3*a* is Israel's complete departure from the OECD pattern from 1977 onwards, for the eight-year period 1977–85. While the horizontal deviations from the GDP trend remain quite similar, it is the vertical coordinate of Fig. 3.3*a*, inflation, which 'lifted off' to a life of its own, in an almost complete dichotomy between the nominal and the real economy (we return to a more formal discussion in the next section).

Prime ministers in Israel almost never dabble in economic matters, and Begin was no exception.[8] He relied on his Minister of Finance, Simcha Ehrlich, from the Liberal Party, to come up with a liberalization package, which confined itself mainly to Israeli citizens' foreign-exchange holdings and capital inflows, did not touch the labour market, and did not get the Prime Minister's support for the absolutely essential concomitant fiscal

[8] The only exception other than Shimon Peres's role in 1985–6 was Levi Eshkol, Prime Minister during the Six Day War, who had come to the job from having been Minister of Finance.

cut.[9] The result of the October 1977 package, which involved a very large devaluation followed by a substantial real wage push, and was exacerbated by the 1979 second oil shock, was disastrous. An independent attempt by the Bank of Israel to use restrictive credit policy, in order to stabilize the growing balance-of-payments deficit and control inflation, failed as imports of financial capital replaced domestic credit as a source of finance. The capital inflow problem was tackled only in 1979, when capital imports were first prohibited and, when later permitted again, became subject to heavy taxation. The foreign-exchange market was to be liberalized again, in a radically different environment, only ten years later.

The parallel developments shown in Fig. 3.3*b* point to cycles of deterioration and improvements in the trade balance under a succession of Ministers of Finance. A deterioration under Ehrlich's failed liberalization (1977–9) was followed by a temporary improvement under the next Minister of Finance, Yigael Horowitz (1979–80), who was determined to reduce the inflation rate and the current-account deficit in the orthodox way, by cutting government demand and pursuing restrictive monetary policy. The budget cut took the form of a sharp slash in subsidies, which caused an immediate jump in inflation. Credit continued to be extended freely to exports, inevitably leaking to the domestic economy. Political support for the maintenance of a contractionary policy, which could eventually have paid off, was weakening in light of the approaching elections and Horowitz was forced to resign at the end of 1980.

Horowitz was replaced as Minister of Finance by Yoram Aridor, who implemented a pre-election, populist, cost-reducing anti-inflation policy in 1981. Subsidies were increased, import tariffs were slashed, and the exchange rate was allowed to appreciate in real terms. While imports of consumer goods rose substantially and the election results paid off again for the Likud Party, there was a temporary fall in inflation (see Figs. 3.2 and 3.3*a*), which may have been a delayed effect of the earlier Horowitz contraction. However, the budget deficit again

[9] Because of President Sadat's unexpected historical visit and the need to attain a cabinet consensus over withdrawal from the Sinai Peninsula, Begin was reluctant to enter a fight over the budget. Ehrlich threatened to resign but later capitulated.

increased sharply and monetary policy continued to accommodate. There was a worsening of the current-account deficit and a concomitant drop in the growth rate in 1982, some of which no doubt had to do with the war in Lebanon.

Aridor ended his career in a major blow-up. A gradualist attempt to move the economy from a monthly inflation rate of 7 per cent to 5 per cent by keeping exchange rates and controlled prices to this monthly rate could not be sustained, given the underlying fiscal, monetary, and wage excesses. A 2 per cent difference between the ongoing inflation rate and the reduced rate of devaluation very quickly built up into a substantial real exchange-rate appreciation and real wages continued to increase. The long-delayed maxi-devaluation took place in October 1983, at the same time as a major bank-share crisis erupted, and Aridor had to resign when the details of a new Dollarization Plan[10] were leaked to the press. From then on the dams burst wide open to a further tripling of the inflation rate. There was an improvement in the current account during the brief spell of the next Minister of Finance, Cohen-Orgad, but a further worsening in the trade-off in terms of growth and inflation. The July 1984 election was now approaching. With expansionary monetary and fiscal policy, and the evident expectation of a post-election correction of the exchange rate, and with widespread uncertainty about election results and post-election policies, inflation remained in the 300–400 per cent annual range. The new national unity coalition government, with both Likud and Labour now sharing power, started the last leap into high inflation (which reached 500 per cent in the first half of 1985). The discussion of that episode is deferred to the next chapter.

Several general features emerge from this description of events. One is the apparent link between the cycle in the trade balance and jumps in the inflation rate, studied by Liviatan and Piterman (1986). The acceleration in inflation that appears to be linked with an improvement in the external balance is closely tied up with the type of corrective budgetary measures adopted (subsidy cuts and indirect tax hikes) as well as with exchange-rate devaluations, both of which constitute price-level shocks which, under

---

[10] Both events are discussed in Ch. 4.

certain conditions (to be described below), lead to jumps in the inflation rate itself.

A similar connection between the dual (government and trade) deficits and the rate of inflation has been found in other countries during that period. For example, in 1982–4 the operational budget deficit in Brazil fell from 8 to 3 per cent of GDP while annual inflation jumped from 93 to 211 per cent. Likewise in Mexico during 1981–4 the deficit fell from 10 to 2 per cent of GDP while inflation edged up from 27 to 62 per cent (it later went up further to 200 per cent; see Chapter 6). The reasons, as in the Israeli case, were the price-level increasing policy instruments, coupled with monetary accommodation and inflationary inertia.

Analysis of the inflationary process in Israel also indicates that there were a number of important landmarks in the process by which the economy lost its 'nominal anchor'. One was in June 1975, when a crawling peg was introduced (involving an almost automatic monthly adjustment of up to 2 per cent in the exchange rate) with the idea of avoiding the political and economic convulsions that inevitably precede and follow large discrete shifts in the exchange rate.[11] As shown by subsequent analysis (see Gottlieb, Melnick, and Piterman 1985), this marked a discrete shift in the inflation expectations-formation mechanism. The second turning-point came after October 1977, when new foreign-exchange denominated liquid bank accounts (called PATAM, a Hebrew acronym) were introduced by Ehrlich as part of the foreign-exchange quasi-liberalization package. This, plus the short-lived opening up of the economy to short-term capital inflow, on top of a discrete devaluation lacking the support of appropriate budgetary restrictions, proved fatal, as did similar experiments conducted in Latin America around the same time.

These two events help explain how the genie was let out of the bottle. The climax came after the failure of the attempt by Minister Aridor to 'manage' a reduction in the inflation rate by announcing a stable 5 per cent rate monthly devaluation, *tablita* style, in the vain hope that prices would follow suit (the Latin American examples from which the term *tablita* originates are

[11] The early lessons and the arguments for and against the choice of the crawling peg from the point of view of the current account and the inflationary process appear in Bruno and Sussman (1979).

discussed in Chapter 6). We now proceed to give a more formal account of inflationary dynamics, starting from an underlying aggregate demand and aggregate supply framework.

3.4 Aggregate Supply and Demand, and the Analytics of Nominal Anchors

Let us now consider more formally a conventional macro-economic model for an open economy with competing exports and intermediate imports. The balance between aggregate demand (AD) and aggregate supply (AS) of goods and services can be written in the following way:[12]

$$Y^s(W/P, P^*_nE/P; z_s) = Y^d(M/P, EP^*/P; z_d) \qquad (3.5)$$

where P = price level; W = nominal wages; E = exchange rate; M = money, P = exogenous imported input prices; P^* = exogenous price of competing exports; z_s = supply shifts (capital stock, productivity, wages, taxes, etc.); z_d = demand shifts (fiscal policy, world demand and interest rates, etc.).

The equilibrium in the commodity market is shown in Fig. 3.4 as the intersection (A) of the upward-sloping aggregate supply (AS) and downward-sloping aggregate demand (AD) schedules, where the horizontal axis measures GDP (Y) and the vertical axis measures the relative domestic to world price levels (P/EP^*, which is the reciprocal of the real exchange rate EP^*/P). An increase in the real wage (W/P) or in the relative world price of inputs (P^*_n/P^*)[13] shifts AS up and to the left. The equilibrium price then moves from A to B. A real appreciation and a fall in output takes place. A contraction in real money supply or a fiscal

---

[12] Formally, the supply schedule $Y^s(\ )$ is obtained from a three-factor production function, equating marginal products of material inputs and of labour to their respective real market prices (see Bruno and Sachs 1985). The demand schedule $Y^d(\ )$ is obtained from a conventional open-economy IS–LM model, reflecting the combination of a money market equation with a Keynesian aggregate commodity demand schedule for consumption, exports, and investments (with substitution for the interest rate).

[13] The relative price P^*_nE/P within the brackets of Y^s in equation (3.4) can be written as a product of the real exchange rate (EP^*/P) and the relative world price (P^*_n/P^*).

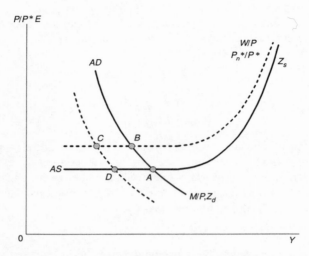

FIG 3.4   Aggregate demand and aggregate supply in the commodities market

cut shifts *AD* down and to the left. Equilibrium will in that case shift from *A* to *D*, and output will fall.[14]

The commodity market will determine the *relative* price $P/(EP^*)$ for given real wage (W/P) and real money supply (M/P). To determine all three real magnitudes we need two additional markets or constraints, the labour market and the current account of the balance of payments. Excess supply (unemployment) in the labour market would be negatively related to real income (Y), and positively related to the real wage (W/P). Excess flow demand for foreign exchange (namely, the current-account deficit) would be positively related to real income (Y) and negatively related to the real exchange rate $(EP^*/P$, or positively related to its reciprocal, $P/EP^*)$. For any given level of excess demand (supply) in the three markets, unique levels will be determined for the three relative prices, which, under conventional assumptions, would also be stable. We confine ourselves here to an explicit discussion of inflation, as it can be derived from the commodity market, assuming, for the sake of simplicity, that the

[14] Whether a real depreciation also takes place depends on the slope of the *AS* curve (along the relatively flat part of *AS*, P/EP^* will not change); see further discussion below.

real wage and real exchange rates are given. We thus leave the labour market and the current account in the background and do not spell them out explicitly here.[15]

The three constraints will, in any case, determine equilibrium levels only for the three relative prices. As in a standard neo-classical framework, this still leaves one degree of freedom for the determination of all four nominal variables (W, E, M, P). Fixing any one of the nominal variables then determines all the rest. This is the essence of the anchoring of a stable price level (P) by either money (M), or the exchange rate (E), or nominal wages (W).[16]

A sustained high-inflation process will usually be marked by all four nominal variables moving more or less together. Otherwise, one or two of the relative magnitudes, that is, real variables, will change and further disequilibrate the quasi-stable real system, as in Fig. 3.4. The case in which all nominal variables move together, leaving the real system (namely, real excess demand or supply functions) invariant, corresponds to what in Monetary Theory is referred to as the '*valid* neo-classical dichotomy'.[17]

It is easiest to consider the relationship between the rates of change of the four nominal variables by log-differentiating equation (3.5) and looking at the logarithmic time derivatives under the simplifying assumption that the goods market balance (3.5) always holds.[18] We get the following linearized equation:

[15] For application of a more complete model to the real developments in the OECD countries in the 1970s and early 1980s see Bruno and Sachs (1985). For an explicit application to the analysis of the real developments in the Israeli economy during the same period see Bruno (1986).

[16] Strictly speaking, the price index itself could play the role of an 'anchor', as in the case of a tight price- (and wage-) controlled Soviet-type economy, in which case inflation would be repressed. For a more detailed spelling-out of the role of alternative nominal anchors within a neo-classical model of the open economy see Bruno (1991).

[17] Patinkin made the conceptual distinction between the 'invalid' and 'valid' classical dichotomies: 'it is fatal to succumb to the temptation to say that relative prices are determined in the commodity markets and absolute prices in the money market. This does not mean that value theory cannot be distinguished from monetary theory. Obviously, there is a distinction, but it is based on a dichotomisation of *effects*, not on a dichotomisation of *markets*' (Patinkin 1965: 181).

[18] Low inflation is usually pictured as a price-*level* adjustment to excess demand in the commodity market. A persistent inflationary process of the kind that is considered here may very well continue even while the commodity market is in continuous balance and does not necessarily require the existence of an excess demand gap $(Y^d > Y^s)$ in the goods market.

$$\pi = a_1\omega + a_2\epsilon + a_3\mu + v, \tag{3.6}$$

where $\pi = \dot{P}/P$ —rate of inflation—and a dot represents a discrete $(P_t - P_{t-1})$ or instantaneous (dP/dt) time change; $\omega = \dot{W}/W$ —wage inflation; $\epsilon = \dot{E}/E$ —rate of devaluation; $\mu = \dot{M}/M$ —rate of monetary expansion; v —supply and demand shocks.

The a_i coefficients, which need not be constant (but empirically seem to be fairly stable—see below), are derived from the various elasticities of Y^d and Y^s with respect to the variables in the brackets, and their sum adds up to one $(a_1 + a_2 + a_3 = 1)$ by the homogeneity of the underlying supply and demand framework.

Equation (3.6) may be rewritten in the form of an *inflation acceleration equation*

$$\pi - \pi_{-1} = a_1(\omega - \pi_{-1}) + a_2(\epsilon - \pi_{-1}) + a_3(\mu - \pi_{-1}) + v \tag{3.7}$$

π_{-1} is the one-period lagged inflation rate $[(P_{t-1} - P_{t-2})/P_{t-1}]$.

Equation (3.7) can be looked upon as the constraint that binds the rates of change of the *relative* prices, appearing in Fig. 3.4, for any given inflation rate. Another direct application of (3.7) relates to the case (discussed in greater detail in Section 3.6) in which one or more of the nominal variables is fully indexed (or accommodating) to past inflation. For example, if wages and money are fully indexed, the first and third terms in equation (3.7) disappear and inflation acceleration necessarily follows from real exchange depreciation with elasticity a_2.

During the period being discussed, expansionary fiscal policy and accommodating monetary policy (making liquid assets, $M2$, rise automatically with P, the price level—see Table 3.3) as well as wage behaviour have generally combined to maintain upward pressure on the price level and the rate of inflation; as a result of the structure of the financial system and the policy choices made, the automatic forces that could have stabilized inflation in response to supply shocks were generally weak. Temporary contractionary policies were undertaken (as in 1975–7 and in 1980), but these were usually accompanied by cost-increasing measures (devaluation, indirect taxes, and a cut in subsidies) that pushed up the price level while the flatness of the AS curve implied that contraction showed up in output, and in the derived demand for imports (thus temporarily shrinking the current-account deficit) rather than in prices. A short-run account of inflationary dynamics will then be dominated by the price-level shocks and the degree of accommodation to them. We now turn to an empirical estimate of equations (3.7) and (3.6).

3.5 Time-Invariance of the Basic Inflation Equation

The cost-side dynamics of inflation have featured in several accounts of the inflationary process in the 1960s and early 1970s, the best known being Artstein and Sussman's (1977) pair of annual wage and consumer-price equations for the period 1958–75. Prices were expressed as a function of wages and import prices plus a small, hardly significant, role for money; wages were made a function of prices, unemployment, and the increased labour supply from the territories (which was an important wage-moderating factor in 1968–72).[19]

With the high degree of correlation between the nominal magnitudes (prices, wages, exchange rates, and money), price and wage equations of the above kind are difficult to interpret statistically, especially during the period 1975–85. Moreover, as inflation accelerated, the inflation–unemployment trade-off gradually disappeared. The problem, however, is not only that of the multi-collinearity of all nominal variables. A related issue arises from the fact that the inflation rates do not represent stationary processes (while their first differences *are* stationary). Inflation equations cannot be estimated in simple level form unless the relevant unit-root condition (namely co-integration) holds. While it turns out that this condition does, in fact, hold in the Israeli case (see below), the problem can also be sidestepped by running the price equation in real terms, namely, in the form of first differences with respect to past inflation as in equation (3.7).[20]

The first equation (1a) in Table 3.4 gives the estimates derived from running the basic form of equation (3.7) for acceleration in consumer prices over the period starting in the third quarter of

[19] A similar wage-moderating role was played in the past by large-scale immigration, as is the case again with the Russian immigration in the early 1990s.
[20] This regression equation first appeared in Bruno and Fischer (1986) and has been updated here. When it was first estimated (in 1983) the econometric literature on co-integration had not yet developed. For a co-integration alternative (or complementary) approach, see below.

TABLE 3.4 *Price acceleration equation (3.7) (quarterly data, consumer prices)*

No. of observations	Estimates of coefficients[a]						Statistics	
	DRW	DRE	DRM_2	$DRPK$	DPN	DPX	$\bar{R}^2$	DW
1. 1964: III–1985: II								
1a 84	0.29(0.08)	0.53(0.05)	0.07(0.06)	—	—	—	0.64	2.33
1b 84	0.15(0.07)	0.73(0.05)	0.10(0.05)	—	0.28(0.12)	0.51(0.11)	0.77	2.50
1c 84	0.16(0.05)	0.37(0.06)	0.07(0.04)	0.43(0.05)	−0.01(0.09)	0.36(0.08)	0.89	2.36
1d[b] 64	0.14(0.06)	0.39(0.06)	0.08(0.04)	0.42(0.05)	—	0.42(0.05)	0.89	2.34
1e[c] 64	0.23(0.24)	0.62(0.20)	0.06(0.17)	0.33(0.18)	—	0.87(0.30)	0.81	2.20
2. 1985: III–1991: II								
2a 24	0.23(0.07)	0.63(0.08)	0.02(0.06)	—	—	—	0.89	2.31
2b 24	0.19(0.08)	0.65(0.08)	0.02(0.06)	—	0.20(0.20)	0.20(0.23)	0.89	2.50
2c 24	0.20(0.05)	0.18(0.11)	−0.04(0.04)	0.45(0.09)	0.17(0.13)	0.15(0.15)	0.95	2.18

[a] The first four (DR) are the rates of change, minus lagged inflation, of nominal wages (W), the exchange rate (E), liquid assets (M_2) and controlled prices (PK); DPN and DPX are the rates of change of import and export prices, respectively. Figures in brackets are standard errors.

[b] Equations (1d) and (1e) relate to the period 1969: III–1985: II to enable use of instrumental variables in (1e) and comparable ordinary least squares in (1d).

[c] Equation (1e) is a two-stage least-squares version of (1d) using lagged variables as well as lagged growth rates as instruments.

1964 and ending in the second quarter of 1985, just before the July 1985 stabilization programme. In version (1*b*) we separately add the rates of change of dollar prices of imports and exports, although the effect of foreign prices, relative to the size of the Israeli inflation, was quantitatively small, except for the years of the oil shocks (1973 and 1979). Equation (1*c*) is an alternative regression in which the change in controlled (or subsidized) goods' prices, net of lagged domestic inflation, is incorporated and it comes out highly significant. However, since many of the controlled goods originate from imports or else their price change is highly correlated with exchange-rate and import-price changes, the coefficients of the latter are in such case substantially reduced (that of import prices disappears). There is an insignificant zero intercept in all regressions which is not displayed in the table. The sum of the relevant first three (or four, in the case in which *DRPK* appears) coefficients in the various equations is not significantly different from unity.

These regressions suggest that, for the period as a whole, inflation (or rather, its acceleration in terms of consumer prices) can mainly be accounted for by looking at the role of the three main factors: increases in wages over past inflation, increases in the exchange rate over past inflation, and price shocks coming from either foreign prices or changes in price controls (or subsidies). There is also a small separate role for money, whose coefficient, however, is often insignificant. We note that a dominant role is played by the exchange rate. The fact that the wage coefficient falls when *DPX* (change in the dollar price of competing tradables) is included may have to do with the fact that in that case the separate role of wages is confined to the part embodied in non-tradables.[21] Regression (1*e*), based on a somewhat shorter period (starting in 1969: III), uses two-stage least squares (applying the lagged endogenous variables and lagged GDP growth rates as instruments).[22] This may point to a higher wage and exchange-rate coefficient and a smaller effect of

---

[21] When running similar regressions, not shown here, based on manufacturing wholesale prices the coefficient for wages comes out between 0.35 and 0.4, and that of the exchange rate between 0.55 and 0.6, with money insignificantly different from zero.

[22] Regression (1*d*) is the same as (1*c*), except that it is run on the shorter sample period, to enable comparison with (1*e*).

controlled prices, but levels of statistical significance are too low to allow a more definite statement.

To examine whether lumping the twenty-one-year period into one equation may be an error, we ran the same equations (not reproduced here) over two major subperiods: the eleven years of low inflation and (rarely adjusted) fixed peg, 1964: III to 1975: III, preceding the introduction of the monthly crawling peg, and the subsequent ten years of high inflation (1975: IV to 1985: II). In spite of the fact that the inflation profile during these subperiods varied dramatically, essentially similar coefficients for wages and the exchange rate apply within each one of the models over the two subperiods. But what is probably the most interesting finding is that very similar coefficients for wages and the exchange rate within each one of the models also continue to apply for the much more tranquil period after stabilization, which is displayed in the lower part of Table 3.4 (compare models (2a)–(2c) with (1a)–(1c).[23]

While we find the time-invariance and the estimates of the above inflation acceleration equations to be of interest in themselves, an alternative, more modern approach to the estimation of time-series of non-stationary variables suggests conditions under which one can estimate equation (3.6) directly, in inflation-*level* form, using ordinary least squares, without having to go through first differences as in equation (3.7).

Consider the time-series for price inflation (π), for nominal wages (ω), for the exchange rate (ϵ), and for the domestic prices of imports (π_n) and exportables (π_x). Upon inspection all of these variables turn out to be unit-root processes (namely their first difference is stationary). Applying the so-called Augmented Dickey–Fuller Test,[24] they are co-integrated, namely an ordinary least-squares regression yields unbiased estimates of coefficients and an error term which is stationary (and whose variance goes

[23] What this implies is that the coefficients of the equation for 1964–85 could be used for a forecast of a post-reform inflation. In fact, a monthly version of this equation was used for the design of the stabilization programme in 1985 (see Ch. 4). Only in model (2c) does the rate of exchange appear to fall, relative to (1c), but, given the large standard error of the coefficient and the smaller number of degrees of freedom of this regression, this may not mean much.

[24] For the relevant econometric theory, see Engle and Granger (1987) and Granger (1986). I am indebted to Rafi Melnick, Deputy Director of the Research Department, Bank of Israel, for introducing me to the application of co-integration tests.

to zero as the sample size increases to infinity). Based now on the whole sample period 1964: III to 1991: II (108 observations), two such alternative equations are:[25]

$$\pi = 0.31\omega + 0.56\epsilon + 0.09\mu + \nu \qquad (3.6a)$$

$$\pi = 0.18\omega + 0.24\pi_n + 0.46\pi_x + 0.11\mu + \nu. \qquad (3.6b)$$

It is no accident that the size of the coefficients is practically the same as the respective coefficients in regressions (1a) and (1b) in Table 3.4 (or to the analogous equations, not shown here, when run over the combined sample period up to 1991). While these equations do not convey new information on the estimates obtained, the implication of co-integration is interesting, because it confirms the relevance of equation (3.6) (and (3.6a) or its alternative extension in (3.6b)) as describing a long-run relatively stable inflation equation which seems to apply across very different inflation regimes in which the various nominal variables tended to move together. While this time-invariance applies to the underlying relationship between the contemporaneous nominal rates of change, this is definitely not the case for the adjustment rules which characterized the constituent nominal variables. It is the changing nature of these rules which gave the overall dynamic process its shocks and accommodation profile, to which we now turn.

3.6 Backward Indexation and Changing Inflation Dynamics

We may now go one step further with the framework underlying equation (3.6) and consider the fact that nominal wages could, in turn, be related to lagged inflation and, similarly, that the exchange rate during the high inflation period, at least, was following a crawling peg in an approximate PPP rule, with occasional step jumps.

An interesting property of the wage-indexation system relates to workers' demands to raise the degree of indexation as the inflation rate increases, and at the same time to reduce the length

---

[25] The DF statistic for the first equation is 6.99 (while the Mackinnon critical value at 1% level is 4.81) and for the second equation it is 6.69 (critical value 5.17). The test applied to a regression of the error term on an intercept and two quarterly lags.

of lag in the formal part of indexation, as a means of avoiding real wage erosion as inflation accelerates. Suppose wage adjustment takes the form:

$$\omega = \alpha\pi_{-1} + (1 - \alpha)\pi^e + \nu_\omega, \qquad (3.8)$$

π^e is the expectation of inflation as reflected in the wage contract, which also incorporates a partial cost-of-living adjustment, and ν_ω are additional wage shocks. Accelerating inflation will tend to motivate an increase in α, which will enhance the inertia of the inflationary process, namely, the dependence of inflation on its past lagged values. However, shortening the lag (embodied in the length of time-period between which π_{-1} and π are measured) actually reduces inertia. Monthly, weekly, and ultimately daily indexation would reduce inertia. It also destroys the quasi-stability of the process and enhances the shift from moderate to high inflation and finally to hyperinflation. At the same time, reduced inertia also makes it easier to reduce inflation quickly, once there is a will to do so, with less real disruption.

The Israeli high inflation experience never reached the stage of less than monthly adjustment (although it came close in 1985), but the evolution of formal indexation arrangements in the course of accelerating inflation does point to a sequence of adjustments both in the coefficient of formal indexation and in the length of adjustment allowed. Starting from a semi-annual adjustment of 70 per cent indexation of prices, adopted after the 1975 reform,[26] the coefficient was changed to 80 per cent in 1979 and to 85–90 per cent in the following four years, contingent on *ex post* inflation rates. During the same period the adjustment lag and the basis for the indexation was gradually moved from six to three months, and finally to one month's lag. As Kleiman (1986) has shown, indexation never caught up with accelerating inflation in spite of these changes. As a result, other endogenous wage indexation methods were introduced into the regular wage agreements. The implication, as one can see from Table 3.3, was none the less a consistent increase in real wages over the high inflation

---

[26] The 70% formula was adopted on the basis of a recommendation of a committee headed by Z. Sussman, in agreement with the Histadruth. This formula was adopted in lieu of a more direct way of estimating the role of external import-price shocks and purging them from the indexation formula.

period, showing that there must have been independent shocks (or attempted over-compensation) on the wage side. [27]

Elsewhere (Bruno 1989) I have estimated the elasticity of nominal wages with respect to inflation lagged one quarter and found a systematic upward shift from around 0.44 in the early 1970s to 0.6 in the second half of the 1970s and 0.8–0.9 in the early 1980s. Likewise, the nominal exchange rate during 1975–85 was indexed to lagged inflation through a crawling-peg rule:

$$\epsilon_t = \beta\pi_{t-1} + (1 - \beta)\epsilon_{t-1} + J_t + \nu_\epsilon. \qquad (3.9)$$

Here J_t stands for discrete devaluations (such as in 1974, 1977, and 1983) and ν_e are additional shocks (e.g. world prices). The β coefficients have likewise been shown (Bruno 1989) to follow an increasing pattern with the quarterly elasticity (β) increasing from very low levels (0.1) to 0.3–0.4 during the 'plateau' (1979–83) and rising to 0.8–0.9 afterwards.[28]

In the Appendix to this chapter we show formally how the assumptions already made on the indexation of all nominal magnitudes, along with adaptive expectations and/or a crawling-peg rule, can lead to an expression in which inflation acceleration in period t can, through a recursive process, be made a function of past inflation acceleration terms with weights that are geometrically declining as we move backwards into the past.

Consider a truncated three-period version of the process under the assumption that $\pi_t = a\omega_t + (1 - a)\epsilon_t$. We look at two cases: in the first we assume lagged wage indexation but take π^e in equation (3.8) and ϵ_{t-1} in (3.9) to be constants. By substitution, the price adjustment equation then takes the form:

$$\pi_t = \gamma\pi_{t-1} + \nu \qquad (3.10a)$$

---

[27] A wage-adjustment equation for the high-inflation period was estimated by David Elkayam (1985) of the Bank of Israel. The only way in which the wage increase can be made consistent with adjustment to inflation is by assuming *ex ante* forward indexation to expectations of accelerated inflation.

[28] My (1991) paper shows (using a suggestion by N. Liviatan) how the crawling-peg rule (3.9) can be obtained from local optimization by a (weak) government. The implied objective is to minimize the weighted squared deviation from a stable (high) inflation rate and from a given *real* exchange rate (to defend the current account). β measures the trade-off between the two objectives. The relative cost (β) of deviations from the real exchange-rate objective compared to absolute inflation deviations from a reference rate can be assumed to increase as this reference rate of inflation rises.

where $\gamma = a\alpha + (1 - a)\beta < 1$ and $\nu =$ catch-all shock variable. In the second case we assume $\pi^e = \epsilon_{t-1} = \pi_{t-2}$. In that case we obtain:

$$\pi_t = \gamma\pi_{t-1} + (1 - \gamma)\pi_{t-2} + \nu \qquad (3.10b)$$

or:

$$\pi_t - \pi_{t-1} = -(1 - \gamma)(\pi_{t-1} - \pi_{t-2}) + \nu.$$

Considering the orders of magnitude for a (= 0.4), for α (0.4–0.8), and for β (0.1–0.9), the size implied for γ must have increased from 0.2 to 0.9 in the course of the decade 1975–85 (see further empirical check below). Equations (3.10a) and (3.10b), however, are fundamentally different processes. In the first the price level is non-stationary but the inflation rate is a stationary process. Any one-time shock (ν) from an initial steady state inflation will cause a price-level increase and a momentary increase in the rate of inflation, which will then decay until it gets back to the initial steady state.

Equation (3.10b), on the other hand, represents a non-stationary (unit-root) inflationary process. Starting with a one-time shock ν from a steady state, the price level and the inflation rate will shift up, and will then recede with decreasing amplitude to a new and higher steady state. It can be shown, by applying the inflation-acceleration representation of equation (3.10b), that the new steady state inflation will be higher than the previous one by a shift of $\nu/(2 - \gamma)$.[29] For $\gamma \sim 0$ the eventual shift is $\nu/2$, while for $\gamma \sim 1$ the shift in the inflation rate is immediate—it is the full impact of the initial one-time price level shock ν.

Fig. 3.5 represents a simulation of the impulse effect for case I: $\nu = 5$ per cent, $\gamma = 0.25$, and we add $0.5\pi_{-2}$ to (3.10a) so that stationarity still holds (initial steady state inflation is 5 per cent per quarter). Cases II–V correspond to the non-stationary case (3.10b) with γ successively increasing from 0.25 to 0.5, 0.75, and 1.00 and leading to a higher permanent inflation plateau.

The stylized picture that emerges is one that roughly corre-

---

[29] Equation (3.10b) can be written in the form of a change in inflation ($\Delta\pi$):

$$\Delta\pi_t = -(1 - \gamma)\Delta\pi_{t-1} + v.$$

This gives an infinite convergent geometric series of alternating positive and negative terms whose sum is $\nu/(2 - \gamma)$.

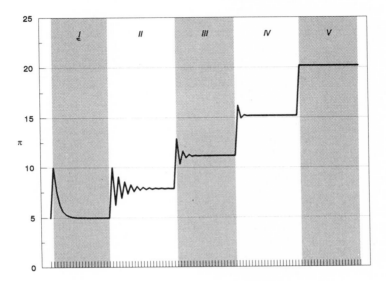

Fɪɢ. 3.5   Shocks and accommodation under alternative regimes

sponds in case ɪ to the effect of a price shock on a typical industrial country (inflationary inertia but a stationary process), while the other cases come closer to being stylized simulations of the shocks-plus-accommodation inflationary profile of Israel (or any other high-inflation country) during the 1970s and 1980s. The shocks came from oil-price increases, cuts in subsidies, and step adjustments in the exchange rate, while the increasing degree of indexation of wages and the exchange rate plus monetary accommodation explain the non-stationary nature of the process underlying equation (A3.6) in the Appendix to this chapter.

In Tables 3.5a and 3.5b we report the estimates obtained from a regression of inflation acceleration on its own lags as well as the acceleration in the exchange rate and of controlled prices[30]

---

[30] In the monthly regressions the acceleration of controlled prices was included only for the period after 1976. Their coefficients are not included in the tables. A corresponding money aggregate (M3) acceleration variable with low (but significant) elasticity was included in the monthly regressions for the period after 1985. Money never appeared significant in earlier periods. On the other hand the exchange-rate acceleration turned insignificant after 1985, probable evidence of the change in the monetary and exchange-rate regime (see Ch. 5).

TABLE 3.5a *Elasticity of inflation with respect to its own lags,[a] quarterly data, 1965–1991*

Subperiod	No. of observations	Average rate of inflation (π)	Elasticity w.r.t. lagged			$\bar{R}^2$
			One quarter $(1 + \gamma_1)$	Two quarters $(1 + \gamma_2)$	One year $(1 + \gamma_4)$	
1965: II–1971: I	24	5	0.27	0.54	1.00	0.59
1971: II–1975:II	17	26	0.67	0.57	1.00	0.91
1975: III–1985: II	40	122	0.88	1.20	1.00	0.85
of which:						
1979: I–1985: II	26	172	0.93	1.27	1.00	0.87
1986: IV–1991: II	19	18	0.02	−0.04	−0.02	0.72

[a] The regression was run separately for each subperiod, in the form:

$$\pi - \pi_{-1} = \sum_{t=1}^{3} \gamma_t (\pi_{-t} - \pi_{-t-1}) + \nu_t,$$

where ν included the acceleration of the exchange rate and of controlled prices. It was tested for homogeneity by adding $\gamma_4 \pi_{-4}$ and finding a zero coefficient for γ_4 (except for the last regression). The resulting equation can also be written in the form:

$$\pi = \sum_{t=1}^{3} (\gamma_t - \gamma_{t-1})\pi_{-t} - \gamma_3\pi_{-4} + \nu_t, \quad \text{where } \gamma_0 = -1.$$

Thus the elasticity for the first quarter is $(1 + \gamma_1)$, the sum for the first two quarters is $(1 + \gamma_2)$, etc.

TABLE 3.5b *Elasticity of inflation with respect to its own lags:[a] Estimates from monthly regressions, 1971–1991*

Subperiod	No. of observations	Average annual rate of inflation (π)	Elasticity w.r.t. lagged inflation				$\bar{R}^2$
			1 month	3 months	6 months	1 year	
Feb. 1971–Sept. 1973	32	15	0.10	0.43	0.57	1.00	0.65
Oct. 1973–Oct. 1977	49	38	0.69	0.66	0.60	1.00	0.53
Dec. 1976–Dec. 1979	27	60	0.65	0.72	0.92	1.00	0.74
Jan. 1980–June 1985	66	165	0.78	0.80	0.91	1.00	0.72
of which:							
Nov. 1983–June 1985	20	287	0.93	0.79	1.20	1.49	0.66
Aug. 1986–Sept. 1991	62	18	0.42	0.21	−0.05	−0.06	0.65

[a] Estimated from inflation-acceleration equations by the same method as in Table 3.5a, except that the regressions were run with eleven lagged terms, testing for $\gamma_{12} = 0$.

over a year of quarterly or monthly data respectively. In all cases we tested for the inclusion of a time trend and found it insignificant; homogeneity was also tested for by separately adding the first lagged inflation term beyond the year (i.e. four-quarter lag or twelve months' lag, respectively). For all phases, except for the post-1985 stabilization phase, we find homogeneity of at least degree one to apply for that length of period.

Table 3.5*a* provides the implied coefficients of inflation on its own lags in the preceding one and two quarters (of the four quarters included in the quarterly regression). We note the monotonic increase in the coefficient of the first quarter and likewise for the sum of the two quarters as inflation edged upward and up to the height of the crisis. This is strong evidence of the homogeneous autoregressive nature of the inflationary process, as we described it, and at the same time it indicates the shortening of the lag in the implicit indexation of all nominal magnitudes. It is also notable that once the economy settles back at a post-stabilization, low-inflation rate, the coefficients revert back to a very low level, even lower than in the mid-1960s, and homogeneity no longer applies.

The analogous elasticities estimated from monthly (instead of quarterly) regressions applied to the period after 1971 are summarized in Table 3.5*b*. While the subperiods used here differ slightly from those in the quarterly regressions, the results are basically the same. Here we have additional information about the first month's lag. There is evidence that in the last spurt of high inflation (after the October 1983 crisis) the adjustment lag shortened dramatically; the first month has a coefficient of about unity, and for six (let alone twelve) months we find a cumulative elasticity of more than one.

In the period after stabilization the coefficients fall to very low levels and linear homogeneity no longer holds. This would seem to show that there was a sharp reduction in inertia after stabilization. It also begs the question, to be raised later, why a moderate inflation persisted after 1985. The difference in findings between Tables 3.5 and the earlier price regressions as to the shift in behaviour after 1985 suggests that while prices continued to be as closely related to wage and exchange rates after 1985 as they were before, the strong backward linkage of nominal wages and of the exchange rate to lagged inflation weakened substantially after 1985. The implications of that for the inflationary process and for the regained inflation real-activity trade-off will be taken up again in Chapter 5.

Finally, we reconfirm a finding in the earlier study by Bruno and Fischer (1986), that during the high-inflation period (at least until mid-1984) there was an asymmetric response to upward and downward inflationary shocks coming from the exchange rate and the changes in subsidies on controlled goods. Positive shocks got significantly positive coefficients (around 0.3), while negative shocks had a zero coefficient.[31] When the general economic climate is expansionary and the government is running a large and persistent deficit that shows no evidence of declining, cost reduction will be perceived as only temporary. That adds to the explanation of the general upward thrust of the inflationary shocks during the crisis period.

3.7 Concluding Note

At the end of Chapter 2 we noted the self-reinforcing elements of the crisis in the real economy. The discussion of the nature of the inflationary process that developed in the course of the period 1977–85 adds a complementary dimension to the deepening of the crisis from the 'nominal' side of the economy. The increased budget deficit and its dependence on inflationary finance as well as the price shocks and the tightening linkages between the components of the price system were shown to lead to the step-wise acceleration of inflation into the three-digit range, just short of reaching explosive hyperinflation proportions by the first half of 1985. Central to this process were the policy responses to the twin deficits in the form of government-controlled price adjustments, primarily of the exchange rate.

On the analytical side, certain elements were left out of the present discussion. One aspect is the need to make for a tighter integration of inflation dynamics with the elements that make the long-run inflation rate determinate (based on the components of deficit finance discussed in Section 3.2). Otherwise, the shocks-

---

[31] A similar finding was recorded in an earlier paper by Bruno and Sussman (1979).

and-accommodation process analysed in the latter sections could be misinterpreted as leading to ever-rising inflation plateaux (like a one-way random walk process), as long as the seemingly exogenous shocks continue. Elsewhere (Bruno 1989) we have considered the incorporation of price and exchange rate dynamics into a seigniorage-based model in which the money demand and supply schedules are explicitly spelled out. The theory and the empirics raise the possibility of the existence of more than one long-run inflationary equilibrium, at any given government deficit, and that, starting somewhere around 1979, a jump across a critical inflation threshold (estimated at around 80–100 per cent annual inflation) took place, beyond which the economy got to the 'wrong side' of the Laffer curve. This is a seemingly 'perverse' state in which the elasticity of demand for money rises above unity and a decrease in the deficit (and the inflation tax) leads to further upward, rather than downward, shifts in the long-run inflation equilibrium. The fact that two such equilibria, low-level and high-level inflation, can be stable, hinges on the fact that the crawling-peg rule for the exchange rate (equation 3.9) has an adjustment coefficient (β) which rises with the rate of inflation, and that sufficiently large discrete devaluations of the exchange rate (the variable J_t in equation (3.9)) could have moved the system across the above threshold. An alternative, or complementary, interpretation of the dual equilibria model is one that follows the Barro (1983) distinction between discretionary government policy (or a non-co-operative equilibrium in game-theory terms), under which such a 'perverse' higher inflation equilibrium could occur, and the case of a strict *rule*, independently of the inflation rate (or a co-operative solution to the game), under which this high-level equilibrium could not occur.[32] While these are interesting theoretical issues on which some additional work also needs to be done, they would take us too far afield in the present context and are therefore left out of this discussion. Suffice it to say, at this juncture, that the specification of the high-inflation process, of the kind analysed here, requires both

[32] The conditions for the existence of dual equilibria and their characteristics under different adjustment rules are analysed in Bruno and Fischer (1990). The possibility that they may both be stable under an exchange-rate crawling-peg rule is studied (with empirical estimates for Israel) in Bruno (1989). The discretion versus rules interpretation is given in Kiguel and Liviatan (1992) and in Bruno (1991).

the existence of a government deficit to start the process and the indexation (accommodation) mechanism to sustain it. Therefore, as we shall argue, to eliminate inflation within a major stabilization programme, both components of the process have to be tackled.

Mathematical Appendix

Inflation dynamics:

Consider equation (3.6) in the text:

$$\pi = a_1\omega + a_2\epsilon + a_3\mu + v. \tag{3.6}$$

Now assume that each one of the nominal variables ω, ϵ, μ to be denoted by x_i ($i = 1, 2, 3$, respectively) is indexed to past inflation (π_{t-1}) and to inflationary expectations (π_t^e) in a linear homogeneous way:

$$x_{it} = \alpha_i\pi_{t-1} + (1 - \alpha_i)\pi_t^e + v_i. \tag{A3.1}$$

Substituting for the three nominal variables on the right-hand side of (3.6) at time t and aggregating we get:

$$\pi_t = \alpha\pi_{t-1} + (1 - \alpha)\pi_t^e + \theta_t$$

or:

$$\pi_t - \pi_{t-1} = (1 - \alpha)(\pi_t^e - \pi_t) + \theta_t \tag{A3.2}$$

where

$$(1 - \alpha) = \sum_{t=1}^{3} a_i(1 - \alpha_i) \quad \theta_i = v + \sum_{t=1}^{3} \alpha_i v_i \text{ (observed at } t).$$

Consider the case of *adaptive expectations* (or a *crawling peg*):[33]

$$\pi_t^e = \beta\pi_{t-1} + (1 - \beta)\pi_{t-1}^e$$

or:

$$(\pi_t^e - \pi_{t-1}) = (1-\beta)(\pi_{t-1}^e - \pi_{t-1}). \tag{A3.3}$$

Substituting into equation (A3.3) and proceeding in a recursive fashion we eventually get:

[33] If we substitute the rate of devaluation (ϵ) for inflationary expectations (π^e) in (A3.1) and assume a crawling peg the formal analysis is exactly the same, except that a foreign price shock must be included separately.

$$\pi_t - \pi_{t-1} = \theta_t + (1 - \alpha)(1 - \beta) \sum_{i=1}^{\infty} [\alpha(1 - \beta)]^{i-1} \theta_{t-i}.$$
(A3.4)

α tends towards unity as inflation persists and the degree of indexation in ω, ϵ, and μ rises and likewise β may be close to 1. When $(1 - \alpha)(1 - \beta)$ becomes small a positive shock θ_t to the price level will be transformed into an immediate *jump in the inflation rate* rather than in the price level.

In the case of *rational expectations* we find

$$\pi_t - \pi_{t-1} = \theta_t + [(1 - \alpha)/\alpha]_{t-1}\theta_t,$$
(A3.5)

where $_{t-1}\theta_t$ is the expectation formed at $t-1$ of θ_t.

In that case α becomes the key determinant of the inflation rate. At the limit, as $\alpha \to 1$, we get the same result as above. The assumption of an initially slow adjustment of expectations as in (A3.3), with β tending towards 1 and the length of the period shortening, would again give a very similar outcome as in (A3.5).

Another derivative of the system (3.6) with (A3.2) and (A3.3) can be obtained by substituting from (A3.3) into (A3.2) in difference form to get:

$$\pi_t - \pi_{t-1} = (1 - \alpha)(1 - \beta)(\pi_{t-1}^e - \pi_{t-1}),$$

and then proceed recursively to get

$$\pi_t - \pi_{t-1} = - (1 - \alpha) \sum (1 - \beta)^\tau (\pi_{t-\tau} - \pi_{t-\tau-1}) + \nu$$
(A3.6)

where

$$\nu' = \theta_t + (1 - \alpha)(1 - \beta)^{N+1} (\pi_{t-N-1}^e - \pi_{t-N-1}),$$

where N is any number of past lags.

Writing $\gamma_\tau = -(1 - \alpha)(1 - \beta)^\tau$ and $N = 3$, we obtain the inflation–acceleration equation that underlies the calculation of Tables 3.5*a* and 3.5*b* in the text.

4

Preparing for a Comprehensive Stabilization Programme 1981–1985: Doctrinal Debates, Politics, and Trial by Error

4.1 Introduction: Ideas, Economists, and Politicians

The analysis of Israel's structural crisis—especially the key role played by the government budget (Chapter 2)—and our discussion of inflation dynamics (Chapter 3) almost invariably leads one to the essential ingredients of a comprehensive stabilization programme for Israel. In fact, much of the analysis of the high inflation process and its policy implications were known to the present author and some professional colleagues by the end of the 1970s. In hindsight, what could sound more plausible and straightforward than following an all-out two-pronged attack: on one flank a far-reaching fiscal and monetary reform and on the other—abruptly halt the momentum of inflation? Life, however, is rarely that simple.

First, ideas take time to mature and take hold as events

In this chapter, more than anywhere else in this volume, a disclaimer of historical objectivity is in order, because of my varying personal involvement in the process (to be clarified here) and the lack of objective measurement criteria for an account of this kind. After a brief nine months' service in 1975–6 as Senior Economic Adviser to Finance Minister Rabinovitz, my involvement in the problems throughout the subsequent period of high inflation (1977–84) was that of an interested (and concerned) academic bystander rather than that of an insider. Only in 1984, after the formation of the National Unity Government, did I return, in stages, to more direct involvement in the economic advisory process. During 1984–6, as an academic, I participated in the policy design on an informal basis and subsequently, a year after the July 1985 programme was installed, I was appointed Governor of the Bank of Israel, a post that I held until Aug. 1991. Although an attempt will be made to give a fair account of the various views and hurdles on the path to the final adoption of the programme, the description will naturally be conditioned by the different hats I was wearing along the way. Supplementary and correcting information from various colleagues, who have read a number of earlier drafts, is gratefully acknowledged.

unfold. It took time to understand and convince others that the high-inflation process was different from anything else that had been known until then. Moreover, a plan of action that may sound intuitively plausible is often initially rejected in the professional arena because its unorthodoxy seems to run counter to existing policy paradigms. Such was the case with the 'hetero' part of what came to be called the heterodox approach to stabilization—in particular, the use of the exchange rate as a stabilizing device and the introduction of temporary price controls. Both these tools had been abused by policy makers in the past, and their record, in different contexts, had been rather poor. Only at a much later stage, once success of a programme has been firmly established, does the subsequent theoretical and empirical analysis give a new approach the stamp of approval of economic science, whereupon the underlying design joins the ranks of 'the obvious'.

Convincing one's professional colleagues to support a certain new line of thought is a very important ingredient in the 'production' side of economic policy, if only because the existence of differing views amongst experts usually convinces politicians to do nothing. But this is a relatively small hurdle in the arduous route through the politics and political economy of a crisis. As we shall see, politicians, rightly or wrongly, will always opt for partial or gradual, seemingly less risky, solutions, as long as they envisage easy ways out. Unlike the economists, Israeli politicians by tradition have never refrained from 'unorthodox' (i.e. administrative) meddling with the price system. They even thrive on such measures. Their problem, rather, is with the need to administer far-reaching and painful reforms, a stage to which they seem to be drawn only by a catastrophe or explosive hyperinflation.[1]

As the crisis deepens, a point may be reached at which one may even succeed in persuading the final 'consumers' of economic policy—the public at large—that there is no escape from a large and painful dose of medicine. Sometimes, as in Israel, politicians and policy makers are the last to realize that all possible partial measures and alternative lines of escape have been exhausted. But even when this stage is reached there are difficult issues of co-ordination and implementation, in which the bureaucracy and

---

[1] The choice of a minimum risk-aversion path by the average politician will be taken up in Ch. 8.

strong vested interests may either collaborate or form an opposition. The co-operation and the prodding of an interested external creditor (the US government in the Israeli case) also plays an important role. In fact, in the long chain that connects a policy proposal with its final implementation there are so many potentially weak links and hurdles to be overcome, and such high odds against success, that it may be difficult to understand what saved the one lucky outcome from having been buried in the vast graveyard of failed attempts to stabilize.

Why comprehensive stabilizations are delayed for so long is an interesting theoretical and practical issue to which we will return at a later stage. The fact is that in the Israeli case it took more than five years from the point (around 1978–9) at which the existing gradualist or partial policies could obviously no longer work until the 'right' programme was finally adopted, based at long last on the fruitful combination of the economists' intellectual input and the politicians' readiness to act.

The evolution of the underlying ideas, the genesis of the programme, the political hurdles on the way to its final adoption, and their interplay with the deepening crisis all merit some discussion before we get to the actual launching of the programme by a broad coalition government in July 1985, almost a year after that government assumed power. In our account we shall attempt to relate the process as it actually occurred, in the context of the information and the uncertainties as they were perceived at the time. In particular, it seems more appropriate to avoid, at this stage of the discussion, the application of theoretical or empirical hindsight. The latter, and the generalizations that may follow from them, will be deferred for a while.

4.2 Economists' Changing Views on Exchange Rates, Inflation, and Stabilization

Let us start with the cumulative recognition, in the second half of the 1970s, that the inflationary process in Israel after 1976–7 set it apart from a simple textbook excess demand pull on the price level. The fact that wage indexation imparts inertia to the inflationary process was well known. Experience had also shown that when formal *ex post* indexation fails to compensate workers for price increases, supplementary ways of endogenous and forward-looking indexation[2] provide part of the lubrication for an inflationary spiral. Nor was the endogenous nature of the money supply a new phenomenon in the Israeli case. What was entirely new was the gradual realization that the shift, from mid-1975 onwards, from an exchange-rate peg to a relatively 'smooth' crawling peg, severed the last ties to a 'monetary anchor' of an economy that could not sustain a serious fiscal restraint effort and whose money supply was almost fully accommodating.[3] The effect on the economy manifested itself primarily in the gradual worsening of the trade-off in exchange-rate policy between inflation, economic activity, and the current account, while the inflation rate was accelerating during 1977-9.

The October 1977 Ehrlich liberalization programme and its aftermath, which sparked a heated debate in Israel, gave the extra push to my own changing views on the role of the exchange rate and the evolving nature of the self-sustaining inflationary spiral.[4] A similar realization of the role of the exchange rate in the accelerating inflation rate in some European countries in 1976-8 subsequently led to the formation of the EMS.[5]

[2] See Liviatan (1983b) for a formalization of endogenous wage indexation through the wage contract.

[3] The introduction of the PATAM (foreign-exchange linked) bank accounts at the end of 1977 enhanced the jointly accommodating property of money and the exchange rate.

[4] These views were expressed in public debates and in the Israeli news media starting from the end of 1977. My conviction of the urgent need to shift emphasis from the current account to inflation deepened as inflation was accelerating to an annual rate of 50 per cent in 1978. A quantitative analysis of the worsening exchange-rate policy trade-off between inflation and the current account, due to increasing inertia and monetary accommodation, was presented as part of my Presidential Address to the Israel Economic Association in 1979. This was done in terms of an open-economy inflation model for Israel, based on Artstein and Sussman (1977) (see Bruno 1980a; some of the arguments also appeared in Bruno and Sussman 1979). This change of view on the role of the nominal exchange rate in the inflationary process was also inspired by my simultaneous theoretical and cross-section empirical analysis of the industrial countries' response to the first oil-price shock (see Bruno 1978, 1980b).

[5] In a recent paper on the changing attitudes towards inflation in Italy, leading to the formation of the EMS, Collins and Giavazzi (1991) mention Italy's accelerated inflation in 1976-8 (which was double the European average) and quote an *ex post* comment by the Governor of the Banca d'Italia on the trade-off between inflation and the current account: 'Though aware of its role in shaping the dynamics of prices, we guided the external value of the lira so as to permit a growth of exports setting the premises of a recovery of accumulation and of

When inflation jumped to 130 per cent per annum by 1979 there was hardly an observer who thought that a 7 per cent monthly inflation rate could be sustained much longer. Yet 1979 ushered in a four(!)-year period in which inflation persisted at an almost constant monthly rate of that magnitude, with all other nominal variables (wages, money, and the exchange rate) increasing at virtually the same rate. A student of Patinkin's *Money, Interest, and Prices* and its rigorous analysis of the neo-classical macro-economic framework (for a closed economy) could only be reminded of the mental exercise that one was asked to conduct in the classroom: 'double the money supply and all prices will double, keeping the real system invariant' (see our discussion in Chapter 3). Inflation now seemed to 'lift off' to a life of its own, quite divorced from the real economy, like a missile escaping the gravity of Earth.

Observation of such a nominal process for a substantial period of time, during which the real economy does not seem to vary much, can easily lead one to a mistaken diagnosis of both its sources and its possible cure. 'Bubble' theories of inflation, according to which the process is merely driven by the inertia of self-fulfilling expectations, were quite popular both in Israel and in some Latin American countries (Argentina and Brazil) where a similar process was taking place (see Chapters 1 and 6). The main implication is that all it takes to deflate a balloon is to let the air out; hence high inflation could be eliminated by a synchronized wage–price freeze. This admittedly requires some coordination, but would seem to be otherwise painless, since no real budgetary or other cuts would be required. The budget deficit, after all, had proved consistent with several inflation rates.[6]

employment less conditioned by the external constraint' (Banca d'Italia, *Annual Reports* 1979, 1980).

[6] On the rare occasions in which I had a chance to express my views to Minister of Finance Ehrlich (in Nov. 1978) and to Prime Minister Begin (in Feb. 1979), and more frequently in the media, a central point made was the need to eliminate the budget deficit both because of its real consequences and because of the role this would play in signalling government's commitment to price stabilization. Such a fiscal step had to be an essential component of a comprehensive stabilization programme in which the stabilization of the exchange rate and other government-determined prices, as a way of quelling inflationary expectations, would form the complementary part. Such a programme would also have to eliminate the distortive asymmetry in the price indexation of government bonds and

A considerable part of the earlier failed stabilization experiments in Latin America, such as the use of the *tablita* as a way of bringing down inflation by slowing the rate of devaluation, were based on such a prescription, whose most extreme (later) example was Brazil's 1986 Cruzado Plan. Israel's own episode—Aridor's experiments with disinflation in 1981–3—also showed signs of an underlying 'bubble-theory' approach, although some lip-service was paid to the need for fiscal prudence.[7]

The polar view is the obvious orthodox one. The only source of the inflationary process, according to this view, is the 'original sin', namely the large budget deficit. The one and only way to eliminate high inflation is to eliminate its source, that is, balance the budget and halt the monetary injection. All else is mumbo-jumbo. Once the budget is balanced, and supported by stringent monetary policy, inflation will fizzle out. According to the orthodox view, any direct intervention in the inflationary process, such as an exchange-rate freeze or price controls, can only lead to serious distortions, loss of reserves, and/or goods rationing.

Most academic economists in Israel around that time tended to side with the orthodox view.[8] This is understandable, in view of the ill effects of the protracted budget deficit on the real economy during the preceding decade. Any other approach was perceived (often rightly so) as an easy way out, which could not work. Past experience with incomes policies in Israel on the whole did not seem to have worked very well. A typical monetarist's view in those days would further argue, in reference to the role of the exchange rate, that causality runs from prices to the exchange rate rather than the other way around. The monetarist view of

the lack of indexation on the lending side. Finally, it was my belief at the time that exports would have to be handled by instruments other than the exchange rate and cheap credit, namely by a return to explicit subsidies based on value added, a method that had worked well in the 1960s, when the formal exchange rate was pegged.

[7] A less crude version of the bubble theory, which contains a grain of truth (also borne out by subsequent developments), would be to argue that part of the budget deficit is endogenous to the inflationary process due to tax erosion (the Olivera–Tanzi effect) and to the implied subsidy on long-term credit. Once prices are stabilized there is a reverse fiscal dividend. Quantitatively, however, this cannot be the whole story. The investment credit factor, at any rate, was no longer present after 1980.

[8] Typically this has been the position of most faculty members at Tel Aviv University (with Assaf Razin being their most prominent spokesman). The views aired at Hebrew University were more varied.

inflation and the balance of payments, as well as a gradualist approach to policy, were very much in vogue in academic circles during the 1970s, abroad as well as at home.

Unfortunately for the strict orthodox view, however, the immediate effect of the few attempts to cut the budget, mainly through a cut in subsidies, was an acceleration of inflation (as at the end of 1979). Besides, even those cuts fell far short of what was considered necessary to escape the quagmire. At the time, the notion of combining the two approaches within a comprehensive programme appealed only to very few professional economists and could make no headway with the politicians because there was no readiness to undertake the extent of fiscal stringency and likely recession that any reasonable programme, be it orthodox or heterodox (the name had not yet been invented), would require. No wonder the accelerating inflation in 1979, coming in the wake of the Horowitz budget cut, paved the way for his successor's (Aridor) new policy in 1980–1, in which he was inspired by the views of Yakir Plessner.[9] The consequences of Aridor's attempt to bring down inflation gradually by use of the exchange rate, without tackling the fundamentals, did little to promote an alternative to the orthodox approach.

4.3 A Digression on the Players in the Political Game

The views of the economics profession in Israel have always had some impact on policy making, the extent of impact obviously varying with the existence of politicians who were willing to listen. Of least impact was the almost unanimous[10] view on the paramount need to cut budget deficits. But whatever the influence (or lack thereof, particularly during the period 1977–84) of leading academic economists or their intermediaries on the fringes of government, the choice of policies and their execution depends primarily on the workings of the broader political market-place. This may therefore be a suitable point at which to digress and consider the major players in this game. I here deal specifically

[9] A newspaper article by Plessner (who is economics professor at the Agricultural Economics Faculty of the Hebrew University at Rehovot) on the inflationary process attracted Aridor's attention.

[10] One could always find at least one, if not more, dissenting view.

with the Israeli 'market-place', although there are obvious parallels in any other democratic system.

It should be stressed, again, that by tradition the Prime Minister of Israel seldom takes an interest or intervenes in economic issues (Peres's temporary involvement in 1985, as we shall see, was only brought about by very special circumstances). His or her preoccupation centres on matters of defence and foreign policy, while economic leadership and the substance of economic policy are usually delegated to the Minister of Finance, who most often is vested with full powers of senior economic decision maker.

The most relevant groups of protagonists are the following: (1) The *Minister of Finance* and his top officials, who are in charge of the design and execution of government economic policy, in particular the various components of fiscal policy; (2) other *government ministries*, whose main objective is to get the largest possible share of the budget pie; (3) the *legislators and members of parliamentary committees*; in Israel, at least, they mainly represent special-interest groups (in particular, there is a relatively vocal populist lobby professing to represent the interests of lower income strata). They tend not to be particularly concerned with stability (of the price level or of macro-economic policies) *per se*, or with the need to increase the size of the pie.

Next come the direct representatives of the private sector: (4) the *workers' unions*: the Histadruth (the Israeli federation of trade unions), and some quasi-independent professional unions (that breathe down the Histadruth's neck). These usually represent the wages and working conditions of the insiders (employed), rather than the outsiders (unemployed). In the Israeli case the Histadruth is also the owner of some large industrial enterprises, the major health service, pension funds, etc. Then there are (5) the *employers' associations*, of which the Association of Manufacturers is the most influential. The latter's main objective has usually been to milk the budget for special investment subsidies, to promote protectionist measures, etc. In the context of the inflationary process (and its stabilization) they have been the strongest pro-devaluation lobby, valuing the protection of the real exchange rate above price stability.

Although both the Histadruth and the employers' associations could exercise influence by lobbying with individual ministers or members of parliamentary committees they were at times boosted into playing an important independent macro-policy role which went beyond their objective political power base. This role gained prominence in a joint 'Economic and Social Council' which was occasionally convened by Prime Minister Peres in 1984 and 1985 in order to elicit recommendations, for example on incomes policy, which would then win public support and indirectly influence decisions in an otherwise hostile cabinet or parliamentary committee.

Next come (6) *members of the economics profession*, including universities, semi-academic research groups, and the occasional 'objective' (as against narrow interest-focused) economists in a government ministry. As noted, the economists were fairly unanimous on the excessive role of government and its distortive effects in Israel, but were divided on some important policy issues such as the role of exchange-rate policy (on this issue the division has persisted) or the exercise of price controls. Finally, there is (7) *public opinion at large*, in whose formation *the news media* play a most important role and which does not always conform to the stance taken by the institutionalized lobbies. That, however, became decisive only late in the game. These groups are by no means monolithic; they often line up against one another in different coalitions and sometimes engage in internal conflict. The resulting game is thus extremely complex; assessing the outcome, let alone affecting it, is an art rather than a science.

I have so far not mentioned the *Bank of Israel* explicitly. Needless to say, the Bank could have been a key disinflationary player early on in this 'game', as a fairly independent central bank should be. One of the problems of the inflationary period, however, was the Bank's inability—owing to both constitutional and personality reasons—to play an independent monetary role. It is very likely that, given the extreme fiscal excesses of the 1970s and early 1980s, neither legislation nor a stronger Governor at the helm could have withstood the pressure to accommodate.

One important aspect of the Bank's traditional standing in the Israeli economy should be mentioned. Because of the statutory role of the Bank's Governor as Senior Economic Adviser to the government (in addition to his conventional responsibilities as a central banker), the BOI's research department has at various times played an important intermediary role in the market for general macro-economic policy advice. The Bank collaborated with the Minister of Finance on the 1975 crawling-peg decision, the 1977 liberalization package, and the resolution of the 1983 bank-share crisis, but was prevented from exerting any direct counter-inflationary influence during Aridor's reign as Minister of Finance.[11] During the following period of mounting inflation the research staff, under the direction of Mordechai Fraenkel, contributed substantially to the new thinking on the nature of the inflationary process and the prerequisites for reform.

The last—and by no means least—player in the game is the *US government*, whose lending and quasi-IMF monitoring role was very important at crucial points along the way.

4.4 Deepening Crisis, Lebanon, and a Dollarization Fiasco, 1981–1984

When Aridor succeeded Horowitz in 1980 inflation was firmly entrenched at a 7 per cent monthly rate. Direct tinkering with the inflation rate by reducing import tariffs and taxes on durable goods just before the 1981 elections helped the incumbent (Likud) party to increase its representation in the Knesset. For a while it looked as if the 'new approach' to stabilization could not only buy time, but might also be a gradualist substitute for a more radical programme. National defence issues and the deteriorating situation in the Lebanon took precedence in government discussions and eventually led to the invasion of Lebanon in June 1982, the first war that Israel ever waged over which the nation was deeply divided.

At any rate, 1981–2 was not the time for a radical economic reform, although the nature of the inflationary process and the potential shape of a comprehensive stabilization programme had

[11] Aridor replaced the two in-house professional Deputy Governors, Sussman and Sheffer, with his own man, Plessner, under a much weakened Governor. According to Israeli law, the President appoints the Governor (who is only nominated by the government), while the appointment of a Deputy Governor (such deputies so far were appointed only during the period 1979–84) is done by the government (albeit 'in consultation with the BOI Governor'). Such appointment could thus be very much in the hands of a Minister of Finance if he is politically strong in relation to the Governor.

by then become quite clear.[12] Neither the political system nor the public at large could be convinced of the dangers lying ahead. As long as inflation remained steady, the various indexation schemes were working, and no specific segment of the population was specifically hurt by inflation (it seemed more like a risky but indiscriminate lottery), the fight against inflation could never generate any mass appeal while unemployment would invite unrest—the aggregate cost to the economy in the form of lower efficiency does not impinge on the individual as long as he or she is gainfully employed and living standards keep on rising.

Public awareness of just how precarious the misleadingly stable economic situation was changed dramatically with the bank-share crisis of October 1983, following closely upon the failure of Aridor's anti-inflation policy. One of the characteristics of the high inflation period was the massive placement of private savings in the shares of the major commercial banks, which seemed to be both the safest and most lucrative asset. Month in and month out these shares were yielding guaranteed real rates of return that were higher than government indexed bonds. This was not due to the long-term profitability of the banks. In fact, the gap between any reasonable estimate of the true underlying net worth of the banks and that of the market price of shares gradually widened, but the public failed to heed the warnings of a few experts. The reason for this paradoxical price behaviour was simple: the banks were manipulating the prices of their own

---

[12] A detailed interview-based article published at the beginning of 1981 in a Labour Party monthly ('A Quick and Determined Blow to Inflation', *Migvan* (Feb. 1981)) for the first time outlined my comprehensive 'shock' programme, centred on the re-establishment of the exchange rate as a nominal anchor, along with a fiscal cut. This was to involve, along with fiscal reform, an agreed, synchronized, temporary freeze of all nominal magnitudes, a number of additional monetary reform steps, such as reducing the liquidity of PATAM accounts (while maintaining them as a means for long-term savings), and elimination of the export credit facility and its replacement by a temporary value added subsidy on exports. In July 1981 an internal seminar took place in the Bank of Israel in which several macro-economists from Hebrew University (Patinkin, Liviatan, and myself) and Tel Aviv University (Berglas and Helpman) participated as well as Stanley Fischer from MIT and Jacob Frenkel, then at Chicago. As a follow-up and summary of this seminar Fischer and Frenkel published a detailed proposal for a stabilization strategy involving fiscal and monetary reform (Fischer and Frenkel 1982). It stressed the need for a concerted, rather than a gradualist, effort, and leaned toward using the exchange rate, at least partially, as a stabilization device.

shares, with the tacit agreement of the authorities, which were held captive by the banks since the latter provided the main channel through which foreign borrowing was funnelled to cover the mounting budget deficit.

As Aridor's failure to reduce inflation by a pre-announced 5 per cent rule on devaluation and government-regulated prices (called the '5–5' policy) became increasingly apparent, the public came to expect a major devaluation and started unloading its holdings of bank shares in massive chunks. This was more than the banks were able to absorb in their portfolios. An earlier attempt by the banks to co-ordinate a phased withdrawal from intervention failed, and the fear of a major run on the banks by foreign depositors made the government, in a fateful late-night meeting, yield to the bankers' pressure and bail the banks out by guaranteeing the price of their shares for the subsequent ten years in what became the Bank Share Arrangement.[13] The step devaluation that did take place, in the wake of the ongoing real exchange-rate appreciation, sparked another jump in the inflation rate and, as already mentioned, the leak of an imminent Dollarization Plan caused the resignation of Aridor as Minister of Finance in November 1983.

The Dollarization Plan was secretly being prepared in the Ministry of Finance during 1983, as the '5–5' policy faltered. This was done at first with the participation of the Bank of Israel and the help of academic advisers (including Berglas, Helpman, and Liviatan)[14] under the direction of the Director-General of the Ministry Ezra Sadan, himself a member of the agricultural economics faculty at Rehovoth. The plan was also discussed with US government officials in Washington with a view to obtaining a substantial stand-by loan for the operation. The leak to the press, which sparked an angry reaction from various politicians, mainly on patriotic grounds ('currency is like a national flag— you don't just give it up'), put an end to another non-orthodox anti-inflation programme.

---

[13] The share crisis eventually brought about the appointment of a public commission of inquiry (headed by a Supreme Court judge), in 1985–6, which led to the dismissal of all major bank managements as well as the Governor of the Bank of Israel in 1986.

[14] A consensus was not reached; some participants left the team once it became clear that the programme was not going to include a significant budget cut.

The new Minister of Finance, Yigael Cohen-Orgad, was an ex-government economist with basic real macro-economics training, which did not include the monetary dynamics of high inflation. He proceeded by attempting, in vain, to cut the budget by an across-the-board slash (the cumulative economic cost of the war in Lebanon reached an extra $2 billion), and tried to prop up export competitiveness through various credit and other subsidies. He ignored overtures by the Histadruth to enter talks about a 'package deal', namely a negotiated wage–price freeze, to avoid the harmful consequences of inflation which now was reaching 300–400 per cent on an annual basis. Various attempts were made at the Ministry to proceed with gradualist stabilization plans, including an abortive attempt to involve the Prime Minister (Shamir[15]), and the first promise of an American conditional commitment to provide a $800 million safety net. However, the approaching elections rendered these attempts futile, and the recently appointed Director of the Ministry, Emanuel Sharon, as well as his economic adviser Mordechai Fraenkel, resigned.

By now (at last) the public was becoming quite nervous about the likely outcome of runaway inflation. The bank-share débâcle, which caused considerable capital losses to those who did not get out in time, suddenly drove home the idea that private savings, which by and large took the form of government debt, might no longer be safe, as the government might have to repudiate its debt. By that time the government was for the first time no longer able to issue new net debt (see Table 3.1). The fear of repudiation instigated summary populist pre-election legislation, in mid-1984, by which private savings would be safeguarded by a two-thirds majority requirement that would henceforth hold for any change in existing savings plans.

In the meantime, the events of October immediately prompted another heated discussion in academia (mainly in internal seminars of the economics faculty in Jerusalem but also in the media) concerning stabilization and the merits of alternative methods of currency reform. Proponents of dollarization, namely a complete shift to the dollar as legal tender, stressed its advantages in enabling a tighter synchronization of all nominal magnitudes through a com-

---

[15] Shamir became Prime Minister after Begin retired.

mon credible yardstick.[16] The main arguments against dollarization were the implied permanent dependence on US monetary policy, the inability to conduct one's own monetary and exchange-rate policy, and the problem of destabilizing capital flows.[17]

My own objection was also premissed on the assumption that eventually, after another election, an alternative comprehensive course of action would present itself. This was expressed in a detailed counter-proposal, circulated in November 1983, and consisted of a comprehensive stabilization package involving the introduction of a new Israeli currency called the 'sela' (an ancient biblical coin, also meaning 'rock' in Hebrew). This would be linked to the dollar or a trade-weighted basket of currencies (an initial one-year linkage to the dollar would be advantageous from a public comprehension point of view), in terms of which wages and maximum prices for non-tradable goods would be determined. The existing PATAM (foreign-exchange linked) bank accounts could form the basis for the new money. At the same time the government would introduce legislation to limit the size of the budget deficit to 3 per cent of GNP, financed only by the issue of new sela-denominated long-term (unindexed) debt, and barring the government henceforth from borrowing from the Bank of Israel. There would be an initial credit freeze to support the introduction of the new exchange-rate 'anchor'. As against a cut in all subsidies on domestic goods there would be temporary subsidies to exports, and taxes on wages were to be reduced. Under a modified version of the programme the actual introduction of the new currency could be postponed to a second stage, and the first stage could be started with an explicit exchange-rate peg based on the old shekel. This would enable an exchange-rate adjustment a few months after initial stabilization, in case of need, without immediate loss of credibility associated with launching a new currency.

[16] The conceptual framework and the various arguments for and against this extreme form of currency reform are discussed in detail by Liviatan (1984). See also Plessner (1984).

[17] An additional argument against dollarization could be the loss of seigniorage income to the government, which would now accrue to the government that issues the currency, namely the USA (see Fischer 1982). Since seigniorage revenue in Israel has been of the order of 2% throughout the high-inflation period, this would not have been a dominant argument against dollarization in the Israeli case.

Since most academic economists agreed that a major budget cut (of some $2 billion) was required to fix the fundamentals, but there was no unanimity on other measures, let alone on currency reform, a petition was sent to the government, and made public, which demanded a fiscal cut of that magnitude. It was signed by twenty-five senior economics professors of all universities.[18]

One of the characteristics of an economy in severe crisis is the abundance of new ideas and proposals brought up almost daily both by professional economists and by well-meaning individuals from all walks of life. In the course of 1984 the research department of the Bank of Israel came up with a number of currency-reform proposals based on the liquidation of the PATAM accounts, similar in spirit to my own proposal but worked out in greater detail (Gal-Yam, Litvin, Meridor, and Rubin in miscellaneous memoranda). Some private individuals proposed innovative ideas, but there were also more ludicrous suggestions such as printing 'real' consumer-price indexed money rather than 'worthless nominal paper'.[19]

4.5 The National Unity Government in its First Year (1984–1985), or The Fine Art of Muddling Through

In June–July 1984 the country prepared for a bitter election campaign. The Labour Party under Peres and Rabin was expected to

[18] Amongst a few others, I did not sign the petition. While obviously agreeing with the need for the fiscal cut, I strongly believed that a much more comprehensive approach involving a broad social compact was required. Also expressed was the need to set up a new emergency broad coalition government for a period of two years with two assigned policy objectives—getting Israel out of the Lebanon and extricating the economy all at once from the quagmire (in a signed article in *Ha'aretz*, a major daily newspaper, 20 Jan. 1984). It also indicated the need for the Prime Minister to be personally involved in the guidance of a comprehensive stabilization programme.

[19] In his description of the events immediately preceding the German stabilization of 1923 Hjalmar Schacht has the following description: 'Not since the spring of 1919 had Germany been so close to the peril of Bolshevizations as in these weeks. It is hard for foreigners to form a conception of the excitement within the country at this time, for Germany was then completely isolated. All who held any leading position in the business or public life of the country tortured their brains day in, day out to find a remedy for the position. Meetings and discussions great and small took place daily, and schemes of reform and appeals for action accumulated one on top of the other' (Schacht 1927). This description fits well what was going on in Israel throughout 1984 and up to June 1985, including the public allusion to the possible need for a dictator to take over for a time.

stage a comeback, based on the public's deep frustrations over Lebanon and high inflation. Strangely enough, the Labour Party at that time had no alternative plan of economic action to be implemented once it assumed power. A self-appointed voluntary team of outsiders, headed by the late David Golan, an ex-government economist turned banker, was formed to discuss proposed courses of action.[20] The plan adopted by the team was based on my updated proposal for fiscal and currency reform. The 'Big Move', as the programme was termed, was presented orally[21] to Shimon Peres on election day (23 July 1984), to enable him, if elected, immediately to expedite its execution.

The programme was now prepared in greater operational detail concerning the composition of the proposed $2.2 billion budget cut (around 6–7 per cent of GNP, of which approximately one-third was to come from defence, one-third from a cut in subsidies to basic commodities, and the rest from a cut in export subsidies; there would also be a cut of half a billion dollars in miscellaneous social services, allowing, however, for an equivalent income-tax relief and a social safety net for the most needy, particularly the inevitable unemployed). There would be an up-front initial devaluation (20–30 per cent) and a capital levy (of the order of 10 per cent). The government would then immediately enter tripartite negotiations over the proposed incomes policy package (involving a temporary suspension of COLA and income-tax relief on wages), including a system of temporary (three to six months) price, wage, and profit controls.

The exchange rate, based on a new currency (the 'sela'),[22] was

---

[20] The other (academic) members were Haim Ben-Shahar and Eytan Berglas of Tel Aviv University, and Yoram Ben-Porath and myself from Jerusalem. Amnon Neubach, later Peres's personal economic adviser in the Prime Minister's Office (and thereafter Economic Counsellor at the Israeli Embassy in Washington), acted as secretary.

[21] Oral rather than written presentation was chosen so as to avoid the likely leakage of sensitive details (such as the proposed capital levy and devaluation) in the course of political negotiations over the formation of the coalition government. I was charged with writing up the full document by the following week if the election results were to turn in Labour's favour. In retrospect it proved prudent that the contents of the meeting were kept secret. By the time that team's programme was leaked and became public knowledge, three months later (*Ha'aretz*, 19 Oct.), the likelihood of its adoption seemed remote and nobody paid any attention.

[22] There was already, at that point, some doubt as to how the technical problem of the issue of new currency could be overcome. Moshe Mandelbaum, the

to be pegged at first to the dollar and by the end of the first year to a trade-weighted basket of currencies (the dollar being a natural unit of account but not a stable measuring rod for Israel's external trade). Details were also given on proposed money and credit arrangements (e.g. use of PATAM accounts). An immediate attempt would also be made to come to an understanding with the US government over a $1–1.5 billion stand-by safety net in deference to the administration's (especially Secretary Schultz's) penchant for an IMF-type surveillance role in a credible stabilization programme. Finally, the presentation of the plan was accompanied by an estimate of the quantitative effects, including the likely inflation and real wage profile starting with the initial implementation (presumed to be September 1984). Using a simple monthly inflation model (very similar to the quarterly version given in Table 3.3), it was estimated that inflation would rise to 22 per cent in October (it was 13 per cent a month when the discussion took place) and drop to 2 per cent a month (and then less) by January 1985. There would be a one-time real wage drop of 22 per cent. Various alternative trajectories involving a smaller exchange-rate adjustment at the beginning and/or up-front wage increases or income-tax relief on wages were also worked out.

This election day symposium, then, was to be the opening move in persuading the leader of a new government to adopt the long-awaited stabilization programme. But this time, again, it all fizzled out, and the programme was shelved. The election that same night resulted in a draw. The Premiership was to be rotated between Peres and Shamir, with Peres taking the first two years in return for the appointment of a Liberal Party, Likud-related politician and businessman, Yitzhak Moda'i, as Minister of Finance. Moda'i had his own ideas on how to run the economy; Peres, who needed the future support of the Liberal Party against its senior partner in the Likud, let Moda'i pick his own path and applied himself to the problem of withdrawing from Lebanon.

Moda'i set off as Minister of Finance by taking a typical 'orthodox' pair of steps: a 9 per cent devaluation and a subsidy

Governor of the Bank of Israel, told me upon enquiry that the only alternative back-up notes the Bank had in its vaults had been printed fifteen years earlier. These were very primitive, reminiscent of notes used in a Monopoly game, and could easily be forged. The issue of new notes, he argued, would take nine months.

cut. These sent prices skyrocketing for the next two months—in the course of September–October alone the CPI shot up by 51 per cent. Panic-stricken, and to regain control over inflation, Moda'i was led two months later to sign a three-month package deal with the Histadruth and the Manufacturers' Association, freezing wages and prices completely from 1 November 1984 to 1 February 1985, omitting the exchange rate, interest rates, and the budget from the deal.[23] For a while, inflation did indeed recede quite substantially. Prices rose by 19.5 per cent in November and then by 3.7 and 5.3 per cent, respectively, in the next two months.

In the meantime, economists in and out of government continued their discussions of alternative solutions. In the course of September meetings took place at the Ministry of Finance and also in the plenary cabinet sessions (19 September), to which a number of academic economists were invited, and the ministers were exposed to the various points of view. Again the academics' views seemed to converge on the need for a substantial budget cut (which Moda'i claimed he lacked the power to undertake) and were divided over the wisdom of directly meddling with the wage–price mechanism. The economists of Tel Aviv University even issued a stern public warning on the morning of the cabinet meeting against '*any* use of wage–price–exchange-rate freezes under any circumstances', claiming that 'these have *never* worked anywhere as an answer to the inflation problem'.[24] I again

---

[23] The originator of the idea was Moshe Sanbar; a fellow mediator in the process was Arnon Gafni. Both were former Bank of Israel governors who, as previous directors of the Ministry of Finance, were well versed in the art of negotiation with the relevant parties, but less so in the macro-economics of the inflationary process. Somehow both Peres and Kessar were convinced by them that this was the least costly way out. An attempt to convince Peres to adopt a more comprehensive approach and a dollar-linked (rather than shekel-based) package deal failed. Moda'i went along with the deal, but at the same time empowered Emanuel Sharon (see below) to prepare a more comprehensive stabilization plan.

[24] The written petition, addressed to the government (see *Yedi'ot Aharonot* daily, 21 Sept. 1984), was signed by ten professors from Tel Aviv, led by Assaf Razin and including, at that time, Elhanan Helpman and Leo Leiderman. Both Helpman and Leiderman later changed their views, once the 1985 stabilization programme, which included such a freeze, proved a success. The view expressed by my colleagues from Tel Aviv at the time was a perfectly legitimate one, especially if one considers the cumulative record of wage–price freezes under low inflations and the fact that there was no precedent to go by for the case of three-digit inflations in which the stakes and likely costs are that much higher. A programme of the kind that Israel finally undertook could equally well have failed.

circulated the essential part of my own version of the proposed comprehensive programme, similar to the one adopted by the Golan Committee three months earlier (in an updated document, under the title 'An Anchor for Stabilization of the Economy', October 1984). The Bank of Israel also prepared a detailed twenty-page memorandum (by Meir Sokoler, Sylvia Piterman, and Mordechai Fraenkel, October 1984) suggesting a similar, but two-stage, approach (first set the fundamentals, then introduce a total freeze).

We do not know if the difference of opinions amongst economists was to blame, or whether it was just plain expediency, but the political leadership opted for the October package deal and bought another three months of time and illusions. The main illusion was that the lower inflation rate during the subsequent two months implied that there still was a relatively costless, gradualist way out.

4.6 *Economists are Finally Given a Chance*

At this point I should mention two important institutional changes that had been taking place and were to become of great significance for the subsequent handling of the stabilization process. The first was the appointment, in October 1984, of Dr Emanuel Sharon as Director-General of the Ministry of Finance. Dr Sharon, a trained operations research economist with ample practical experience,[25] had resigned from the directorship of the Ministry just before the elections over lack of a coherent strategy, and now became active in promoting a comprehensive approach to stabilization.

Emanuel Sharon skilfully led the whole government design and implementation process in the next three years, including the politically tricky co-ordination between the Ministry of Finance and the Prime Minister. He initiated the involvement of outside academic advisers as well as handling the close co-ordination

---

[25] Emanuel Sharon, a reserve colonel in the Israel Defence Forces, had served as Deputy Head of the Internal Revenue Administration, had taught at the Hebrew University Business School, and had been Chief Executive of Control Data Corp. in Israel.

with the US administration, with which he had already established his high credentials. The latter aspect ties in with another important institutional innovation—the active deployment of a Joint American–Israeli Economic Development Government Committee (JEDG) based on an agreement between George Schultz and Shimon Peres.

JEDG consisted of a group of officials and independent economists from each side, headed by Emanuel Sharon and Under-Secretary of State Allen Wallis, respectively.[26] The committee was scheduled to meet at least twice a year (once in each of the two countries) and its first regular meeting was to take place in Washington in the second half of December. This meeting was preceded by a November 1984 visit to the USA by Sharon, in which a possible aid package, contingent on comprehensive stabilization, was discussed.[27] The US government, both in Washington, DC, and through Ambassador Lewis in Israel, expressed its dissatisfaction with the 'package deal' policies.

At this time, as the first package deal was about to expire (on 1 February 1985), there was renewed discussion of the stabilization regime that should be adopted (and negotiated with the Histadruth) for the next stage. The economists on the Israeli team, who were now meeting more regularly, adopted a version of the suggested comprehensive monetary reform, and an attempt was made by both Sharon and myself to get the Prime Minister to empower the team to come up with the programme in the Washington discussions where the question of a stand-by or

---

[26] The economists on the Israeli side at that time were Berglas and myself, with Nissan Liviatan also participating during part of the time (Mordechai Fraenkel, head of research at the Bank of Israel, was an unofficial member of the team, since the Governor of the Bank was not formally involved in the process). Our counterparts on the American side were Herbert Stein and Stanley Fischer. Herbert Stein brought with him a wealth of practical experience as senior economic adviser to several US administrations. Stanley Fischer was well versed in the problems of the Israeli economy on which he had done considerable work. Specifically, he had already substantially contributed to the 'new' view of the inflationary process and its cure—much of it appeared in our joint research papers. Both Stein and Fischer played an important role in the subsequent persuasion process with both Peres and Schultz.

[27] A very special role was played by Dan Halperin, Israel's Economic Counsellor in the Washington Embassy, whose aid-lobbying talents were priceless (quite apart from his valuable previous experience as economic commentator and media expert).

stabilization fund would again be negotiated.[28] Peres vacillated between adopting our programme right away and opting for another period of muddling through, with yet another old-style package deal, before the adoption of a more far-reaching programme.

There appeared to be two reasons for adopting the second option—one was the apparent success of the existing package deal in reducing inflation and giving the new National Unity Government what appeared to be its first boost of public credibility. The other—political—reason was the impending election campaign in the Histadruth, scheduled for April 1985 (the elections were eventually held only in May, which may explain the subsequent timing of events). With Kesser seeking re-election as Secretary-General against an increasing representation of the Likud in the governing body of the Histadruth, he would be less amenable to drastic moves.[29] Peres did, however, give the impression that if the expected stand-by from the USA were made conditional on the comprehensiveness of the programme he might none the less opt for it right away once the team got back from Washington.[30]

The meetings in Washington helped to convince our professional counterparts in the USA of the seriousness of the proposed comprehensive programme. The outcome on the aid package, however, given the objections of the US Treasury

[28] The new version, prepared on 1 Dec., when the exchange rate stood at 580 (old) shekels per dollar, envisaged an exchange rate of 750 on 1 Feb., upon the termination of the first package deal, and the announcement of a shift to the dollar as the accounting yardstick for controlled wages, prices, credit, and the budget (after a massive subsidy cut) on that date. The actual new currency (sela) was to be introduced at the second stage, on 1 Apr. 1985 (which coincides with the beginning of the fiscal year), by which time a nice round number for the new pegged rate of 1,000 (old) shekels or one sela per dollar would be made to match the required relative wage, exchange rate, and price systems. A cost-of-living payment (based on sela prices, if they were to rise) would be promised for June, and by Oct. 1985 there would be a shift to a currency basket.

[29] My own informal talks with Kessar and his political associates in the Histadruth indicated that a dollar linkage of wages could be quite an acceptable alternative basis for a renewed social compact. The broader policy package, including the touchy problem of the Histadruth-owned pension funds within a capital market reform, could, of course, not be discussed openly at that time.

[30] According to one of the participants in the process it was an unveiled threat made by the academic economists, that they would not go to Washington if prevented from presenting the comprehensive programme, which convinced Peres to adopt the programme at that stage, while continuing to play for political time.

(staunchly represented by David Mulford), remained ambiguous. So did the resolve of the Prime Minister by the time we got back from Washington, which in turn made the US team rightly doubt whether an extra aid package was justified. The Prime Minister's vacillations could, if necessary, receive convenient support by a further division of opinion amongst the economists and some of his other advisers. Particular favour was given to the 'administrative' solutions put forward by Sanbar and Gafni (both ex-BOI governors) to the objections raised against exchange-rate freezes (by Professor Haim Ben-Shahar of Tel Aviv University, who had been Labour's candidate for Minister of Finance before the elections), as well as to some alternative micro 'gimmicks' suggested by a number of bankers and businessmen to whom Shimon Peres liked to listen.[31]

At the beginning of 1985 yet another concerted attempt was made to persuade the Prime Minister to adopt a comprehensive monetary reform. It failed, and another partial way out was adopted.[32] A new package deal was signed with the Histadruth and the Manufacturers' Association, this time in terms of a freeze of a *positive* inflation *rate*. This soon proved impossible to implement. You can ask consumers to monitor price levels of goods and to submit complaints to the controlling authorities about any increases in price *levels*. There is no way in which they can monitor the increase in prices from one date to another. In spite of this basic weakness of the second package deal, political

[31] For example, Zadik Binu, a successful banker, every now and then came up with creative innovations in the area of private and public finance. The flow of such micro-suggestions at times deluded Peres into thinking that financial or taxation 'gimmicks' could substitute for a serious macro-economic fiscal and monetary reform. This syndrome repeated itself again and again up to the crucial decision-making stage before 1 July 1985. Occasional derisive remarks about 'the crazy ideas of these university professors who never managed a business in their lives', made by businessmen and heads of major concerns who had the Prime Minister's ear, often helped in the same direction. There are, of course, quite a few exceptions, the most notable one being the then President of the Manufacturers' Association, Mr Eli Hurwicz, manager of Teva, a major pharmaceutical concern. His role in eventually getting the programme rolling was very important.

[32] The Ministry of Finance at that time secretly commissioned two additional programmes (other than the one that was finally adopted). One was a return to the idea of complete dollarization and the other related to a 'doomsday scenario' for the case in which the market system could collapse and there would be need to introduce emergency rationing of foreign exchange and of vital goods (this information was conveyed to me only much later).

circumstances dictated its succession by a third, even weaker, deal three months later.

The first half of 1985 saw a gradual worsening of inflation (prices doubled between December 1984 and June 1985), the rapid dwindling of foreign-exchange reserves, and a renewed perception by the public that the authorities had completely lost control over the economy. In March, Herbert Stein and Stanley Fischer were sent to Israel to figure out what Israel might do and what conditions for aid might be relevant.[33] By the beginning of June the chips were down. The first major objective of the National Unity Government—a successful pull-out of most of the army from the Lebanon—had been achieved. The Histadruth elections, in May 1985, were over. But the most relevant fact was that, with the badly deteriorating economy, Peres's personal standing and credibility, both internally and no less in the eyes of the US administration, was at a very low ebb. Only then, after all partial policy alternatives had been exhausted, was the Prime Minister, with some delicate external pressure from the visiting JEDG team, and with his back to the wall, ready to give the alternative route, twice rejected, a fair chance. On 5 June Peres and Moda'i gave their blessing to a small informal five-member expert team which was expected secretly to prepare a detailed plan of action, which would be presented to the government within three weeks.[34]

Given the composition of the team and the previous groundwork, as well as discussions amongst its members, there was by

[33] They also handed Peres a memo, subsequently termed 'Herb's Ten Points', in which the outline of a comprehensive stabilization programme was laid out. For the view from the US side see Stein (1990). At a later stage this led to the rumour that the stabilization programme was both conceived and imposed by the US administration. Actually, there was apprehension among private economists on either side that an extra aid package might be approved by the US Senate before the adoption of a comprehensive programme and without adequate conditionality being attached.

[34] The insiders were Emanuel Sharon, Director-General of the Ministry of Finance, who both initiated and headed the team; Mordechai Fraenkel, Director of the BOI Research Department, who could tap the expertise of the Bank (without implicating a reluctant BOI Governor) and Amnon Neubach, who was Peres's personal economic adviser and filled an important liaison role with Peres and the political system. The two outsiders, Eytan Berglas from the University of Tel Aviv and the present author, were completely independent and were not even formally appointed (or paid) consultants. This had the advantage of our being

now a hard core of common conceptual ground to build on.[35] The only new data to come in since the previous planning phase (December–January) were the positive and negative lessons of the preceding seven months of package deals. These formed an important input into the way the wage–price–exchange-rate freeze was to be set up. Most of the time and effort could be spent on carefully laying out a balanced plan and its sequential implementation.

Differences of opinion on some crucial issues, mainly between the team and other advisers of the Prime Minister, were discussed in frequent evening meetings at the Prime Minister's residence in which he now, for the first time, took the lead. From that stage on, and for a period of at least six months, it was Peres's political determination and leadership that provided the major push of the programme through its fragile early stages. Some fruitless debates were spared as a result of the absence abroad of some influential dissenters at a crucial phase, but one or two important elements were none the less left out. One of these was the proposed capital levy, part of the original plan, which had been vetoed by two of Peres's political-economist party members in the discussions. The credibility argument brought up by the dissenters did not seem relevant. Once a one-time broad-based levy was introduced as part of a comprehensive emergency programme, the government could credibly commit itself not to do the same thing again. The more convincing argument was a practical one. Due to the last minute pre-election legislation, in the preceding year, a two-thirds majority in the Knesset (parliament) was now required to make the change. Given the populist sentiment among many MKs, the chances of gaining such a majority seemed dim.

The programme was ironed out by 29 June in almost complete secrecy[36] and brought before the cabinet the next day. The

able to exercise considerable moral pressure on the PM, including a threat to withdraw completely from the plan at a crucial moment during the cabinet meeting on the night of 1 July.

[35] Nissan Liviatan, who was absent from Israel in June, could not join the team, but was a very active participant in various internal discussions prior to the team's formal deliberations.

[36] The team conducted its work in two 'hide-outs'—a flat in the busy central area of the city and a room in the Israel Academy of Arts and Sciences which no one suspected could have anything to do with practical policy matters. The Prime

'fundamentals' part of the programme (subsidy and other budget cuts plus the initial devaluation and financial arrangements) was approved at the end of a stormy twenty-hour cabinet session in the early morning hours of 1 July. There ensued another turbulent fortnight of strikes and labour unrest which eventually led to a tripartite agreement on the temporary wage–price freeze. The latter, on 15 July, clinched the initial political launching of the programme. We now return to the substance of the proposed programme.

4.7 Outline of the July Programme

The declared aim of the programme was to reduce inflation at once from a monthly rate of around 15–20 per cent to virtually nil. Given some inertia and tail-end effects, this would in effect imply a reduction of inflation at first to no more than 2–3 per cent a month and hopefully, within a few months, to even lower rates. The programme was also designed to permit a significant improvement in the balance of payments. The hope was also expressed that 'the new programme would lay the foundations for a return to growth'. In line with our analysis of the origins of the crisis, the programme had to be both comprehensive and drastic in its effect on public expectations and confidence. It therefore simultaneously tackled the real crux of the problem, namely the government budget, as well as the establishment of a nominal anchor or, rather, several synchronized nominal anchors. A reduction of the budget deficit by $1.5 billion (7.5 per cent of GNP) below the 1984 budget was announced. At the same time, the shekel was devalued by 19 per cent (on top of a cumulative crawling devaluation of about 6 per cent in the preceding week), along with partial reduction of existing import duties and export subsidies.

Minister kept the contents of his evening meetings secret from all but his closest political allies and only on the last evening before the crucial cabinet session were a few of the ministers as well as Israel Kessar, Secretary of the Histadruth, and Eli Hurwitz, President of the Manufacturers' Association, brought into the programme. The cabinet was first called in to a 'smoke-screen' morning session on 30 June, to discuss an innocuous programme by Gad Jacobi, Minister of Economics and Planning. The secret would have been complete were it not for a major leak, caused by a disgruntled senior official who was not invited, two nights earlier. This brought the press to the Prime Minister's house, but with so many confusing signals only little damage was caused.

Simultaneously the government declared its intention to freeze all shekel-denominated aggregates: wages, prices, exchange rates, and credit (after an up-front adjustment). The exchange-rate peg was made dependent on preserving the required level of nominal wages.[37] The latter, including the temporary suspension of the COLA agreement, remained to be determined through negotiations with the unions and the employers. The Bank of Israel undertook to restrict the nominal size of bank credit, and the Ministry of Commerce and Industry remained responsible for price controls, learning from the experience of the three preceding package deals.[38] The government also announced its intention to limit the nominal budget level planned for the subsequent quarter.

For the capital market the guiding principle was clearly to ensure the preservation of long-term (indexed) savings while at the same time reducing the liquidity of linked assets, in a clear departure from the previous regime. Current PATAM (dollar-linked) accounts would henceforth be 'one-way': free withdrawals were permitted but new deposits would be accepted only for periods exceeding one year. Furthermore, the government would undertake to make all its bonds fully tradable (with the temporary exception of bonds held against the pension funds) so as to widen the basis for open market operations. The announced time-span for the stabilization programme was one year, whose first three months were declared an economic emergency period.

A few additional remarks on the details of the programme are in order. *On the budget cut*: at the core of the 'real fundamentals' part of the programme lay the desire to reduce the budget deficit

[37] The announcement of a conditional exchange-rate peg was considerably more ambiguous than I, for one, had wanted. The degree of insistence on the exchange rate as a firm nominal peg fuelled much of the ongoing debate both within the economic team and outside it. Moda'i wanted the more lukewarm commitment and received continued support from many of my colleagues. That debate obviously continued in many different forms in the following months and years.

[38] This turned out to be one of the most skilfully handled parts of the programme. The conceptual basis and planning was done by David Brodett, at that time in the Ministry of Trade and Industry (later head of the Budget Division in the Ministry of Finance), who used an input–output type framework to work out the initial price ceilings, after allowing for an across-the-board 'safety cushion'. The number of supervisors used for the actual controls was very small and the main vehicle for the monitoring was through public complaints and a summary court procedure.

to the point at which (quoting from the programme) 'the government's internal and external debt would no longer grow in
absolute real magnitude', so that subsequent GDP growth would
entail a gradual reduction in the debt/GNP ratio. This formula
would have required a cut of $2–2.5 billion (10 per cent of GNP)
in the budget deficit from the 1984 figure. A top-level compromise decision between Peres and Rabin (Minister of Defence and
Peres's arch rival in the Labour Party) barring substantial cuts in
defence expenditure reduced the planned reduction to $1.5 bil-
lion, in the hope that complementary cuts would be introduced in
the 1986 budget. The reductions included a substantial cut in
subsidies to basic commodities (whose prices, as in the case of
dairy products and bread, immediately increased by 60–75 per
cent). There were a few increases in direct and indirect taxes.
Only 20 per cent of the planned cut in the deficit was to come
from public expenditure on services and social transfers—the
price of maintaining a minimum coalition of ministers for the
crucial vote in the cabinet.[39] The programme also stipulated compensation for price increases in the lower income brackets
through the social security system.

The *ex ante* planned (and finally adopted) cut in the deficit was
obviously lower than was objectively required. This fact alone led
most of my academic colleagues to criticize the programme when
its details were first divulged to them (on the day of the cabinet
session). However, the expected extra financial aid from the US
government ($750 million in each of the budget years 1985 and
1986) was expected to bridge over both the likely budget deficit
and the eventuality of a balance-of-payments difficulty. As it
happened, the reverse Tanzi effect on both the revenue and the
expenditure side (see discussion in Chapter 5) fortunately helped
in reducing the domestic deficit to considerably below the level
expected on the basis of the formal cut alone. Finally, the government also announced a reduction in its own manpower by
about 3 per cent (10,000 employees);[40] it was an important signal

---

[39] The twenty-hour debate consisted primarily of long monologues by each of
the twenty ministers, each explaining what a disaster a cut in *his* budget would
cause.

[40] Moda'i insisted that both the suspension of the COLA and the reduction in
government employees be done by a unilateral government Emergency Decree
(based on a law dating back to British Mandate times, which is not subject to
parliamentary approval). This, more than anything else, angered Kessar and the

of intent but, strictly speaking, was carried out only at considerable delay while the rest of the public sector (local authorities) continued to grow (the absolute number of employees in the public sector as a whole did, however, stop growing for a while).

A word on the *size of the devaluation*: the devaluation was smaller than the one required to permit the total abolition of export subsidies.[41] The latter would have required an additional 10 per cent devaluation. The envisaged initial price shock and its likely effect on real wages was already too high in the eyes of the decision makers (for a less moderate handling of this issue in a recent East European context see Chapter 7).

On the *choice of multiple nominal anchors*: the exchange rate, as already argued, was considered a more appropriate central nominal anchor than either money or credit (which would be highly unstable during disinflation). On the other hand, it would have been inconceivable to freeze the exchange rate unless a nominal wage freeze could also be guaranteed. For that, the co-operation of the unions, though not sufficient, was certainly necessary (at least for the part necessitating the suspension of the COLA agreement and a wage freeze in the public service sector). The unions, in turn, demanded a price freeze. Thus, even for political reasons, a multiple anchor approach was required. However, there was more to it than that. In a neo-classical system we know that in equilibrium the setting of one nominal variable will fix all the rest. But given a disequilibrium and situation of uncertainty, at least an intuitive argument in favour of attempting an *ex ante* nominal freeze on all four nominal variables could be made.[42]

---

trade unions when they called for strikes against the programme. They insisted on, and obtained, a voluntary negotiation process on COLA. For the reduction in employees a Decree was none the less used, but not fully implemented. The Israeli tradition of decision by consensus is deep rooted.

[41] Subsidized credit for exports was mostly abolished, as were some other special export subsidies. Some version of government exchange-rate insurance (analogous to an 11% subsidy to value added) was maintained. This was later curtailed in stages with each new exchange-rate alignment.

[42] The notion of 'multiple anchoring' is suggested by the analogy of securing a ship with several lines so as to distribute the load in rough weather, with at least one of the lines taking the strain at any point in time. Should one of the lines part, the others can take up the extra burden, but it is none the less important to co-ordinate the lengths of the different lines ahead of time. This analogy came up in my discussion of the idea with Mordechai Fraenkel some time in 1983 or 1984.

4.8 Politics and the Social Wage Contract

The programme was approved by the cabinet on the morning of 1 July, amid considerable resentment and with quite a few dissensions, notably by most of the Likud ministers, to whom the whole thing looked like an unholy coalition of the Labour Party with Liberal partners, headed by Moda'i. Outside, in the public domain, all hell broke loose. The price hikes, the imminent sharp wage reduction, and possible unemployment gave some of the more militant trade union leaders an easy excuse for wildcat strikes and demonstrations. In one instance Peres was prevented from appearing on TV because the electricity was cut off by the powerful (and extremely well-paid) electric power union.

What eventually won the Histadruth and Kessar over in favour of a negotiated settlement was a basic grass-roots sentiment that this government should be given one more chance to try another way. An enormous effort was made by everyone involved in the programme and our colleagues in academia to explain its details and underlying philosophy in public appearances immediately after the programme's inception.[43] Backstage, the elements of another tripartite agreement were being ironed out.

On the assumption that the real net take-home pay prior to the programme's inception had already been eroded to the 'right' level, all that the plan had to stipulate was that any further reduction in the net real wage (which was inevitable given inflationary dynamics) would be temporary and could be corrected by the end of the 1984/5 fiscal year (March 1985). Given the relatively strong position of the unions and the relatively weak starting-point of a government that had to deliver price stability from a base of a very poor past record, it was clear that the workers would ask for initial compensation as well as for some kind of additional insurance in return for a three months' suspension of the COLA agreement.

Finally, on 15 July, at the end of a stormy fortnight and some tough bargaining, a wage agreement was signed between workers and employers in the private sector:[44] an immediate up-front

---

[43] A special series of programmes on television and in the other media was devised. At some point an economic 'model' in the form of a flow-chart of the elements of the programme, used in the presentation to the cabinet, was also successfully reproduced on television.

[44] In Israel the government is formally not party to the COLA agreement,

bonus (14 per cent of the July wage) was promised, payable on 1 August. Likewise, a one-time increase of 12 per cent was promised for 1 September. The least satisfactory part consisted of another 12 per cent wage correction to be spread out in the form of consecutive wage increases of 4, 4, and 3.5 per cent for 1 January, 1 February, and 1 March. The employers undertook to absorb all these increments within the established price ceilings and the agreed export subsidies. Finally, the existing COLA arrangement (80 per cent of last month's rise in the CPI) would be renewed on 1 December (November's wage) according to the price rise in October, with a minimum inflation threshold of 4 per cent (replacing the 12 per cent threshold before stabilization). The extension of this arrangement to the public sector was eventually secured by the Histadruth from the government in return for a postponement of certain previously negotiated wage increases, due in October 1985, until after March 1986.

The succession of projected monthly wage increases at the end of six months, and in particular the renewal of monthly COLA adjustment with a very low threshold, seemed extremely problematic. These were, presumably, the insurance costs that were required for achievement of the crucial temporary suspension of the built-in inflationary spiral. An unsatisfactory bargain it was, and, as we shall see, it caused considerable difficulties at a later stage. But by mid-July 1985 the programme was at long last on its way, with a very uncertain future; it was a big gamble on the part of everybody directly concerned, this time shared by economists and politicians alike.

The fact that it took the Israeli programme several years to mature before full-fledged adoption reflects in an interesting way on various political-economy facets of reform in a democracy, a subject to which we return in Chapter 8. Some of the hurdles and conflicts, as we shall see in the next chapter, continued well into the implementation stage.

which is traditionally signed by the Manufacturers' Association and the Histadruth and then adopted by the government and applied to the public sector. In this particular case Eli Hurwitz, President of the Manufacturers' Association, was the chief liaison with the Prime Minister rather than Kessar. This indirect negotiation process may explain why the contract had some obvious drawbacks for stabilization policy (of which Hurwitz was made aware but in which he apparently had no choice). In particular, a considerably better contract would have been to make the subsequent extra compensation contingent on *ex post* stabilization outcomes.

5

The Fight over Stabilization and the Structural Adjustment Process, 1985–1991

5.1 Introduction and Overview

The period 1985–91, after the inception of Israel's July 1985 stabilization plan, was marked by a swift reduction of inflation from 300–500 per cent to a 15–18 per cent annual rate (down to 9–10 per cent by mid-1992) and by a substantial alleviation of the foreign-exchange constraint, as represented by the sharp drop in the ratio of external debt to GNP from around 90 to 25 per cent, both of which were supported by a balanced government budget. At the same time growth picked up, as shown by higher average business-sector GDP growth (close to 5 per cent per annum) as well as improved employment and productivity (see Table 5.1).[1] There is no doubt, therefore, that from a broad-brush perspective July 1985 marks a turning-point at which the economy moved from a prolonged crisis, or 'bad equilibrium', to what seems to be a new, substantially improved, mode of macro-economic behaviour.

These performance indicators are clearly significant. Averages, however, hide the more interesting developments both above and below the surface, and they do not permit a more detailed evaluation of the policy options and challenges posed by the aftermath of a sharp stabilization. From several points of view, particularly the policy lessons for future reference, the unexpected difficulties and policy surprises encountered along the way are more illuminating than the average performance indicators. The most important point that must be made right away is the fact that a successful stabilization and an associated reform process—even if they appear to be the result of 'shock treatment' or a one-time

---

[1] These data were illustrated in Ch. 2 (Figs. 2.1–2.4).

'big bang'—are really a very prolonged and arduous process, beset with pitfalls and potential failures. In hindsight, the post-stabilization strategy, as it evolved over time, is no less important for success than the ingredients that went into the initial policy package. In essence, this strategy involves a fight over the sustainability of the two main pillars of stabilization: first, the real fundamentals, that is, the budget balance, and second, the nominal anchor, that is, the exchange rate, along with the supporting monetary and incomes policies. Each one of these has constituted a separate, though mutually supporting, ongoing test of the seriousness of the government in its stabilization effort. But the toughest problem of all is how to move the economy back to a sustainable growth process. During the period analysed Israel successfully accomplished the first two tasks, but at the time of writing had not yet fully achieved the sustainable growth goal. As we shall see in later chapters, these sets of issues, even in the aftermath of even a successful stabilization, have also been central to other recent reform episodes, both in Latin America and in Eastern Europe.

In the Israeli context the post-programme period can be divided into roughly four major subperiods marking different phases in the transition from the adoption of the programme to successful inflation stabilization and the structural reform process.

Phase 1 (sharp stabilization). The first six to eight months from July 1985 to early 1986 were marked by a sharp reduction in inflation and a substantial recuperation of foreign-exchange reserves, coupled with an initial recession in economic activity. This phase, which is beset with many obstacles, is the critical first credibility test that any sharp stabilization must pass before it can be considered even partly successful. This was followed in Israel by a surprising boom period.

Phase 2 (boom). This consisted of eighteen to twenty-four months, lasting until mid-1987, of an increase in economic activity and a substantial drop in unemployment, fed mainly by a private consumption boom. The monthly economic activity index (Fig. 5.1) summarizes the evolution of the various phases. An evaluation of events up to that point in time might have given the impression that a sharp stabilization at the end of a long

TABLE 5.1 *Key indicators, 1980–1991*

	Rate of inflation (annual %)				Nominal interest rates (annual %)				Labour market			GDP and employment, business sector (% growth)		Debt and government deficit (% ratio)		
	Con-sumer prices	Net CPI[a]	Wage rate	Exchange rate	Money M3	Overdraft	Fixed term debt	Time deposits	Real wage (% growth)	Unit labour cost (% growth)	Unem-ployment rate (%)	GDP	Employment	External debt/ GNP	Internal debt/ GNP	Deficit[b]/ GNP
1981–5	195	192	200	186	215	495c	257c	255c	1.6	2.5	5.4	3.4	1.6	68	117	−12
1986–91	18	16	20	11	26	44	31	15	2.9	1.1	7.2	5.2	2.6	43	89	−1
1986	48	55	61	37	44	62	38	17	9.0	6.0	7.1	5.7	1.6	63	126	3
1987	20	22	30	14	37	62	43	18	8.0	4.0	6.1	7.8	4.5	53	114	0
1988	16	17	22	2	19	46	33	13	5.0	−2.0	6.4	2.5	3.0	44	99	−1
1989	20	15	18	16	21	34	27	12	−1.0	−2.0	8.9	2.0	−0.4	38	93	−4
1990	17	11	15	11	23	30	23	13	−1.0	−1.0	9.6	6.6	2.1	31	91	−3
1991	19	14	13	12	28	30	22	13	−2.0	−7.0	10.6	7.0	4.7	27	81	−3

[a] CPI excluding housing and controlled goods.
[b] Total deficit (−) for the public sector (1986 had a surplus).
c Figures are for 1983–5.

Sources: BOI, *Annual Reports*, and CBS, *Statistical Abstracts*.

crisis period could be almost costless.[2] However, as Fig. 5.1 shows, a more painful transition period followed.

Phase 3 (slump) marked two years, from mid-1987 to mid-1989, of sharply reduced economic activity and an increase in unemployment, representing the delayed cost of adjustment. Considerable structural change was under way and several new important reform steps were initiated, particularly in financial markets and the exchange-rate regime.

Phase 4 (take-off), since mid-1989, has brought about a rapid increase in economic activity whose timing and scope in relationship to the stabilization process cannot be exactly determined, owing to an important external development—the beginning of mass immigration of Jews from the former Soviet Union.

In the following sections we first analyse the unfolding of the initial stabilization phase in greater detail, and then consider various alternative interpretations of the particular business-cycle phenomenon mentioned above. Next we take up, in Section 5.4,

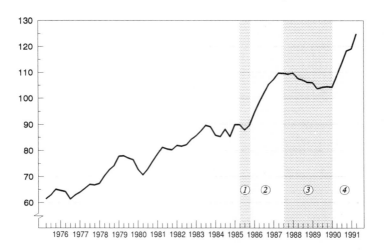

Source: BOI.

FIG. 5.1 The state-of-the-economy index, 1975–1991

[2] At the time my Clarendon Lectures, on which this book is partly based, were actually delivered, the dominant post-stabilization developments described in my second lecture were phases 1 and 2. The rest, which came somewhat as a surprise, unfolded later.

the defence of the real fundamentals, namely the establishment of credible fiscal discipline. This is followed by an analysis of the struggle led mainly by the Bank of Israel, over the defence of the nominal anchor, including the evolution of the exchange-rate regime in the aftermath of stabilization, and the gradual, and costly, learning process it entailed in wage and labour-market behaviour. In Section 5.6 we digress on a subject in which Israel is unique—the successful introduction and gradual phasing out of price controls. The last section (5.7) deals with issues of financial restructuring in ailing enterprises, the reform process in the financial markets, which has made substantial progress, and the less satisfactory pace of structural reform in the real economy.

5.2 Phase 1: Early Tests of Fiscal and Exchange-Rate Credibility

As mentioned at the end of the previous chapter, the first weeks of July 1985 were marked by considerable confusion. The vehement debates between the Histadruth and the government, the strikes, and the lack of clarity as to the government's intentions, cast the very launching of the programme in doubt. However, several factors helped to correct course. On 15 July, June's pre-programme CPI was announced and pointed to a lower price increase than was expected by the Histadruth (14.9 instead of 18 per cent). While the wage contract in the private sector caused subsequent adjustment difficulties, the timing, and the fact that it was signed, served as an important signal in the process of establishing an initial nominal anchor for the system. The dollar exchange rate—the only price quoted on a daily basis—remained stable during the early weeks of the programme[3] and foreign-exchange reserves started rising. Neither the stability of the exchange rate nor the increase in reserves was surprising, as both could be expected after a sizeable devaluation and an exchange-rate freeze, but they certainly helped in attenuating the effect of

---

[3] While the black market for foreign exchange is relatively thin, the fact that the black-market rate stabilized also helped psychologically. As we shall see, the dollar exchange rates eventually remained stable for a very much longer period—eighteen months—until Jan. 1987.

the CPI for July (27.5 per cent), announced on 15 August, which, as expected, was dominated by the initial price-level shock.[4]

At that time, however, bi-weekly indices measured both by the Central Bureau of Statistics and by private institutions were pointing to a levelling-off of prices by the beginning of August. In anticipation of a prolonged period of price control producers tend to overshoot prices ('preparing a cushion') to a level which could, with the ensuing recession, be kept fixed for some time. There were even some instances of downward price adjustments whose public signalling greatly helped in the process (more on price controls in Section 5.6).

This and other issues came up for discussion in a follow-up committee appointed by the Prime Minister and the Minister of Finance. The committee included members of the team that pre-pared the stabilization programme with some additional econo-mists representing various ministries. It continued to be headed by Emanuel Sharon, Director-General of the Ministry of Finance, who at the same time also headed the Price Committee (see below). The committee's weekly closed (and leak-proof) meetings over a period of two and half years played an important role in collecting up-to-date published and unpublished information about developments in the economy, in co-ordinating activities across ministries, and in getting swift ministerial response (mainly at the level of liaison with the Prime Minister and the Minister of Finance) to the inevitable flow of policy changes. This committee also co-ordinated efforts to explain the programme and the pro-nouncements on the development of the stabilization process, all of which would otherwise be highly problematic in view of the inter-ministerial rivalry and infighting that characterize public life in Israel.

A central ingredient in the initial success of a stabilization pro-gramme is the public's attitude towards it. One rough measure is given by public opinion polls. A poll taken for *Yedi'ot Aharonot*, Israel's most widely circulated daily newspaper, showed an

---

[4] An internal assessment of the price-level shock made on 7 July estimated a price increase of 25% for July and 5% for Aug.; it assumed a better wage bargain than was actually signed a week later. The actual rates of price increase were 27.5 and 3.9%, respectively, for July and Aug. This relative accuracy in prediction of the initial price shock will later be contrasted, in Ch. 7, with the sizeable price 'overshooting' during the implementation of 'heterodox' programmes five years later in Eastern and Central Europe.

increase in the number of respondents supporting the programme from 45 to 64 per cent between the beginning and the end of July, whereas the number of those opposed declined from 51 to 31 per cent in the same period; the number of respondents favouring a real wage erosion rose from 28 to 44 per cent (published in the same newspaper, 9 August 1985).[5] Another facet of public confidence in the successful reduction of inflation is represented by the expected inflation measure which is implicit in the market price of indexed bonds approaching maturity.[6] By this measure, expected monthly inflation for the next quarter came down from 18 per cent in June to 11–12 per cent in July-August and then gradually declined through 8, 6, 4, and 2 per cent in the course of the remaining months to December 1985. Actual monthly inflation (known with two weeks' delay) dropped to 3.9 and 3 per cent, respectively, in August and September. As Table 5.2 shows, the multiple wage and dollar exchange-rate anchor in those two months, at least, resulted in almost complete stability.

Weathering the month of October 1985, three months after the initiation of the programme, was a crucial test for it, since it was expected to incorporate a seasonal price increase of at least 3 per cent (on account of the price increase of fruits and vegetables and of clothing). This seasonal increase turned out to be 4.7 per cent, mainly because of a three-monthly update of housing prices. A threshold price increase of 4 per cent triggered the renewal of an 85 per cent COLA for the November wage— payable on 1 December—on top of the first instalment of three successive nominal wage increases (of 4 per cent each) agreed upon in the original, very precarious, wage bargain. Since the essence of the problem (though not its exact size) was known in advance, it was widely believed that a pre-emptive exchange-rate

---

[5] The government also commissioned a series of public-opinion polls from the Israel Institute of Applied Social Science, which provided a guide to the follow-up team. The poll for the first week of the programme showed that approximately half of the respondents believed the programme should be carried out in full (i.e. without making concessions to pressure groups) and that it would indeed 'improve the state of the economy'. This percentage was positively correlated with the level of education of the respondents. Subsequent polls showed an increasing measure of credibility in the government as time progressed.

[6] Based on a study by Yariv (1986) which uses the fact that, at maturity, the bond is indexed to the preceding month's index, which is announced in the middle of the current month (or, effectively, a one-month average delay). Comparison with the price of an alternative nominal asset gives the implicit price expectations.

TABLE 5.2 *Traverse into stabilization, January 1984–June 1987*

	Rate of inflation (monthly %)				Money growth and interest rate (monthly %)			Relative price levels (1980 = 100)			Private consumption per capita (1980 = 100)	Unemployment rate (%)	Budget deficit (% of GDP)
	Consumer prices	Exchange rate ($)	Exchange rate (basket)	Nominal wage[a]	Liquid assets (M3)	Means of payment (M1)	Interest rate (end of period level)	Real exchange rate[b]	Real wage (gross)	Net real wage (after tax)			
1984	15.2	15.9	15.3	16.5	15.9	13.4	16.1	92	116	114	115	5.9	15
1985													
Jan.–July	14.0	13.6	15.3	11.0	13.0	11.8	21.0	103	116	116	113	6.0	12
Aug.–Sept.	3.5	0.2	0.7	0.3	3.5	16.2	14.1	110	95	99	112	7.8	5
Oct.–Dec.	2.1	-0.1	2.0	4.5	1.9	6.7	7.2	105	95	103	117	7.2	4
1986													
Jan.–June	1.4	0.0	1.0	5.4	0.7	8.0	3.8	101	111	119	122	7.1	2
July–Dec.	1.6	0.0	0.0	0.6	3.3	5.6	3.8	95	116	123	133	7.0	1
1987													
Jan.–June	1.4	1.3	1.9	2.3	2.9	1.5	4.6	97	119	126	135	5.6	0

[a] Nominal wage in the business sector.
[b] Relative industrial wholesale prices (P/EP*)—based on trade-weighted basket.

Sources: BOI and CBS.

adjustment would be made in October. This was the reason for opting not to introduce a new currency in the opening move of the programme.

The handling of exchange-rate policy continued to provoke debates among economists and policy makers almost immediately after the programme's initiation. The Governor of the Bank of Israel (Mandelbaum), who had not fully participated in the programme and did not have much faith in its success, attempted to carry out a 'flexible' exchange-rate policy: first the Bank let the exchange rate appreciate for a while (this was consistent with sticking to a very high initial interest rate, a subject to which we shall return below), and later the rate depreciated by over 2 per cent in the course of August (all within limits, permission for which was asked and obtained from the Minister of Finance, but against the views of most members of the planning team). This explains the small deviation from zero, during October–December, in Table 5.2 (col. 2). The opponents of pegging made their views known both in the press and in an internal discussion convened by the Bank's Governor and quickly made public.[7] This led to a crucial policy debate (involving the Minister of Finance and the Prime Minister) in August, which settled the issue for a while. A pre-commitment to continued pegging of the nominal exchange rate through the 'dangerous' month of October and beyond, which was espoused by Emanuel Sharon and myself, won approval against the opposing view of a real exchange-rate peg (to which all the previous players, who had earlier opposed the stabilization programme, adhered).

What tipped the scales was the surprisingly good budgetary performance in the first few months of the programme, in spite of public-sector wage concessions that Kessar, Secretary-General of the Histadruth, succeeded in extracting from the Prime Minister in August (the budget none the less showed balance on a cash basis, reflecting the Tanzi effect at its best—see below). It was also hoped that, given the initial recession in the commodity market, price-setters would use their 'cushion' to absorb the impending cost increases in the private sector and not attempt to violate the price controls. The arrival of the first extra instalment

[7] This discussion was conveniently leaked to the press: a full account with names and contents of the debate appeared in two daily newspapers, *Ha'aretz* on 10 Aug., and *Davar* on 11 Aug.

of $750 million in US government aid, which helped boos
eign-exchange reserves, was no less important in supporting
decision.[8] This decision to stick to the initial peg was the
important signal in a long series of deliberations and arguments
over the exchange-rate anchor which were to characterize the stabilization process in the years ahead (as well as my own subsequent personal involvement as Bank of Israel Governor after
June 1986).

In the meantime, one element of a currency reform—previously
left out of the initial programme (for fear of the need to
devalue)—was announced by the Bank at the end of August: one
New Shekel replaced 1,000 old shekels.[9] Pegging the shekel to the
dollar in the following year and a half, bolstered by fiscal discipline, certainly helped anchor a relatively stable price level, at
least psychologically, although the more relevant trade-weighted
exchange rate was implicitly being devalued as a result of the
strengthening of European currencies while nominal wages were
rising quite substantially from October 1985 onwards. The combination of ongoing import and wage cost increases may also
explain why inflation 'settled' on an 18 per cent annual rate
almost from the beginning, rather than on a single-digit level. By
August 1986 the time was deemed ripe to carry out the earlier
plan to switch to a trade-weighted basket as a basis for the peg
(we return to the exchange rate in Section 5.5). The wage push,
as we shall see, took much longer to quell.

While the nominal wage did continue to increase from October
onwards, the sharp recession of August–September (both the real
wage—gross and net of tax—and private consumption per capita
dropped initially; see Table 5.2, cols. 9, 10, and 11) helped keep

[8] Even though interest rates were excessively high (see below) the monetary
crunch also helped keep exchange rates credibly stable without any pressure from
the market.

[9] The diminutive new one-shekel coin, nicknamed the 'chip', provided comic
relief. Smaller in diameter than one US cent, it was worth 66 US cents at the
time. Its value in 1992, seven years later, was still around 40 cents (which says
something about the depreciation of the dollar over this period). Its minting had
been ordered several months earlier by the Bank of Israel with the cost-saving
rationale that, at a time of high inflation, it would soon have to be replaced anyway. The decision to go ahead with the introduction of the new currency was
justified by the BOI as required in view of insufficient supplies of the old currency. Its introduction seemed to me inopportune, but I was proven wrong *ex
post* as it seemed to give a psychological boost to the perception of relative price
stability.

inflation within bounds, with rates of 0.5 for November (which is a seasonally low month) and 1.3 per cent for December, which, more or less, became the new 'steady state rate'.

In November–December the debate on the 1986/7 budget unfortunately failed to yield the hoped-for additional cut in expenditure, mainly on defence.[10] Amongst other advantages, such a cut would have enabled a reduction in social security taxes to alleviate expected additional cost pressures from wages. At the same time pressure was mounting on the Ministry of Finance to give subsidies and public credit to ailing enterprises. This culminated, after a short while, in a statement by Prime Minister Peres that 'now that we have beaten inflation it is time to embark on growth', by which he implied a desire to bail out ailing enterprises (in the construction and manufacturing industries) in the Histadruth-owned sector. He was successfully resisted by Finance Minister Moda'i, with some backstage help and a public debate.

Turning to the initial monetary developments: a shift from rapid inflation and a high rate of devaluation to a stable exchange rate and relative price stability will, in and of itself, bring about dramatic monetary changes in an economy accustomed to dollar-linked *plus* nominal and real shekel assets. The effective monthly rate of interest on dollar assets was 17 per cent (in shekel terms) just before the programme was introduced, dropping the following day to 3 per cent; the monthly shekel borrowing rate was 20 per cent and the rate on time deposits was 11–14 per cent on the eve of the programme. The Bank was reluctant to bring down shekel borrowing rates too rapidly. The monthly rates for August and September were 16 and 12 per cent, respectively, later going down more rapidly to 9, 7, and 5 per cent in the last three months of the year (the quarterly averages are given in Table 5.2, col. 7).[11]

---

[10] During that debate the possibility was first raised, by Defence Minister Rabin, that the Lavi aircraft project might eventually have to be terminated, if additional budgets were not allocated. It took another two years of hot debates and wasteful additional expenditure before this painful decision was finally taken (see s. 5.4).

[11] The slow adjustment of the shekel interest rate (in contrast to the dollar rate) could have been avoided if Israel had adopted an interest-rate conversion table of the kind introduced with the Austral Plan in Argentina (see discussion in Ch. 6).

Given the sharp reduction in inflation and in inflationary expectations the implied real interest rates were extremely high, averaging between 60 and 170 per cent in annual terms in the second half of 1985, depending on whether the above inflationary expectations or actual *ex post* inflation rates are applied. The interest rates on time deposits came down more quickly. As expected, there was an immediate sharp drop in PATAM (dollar-linked) deposits, whose share in M3 exceeded 80 per cent by the end of 1984, while both the quantity of money and short-term shekel deposits increased steeply.[12] Because of the difference in liquidity ratios (the PATAM ratio was 100 per cent), the Bank had to raise liquidity ratios on shekel deposits so as to avoid a credit increase. Total liquid assets (comprising money, time deposits, and PATAM) declined by 11 per cent in real terms in July, remained stable in August, and dropped again in September. Total bank credit decreased by 9 per cent in real terms in July and rose slightly afterwards, while the share of 'directed' (subsidized) credit, which had been 50 per cent, started sliding from August onwards (more on financial deregulation in Section 5.7).

5.3 Phases 2 and 3: The Post-Stabilization Business Cycle

Figs. 5.1 and 5.2 reveal that there was only a short and relatively small dip in economic activity (in terms of the state-of-economy index as well as the industrial production index) while unemployment continued to rise only up to the second quarter of 1986 (reaching close to 8 per cent before the turnaround). From the beginning of 1986 or thereabouts the economy embarked on an exceptional boom which lasted until the middle of 1987. This was followed by a substantial drop in economic activity in the following two and a half years, and a steep rise in unemployment (the latter trend continued even when output started rising again quite rapidly from the end of 1989, mainly on account of large-scale immigration—see below).

First of all it is important to stress that none of these turning-points was anticipated, although, in hindsight, one can always

---

[12] For more detailed analyses of monetary developments after stabilization see Piterman (1989) and Patinkin (1991).

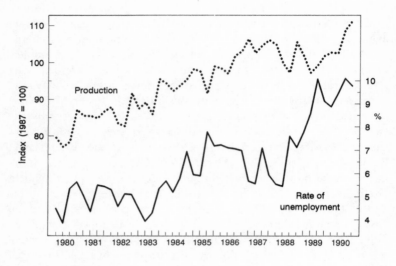

Source: CBS.
Fɪɢ. 5.2   Industrial production and unemployment, 1980–1990

find good reasons. Of the two parts of the cycle it now seems that the initial boom is the one that requires more explaining. To what extent is this rather extreme cycle connected with the nature of the stabilization process? Was it due to some special events? Experience from past moderate stabilizations in Latin America points to a business cycle with an initial boom following in the wake of exchange-rate based stabilizations that are perceived as not credible (see Kiguel and Liviatan 1990*b*; Calvo and Vegh 1991). The argument is that lack of credibility makes the public expect a policy reversal in the future. Thus the fall in nominal interest rates, under interest parity and a fixed exchange rate, is perceived as temporary. This makes present consumption cheaper relative to future consumption and, by intertemporal trade-off, fuels a consumption boom. At the same time, lack of credibility makes inflation stay positive, while the exchange rate stays pegged, and the resulting real appreciation causes a recession.

A look at the data for Israel shows that the boom was indeed fed by a consumption spree. At the same time we know from our previous discussion that it was unlikely to have resulted from lack of credibility at the initial stage. Consumption per capita, which dropped only slightly immediately after inception of the July 1985 programme (see Table 5.2, col. 11), increased by about 20 per cent in one year and then levelled off. A glance at the figures for the net, after-tax real wage (col. 10 in the same table) shows a similar rate of increase starting in August–September, except that the initial dip from which this net wage increase started was considerably larger (a 15 per cent drop). It is therefore not clear whether the wage increase by itself could explain the size of the consumption increase. There may be another, more interesting reason for this large increase in consumption per capita, based on a one-time increase in permanent income or perceived wealth that the stabilization programme may have brought about.

Most of net household financial wealth in Israel, we have argued, takes the form of government (indexed) debt. The bank-share crisis of 1983 made households very apprehensive of the government possibly defaulting on its debt. Perceived household wealth, one assumes, would have fallen as a result. In the next year (1984), as we have seen (Table 3.1), for the first time there was no net purchase of government debt, even though there was an increase in private savings. A sharp drop in private consumption per capita occurred immediately after the bank-share crisis, accompanied by a one-time sharp increase in the private savings ratio. Between the third quarter of 1983 and the July 1985 programme private consumption dropped by 12 per cent. The successful stabilization could be expected to reverse this move, as in fact it did, since individuals and households could now be more confident that the government would not renege on its debt. In other words, perceived net financial wealth may have increased after the programme proved a success. One result there would be an upward adjustment in consumption per capita and a downward adjustment in the private savings ratio, and this is precisely what happened immediately after the programme started.[13]

If this argument is correct, one would expect to observe a fall in the market value of government debt during and after the

[13] A moving quarterly average of consumption per capita (C/N), in log form, appears in Fig. 5.3, based on the third quarter of 1983 as a zero level. Thus, the scale on the right roughly corresponds to percentage changes in C/N from that period on.

bank-share crisis (i.e. a rise in the now riskier rate of return) while the reverse would be expected to take place after 1985. The time profile of the rate of return on government bonds (see Fig. 5.3) seems to substantiate this argument—there is a steady increase through 1984, reaching a peak in the third quarter of 1985, after which there is a sharp drop in the rate of return. While these data may also be partly affected by the monetary crunch in the immediate aftermath of the July programme, the behaviour of the short-term real rates is sufficiently different from the long-run rate to suggest that more basic factors affected the long-term bond market, including the argument mentioned here. The time profile of consumption per capita, which appears in the same figure, seems to fit this theory quite well. In summing up, the above explanation of the consumption boom rests on the perceived credibility of the programme, rather than on any lack thereof (which was the Kiguel–Liviatan argument).[14]

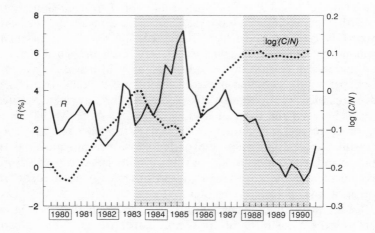

Fig. 5.3 Rate of return to government bonds and consumption per capita, Israel, 1980–1990

[14] Two other arguments might explain the more sustained reduction in the private savings rate throughout 1985–9 by some 5–6% of national income. One is based on the established positive empirical relationship (see Deaton 1990) between the degree of uncertainty and the private savings rate. Past high private savings rates in Israel seem to be associated with the greater price fluctuations that go with high inflation. An alternative argument links the changes in the private savings rate with changes in the opposite direction in the rate of public sav-

The argument that the 1986–7 boom was a one-time demand-side consumption adjustment links up with the subsequent downturn (phase 3). While some special factors may have deepened and lengthened the slump (see below), we believe that it was an inevitable delayed supply-side consequence both of the long structural crisis period of the 1970s and of the early 1980s as well as the result of real factor price increases (and an associated profit squeeze) in the aftermath of the programme. Of these, the most important was real wage overshooting; to a lesser extent, high real interest rates have also played a role.

All these factors would have caused unemployment to increase much earlier on in the stabilization process were it not for the temporary large consumption spree, which not only postponed the slump but even brought about a temporary reduction in unemployment. From a political-economy point of view this may have saved the programme from succumbing to demands for budgetary reflation at an early stage, as unemployment would have surged beyond the politically dangerous 8 per cent mark. As we shall argue below, stabilization involves a prolonged social and political learning process. By 1989, having gone through a new period of relative price stability and some painful structural adjustment, Israel's citizens were probably more ready to live with a 9 per cent unemployment rate. In the next two years unemployment rose further, to 11 per cent, but this time massive Russian immigration was the primary cause. At any rate, the perception on the eve of the 1985 programme had been that any increase in unemployment to more than 8 or 9 per cent would be politically unsustainable, coming on top of what was perceived to be the great sacrifice of across-the-board real wage cuts in return for an elusive promise to stabilize the price level.

Let us return to the possible explanations for the slump, starting with the 'special factors'. The excessive private consumption boom of 1986–7 showed up in a cumulative consumption increase of 24 per cent and led to GDP growth of over 13 per cent in the two years 1986–7 taken together (see annual growth rates in Table 5.3). This in itself was expected to lead to a lower growth rate in 1988. Two special factors played a role in exacerbating the

ings, invoking Ricardian Equivalence (see Meridor 1985) (cf. the last two columns of Table 2.4). Anyway, the existence of several competing or supplementary explanations points to the scope of work remaining on the issue.

slow-down. One was the beginning of the uprising in the administered territories (the *intifada*), in December 1987, which temporarily reduced international tourism and disrupted trade in goods and labour services with the territories. The *intifada* is estimated to have accounted for a loss of close to 2 percentage points of GDP growth over the two years 1988–9. To this one might add 1 percentage point on account of an investment shortfall due to greater economic and political uncertainty.[15]

TABLE 5.3 *Resources and their uses, 1981–1991 (at constant prices)*

	NIS bn. 1991	Average annual rate				
		1981–5	1986–7	1988–9	1990	1991
Resources						
Gross domestic product	135	3.0	5.0	2.2	5.4	5.9
Imports of goods and services[a]	62	3.8	14.2	–4.6	9.0	15.8
of which civilian	57	4.5	13.7	–0.6	8.5	15.8
Total resources	196	3.3	8.3	–0.3	6.6	9.0
Use of resources						
Private consumption	82	4.4	11.8	2.1	5.3	7.6
Public consumption						
Total	40	1.1	3.4	–5.6	4.9	3.4
Excl. direct defence imports	35	1.6	0.7	1.6	3.2	1.8
Gross domestic investment						
Total	33	0.0	6.4	–1.9	22.6	43.4
Fixed	32	0.3	6.3	–2.1	19.6	41.8
Domestic use of resources[b]	150	2.7	7.9	1.3	7.6	12.4
Exports[a]	41	5.2	8.4	1.0	3.0	–2.3
Gross product of business sector[c]	92	3.5	7.1	2.2	6.6	7.0

[a] Imports (c.i.f.), exports (f.o.b.), excluding factor payments and general government interest from or to rest of world. Exports at effective exchange rate.
[b] Excluding direct defence imports.
[c] GDP *less* gross product of public services and ownership of dwellings. At market prices.
Source: BOI *Annual Report 1991*, table 2.1, based on CBS.

[15] The estimates and the discussion are based on Bruno and Meridor (1991).

The other special circumstance has to do with the policy disruptions and uncertainties of an election year (national elections were held in November 1988, and municipal elections four months later), one of whose major manifestations was the postponement of a decision to adjust the exchange rate, a subject to which we return in Section 5.5. The fall in revenues from tourism and the delayed adjustment in the exchange rate contributed to a real 2 per cent fall in export receipts in 1988, compared with an 11 per cent increase in 1987, when substantial growth in private consumption also took place. Together with the fall in investment and private consumption, total expenditures dropped and business-sector GDP growth slowed down further in 1989 (to 1.5 per cent, after dropping to 1.8 per cent in 1988).

When these special factors—the *intifada* and the delay in adjusting the exchange rate —are taken together, however, they account for about one-half of the cumulative 6.5–7 per cent drop in GDP from a hypothetical 10 per cent 'back-to-normal' growth rate that could be expected over the two years 1988–9. This leads one to look for deeper, underlying supply-side factors that are related to a protracted structural crisis in the real economy and its resolution.

The July 1985 programme dramatically changed the economic environment in Israel, and the ensuing drastic decline in inflation required firms to adopt a pattern of conduct very different from the one that had prevailed for over a decade. As we have seen, during the inflationary era firms could over-invest (thanks to cheap government credit) and ignore inefficient real activities. High inflation enabled firms and households to achieve high profits mainly through successful financial manipulations.[16] Low inflation brought to light the real inefficiencies, necessitating structural adjustment and restoring the importance of technical and marketing experts rather than the financial 'wizards' who throve (together with their firms) under high inflation. Moreover, the government's new attitude toward fiscal balance meant not

---

[16] Like all generalizations this statement is, of course, not universally applicable. We pointed out the fact that, during the years of crisis, manufacturing exports successfully continued, thanks to more or less stable real exchange rates. Export industries were hurt mainly by the real appreciation. Even export industries, however, enjoyed the 'benefits' of inflation coming from special access to cheap credit for both working capital and longer-term investments.

only a reduction in current public-sector activities and expenditures, but also a sharp decline in the government's willingness to bail out failing enterprise (except for a few sectors and under very strict conditionality; see Section 5.4). This forced firms to bear the responsibility for their own activities, and changed patterns of management and corporate governance (also bolstered by a more stringent legal framework). While such change in the environment eventually yields large productivity pay-offs, the initial effect is one of a slow-down in supply.[17]

All of this was obviously considerably exacerbated by real cost increases and the resulting profit squeeze resulting mainly from the excessive increase in wages that ensued with stabilization. Real labour costs per unit of output increased by 20 per cent between 1984 and 1988 and the increase in the manufacturing sector even reached 25 per cent. Although this was the dominant factor in the erosion of profitability, aggregate supply and net profitability were also adversely affected by taxation and the costs of finance.

The increase in effective tax collection coming in the wake of stabilization (the so-called reverse Olivera–Tanzi effect) naturally has a greater effect on taxpayers who, under high inflation, had gained from a lag in tax collection, namely the self-employed and the corporate sector.[18] Effective tax rates in the business sector increased from a low of 18.4 per cent in 1984 (25 per cent on average during 1982–4) to a peak of 33.3 per cent in 1986, stayed more or less at that level in 1987–8, and then came down (after some reductions in marginal and company tax rates) to 26 per cent in 1989–90. The sharp increase in net indirect tax rates (due to the cut in subsidies and an increase in the value added tax), from 4 per cent of GNP in 1980–4 to an average of 10 per cent in 1986–90, though in large part falling on households, no doubt also contributed to the reduced net profits of the business sector.

Finally, high real interest rates are a common feature of post-stabilization periods, especially when monetary policy is aimed at supporting an exchange-rate peg against speculative attacks. Real

---

[17] A similar, though clearly much more dramatic 'management shock' has afflicted the liberalizing East European economies since their 1990 and 1991 'big bang' programmes (see Ch. 7).

[18] The other side of the same coin is the relative gain of wage earners whose taxes, by and large, are withheld at the source.

interest rates, which reached a record high during the first few months, decreased later, but remained high (the marginal real rate on overdraft facilities, a common source of business finance in Israel, averaged about 35 per cent during 1986–7; average rates, however, were only about 12 per cent, ranging from 7 per cent in 1986 to 16 per cent in 1987[19]). Since 1988 these rates have come down substantially, but the difficulties arising from the cumulative financial burden remained quite marked for some sectors, notably in agriculture (less so in manufacturing, since it had enjoyed a large component of subsidized export credit).[20] Issues of financial restructuring are discussed further in Section 5.7.

In ending this section we should note again that there is some evidence to the effect that a post-stabilization recession can take place even when there is better synchronization of nominal magnitudes in the process of stabilization. Garber (1982) pointed out the emergence of a sharp recession in Germany two years after the 1923 stabilization, for reasons that have to do with the distorted pricing of capital goods during the inflationary period. Fig. 5.4 for Germany (based on Garber's data) and Fig. 5.2 for Israel do, in fact, look remarkably alike. In Germany of the 1920s, unlike Israel, inflation declined instantaneously and the exchange rate remained unchanged for a long period with no substantial real appreciation (presumably due to lack of inflationary inertia, a term and a phenomenon that were not known at the time). Similar delayed recessions were recorded after the stabilization of some other European hyperinflations.[21]

---

[19] When the first exchange-rate adjustment after stabilization was made in Jan. 1987, interest rates were raised again temporarily for fear of a loss of credibility. The evolution of exchange-rate and monetary policy is discussed in greater detail in s. 5.5.

[20] An interesting point, first raised by Piterman (1989), may mitigate the severity of the liquidity crunch in the early phase of stabilization. A sharp reduction in nominal interest rates creates a one-time automatic 'debt-rescheduling' effect resulting from the fall in the relative interest-payment burden or a rise in its reciprocal, the average loan-repayment period. Assuming that principal is rolled over while interest payments are made on a current basis, the average repayment period of short-term debt (i.e. the ratio of principal to the interest rate) rose from 5.5 months in the first half of 1985 to 10.6 months in the second half and to 31.9 months in 1986. It stayed more or less the same in 1988 (29.2). This interest-rate effect is thus a one-time effect. In the long run, such a 'rescheduling' effect hinges on the real interest rate being below the profit rate.

[21] In Austria and Poland of the 1920s there was a similar delayed recession a few years after stabilization (Wicker 1986), likewise after the Hungarian

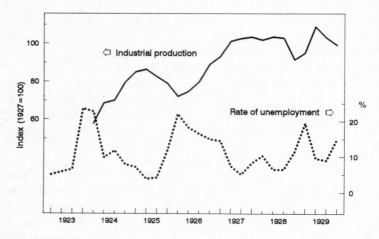

Source: Garber (1982).
FIG. 5.4   Industrial production and unemployment in Germany, 1923–1929

5.4 Establishing Fiscal Credibility

A necessary condition for successful stabilization is the sustainability of fiscal balance over a longer period of time. Whether
this condition has actually been met in a particular case can only
be tested *ex post*. Since divergence from governments' bad past
track record could also prove to be only temporary, the signalling of the seriousness of government's intentions along the
way is a very important part of the stabilization process. Let us
start with the components of the *ex post* fiscal record and then
go on to discuss important policy decisions along the way.

Table 5.4 compares the average structure of the total public-
sector budget during the six years 1986–91 with that of the five
years preceding the programme (1980–4). The main difference is
a net reduction of about 9 percentage points of GNP in public
domestic expenditure, which enabled an 8 per cent reduction in
the domestic deficit-to-GNP ratio and a 1 per cent reduction in

hyperinflation of the 1940s (Siklos 1989). As argued by Vegh (1992), however,
these recessions after a hyperinflation may not, necessarily, have resulted from
stabilization *per se*.

the total tax revenue. Of this, about 4 percentage points consisted of a cut in domestic defence expenditure (which was down to an average of 10 per cent of GNP) and about 6 percentage points are accounted for by cuts in subsidies of various kinds, including the inflation subsidy that was implicit in investment credit. The 1 percentage point difference is made up by an increase in average interest payments.[22] Domestic expenditure on social services and on transfer payments on average stayed more or less stable. Since the net surplus on foreign transactions increased by close to 2 per cent (due to a drop in defence and the interest-rate burden over and above the drop in the average foreign transfer ratio), the combined total drop in the public-sector deficit between the two periods was about 10 percentage points, from 11 to 1 per cent. There is no doubt that this cut was the fundamental factor in the sustainability of the stabilization process.

There is room for a few additional comments, however. A more detailed year-by-year analysis of budgetary developments suggests that part of the immediate cut in the deficit, which exceeded the planned initial cut (recall the insufficiency mentioned at the end of Chapter 4), came from the so-called reverse Olivera–Tanzi effect. We have already mentioned the enhancing effect of stabilization on tax receipts from non-wage income (the fact that there was no overall average increase in the tax burden resulted from a compensatory cut in income-tax rates). But it is important to point out that price stabilization itself also cuts real effective expenditures since it improves the control of the fiscal authorities over effective expenditure of individual ministries.[23]

Next we should note that there were considerable fluctuations in the deficit over time. Fig. 5.5 gives the quarterly developments in central government's (excluding local authorities and the Jewish Agency) domestic deficit on a cash basis. Interestingly, it reveals the fact that the correction of the budget (namely the 'fundamentals') had already started by the end of 1984. Much of

---

[22] The average for 1986–91, however, conceals the fact that over the period the interest-rate burden has come down from about 8 % to 4% of GNP.

[23] Part of the immediate cut in defence expenditure came from the fact that the financial degrees of freedom (e.g. obtaining one's budget allocation earlier in the year and thus 'earning' the inflation differential) that high inflation provided were no longer available. This was also the source of an effective budgetary crunch in several non-profit sectors that are largely financed from the public budget (e.g. universities).

TABLE 5.4 *Principal components of general government income and*
expenditure, 1980–1991 (% of GNP)

	1980–4	1986–91
Expenditure		
Domestic		
Civilian	17.6	16.8
Defence, net	14.2	10.3
Investment	2.4	2.4
Subsidies	5.7	2.9
Transfer payments	11.2	12.5
Credit subsidies	4.5	0.9
Real interest payments	4.2	5.2
Total domestic expenditure	**59.8**	**51.0**
Expenditure abroad		
Direct defence imports	6.9	4.1
Nominal interest payments	4.0	3.3
Other	0.7	0.5
Total expenditure abroad	11.6	7.9
Total expenditure	**71.4**	**58.9**
Receipts		
Domestic	48.6	47.5
Foreign	12.4	10.3
Total	**61.0**	**57.8**
Deficit (−)		
Domestic	−11.3	−3.5
Foreign	0.8	2.4
Total	**−10.5**	**−1.1**

Source: BOI, *Annual Report 1991*, tables 5.1 and 5.2, based on CBS and National
Accounting definitions.

this was due to a consistent attempt by the new National Unity
Government, from September 1984, to reduce government subsidies, a process that received an extra push in the July 1985 programme. The irony of subsidy cuts, however, is that under
inflationary inertia the resulting price increases tend to cause an
acceleration in inflation, a problem that will be encountered
again in the experience of other countries (see Chapters 6 and 7).
This is precisely why the combination of the two prongs of a heterodox programme becomes so central.

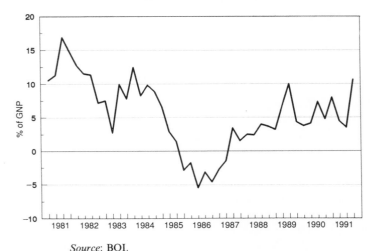

Source: BOI.
FIG. 5.5   Domestic public-sector deficit, 1981–1991

Fig. 5.5 also shows the very sharp further reduction in the deficit, after the beginning of the programme, to the point of a surplus in phases 1 and 2 of the programme. This is where the Olivera-Tanzi effect was most pronounced. Part of the apparent increase in the deficit in phase 3 (mid-1987 to the end of 1989) should be corrected for the slump in economic activity.[24]

Our discussion of the credibility of the sharp fiscal adjustment would be incomplete without mention of two central milestones in the process. The first was the implementation in 1986 of an important legislative step, cutting the automatic central bank budget financing link, which had characterized relations between the Bank of Israel and the Ministry of Finance for decades. The proposal to cut this link had been a key feature in earlier monetary reform proposals (see discussion in Chapter 4). The legislation was drafted by the Bank of Israel, the bill was tabled by Moda'i, and became law early in 1986.

The law (called in Hebrew the 'non-printing' law) stipulates that there can no longer be direct budget borrowing from the Bank of Israel, except for limited bridging loans (to the tune of

[24] Estimated in Bruno and Meridor (1991) at around 1 percentage point in 1988 and 5 percentage points in 1989.

2.5 per cent of expenditures) repayable within the fiscal year. But the law left two potential monetary loopholes. The first lacuna enabled the government to borrow abroad (even short-term) and then monetize the loans by selling the foreign-exchange proceeds to the Bank (which would then have to introduce compensatory monetary measures). This option was deliberately left open, because at the time the bill was being drafted (during 1984) the external financial constraint seemed too binding to give up this degree of freedom. As it turned out, this problem never arose during 1985–91 because the government had a net surplus in its foreign-exchange transactions.

The other quasi-loophole was the potential use by the government of its deposits with the Bank of Israel, accumulated in one year, for free disbursal in a later year. Such an eventuality, not envisaged when the law was being prepared, actually came up in 1989–90 when the government inadvertently over-sold indexed bonds (at too low a price) as mandatory backing for commercial bank savings schemes in a recession year (1989) and then wanted to draw on its deposit in a boom year (1990). This extra degree of freedom, which in this case allowed automatic procyclical budgetary (and thus also monetary) expansion, is obviously undesirable and was vehemently opposed by the Bank when the subject came up in 1990.[25]

The other milestone in establishing a new norm of fiscal discipline came with the decision, at the end of 1987, to scuttle the Lavi fighter aeroplane project. This project had been a source of national pride and the most prestigious development project of the defence establishment and of the aircraft industry, itself the biggest single employer in the country (21,000 employees in 1985). By mid-1987, when the subject came up for review and was being hotly debated in government and in public forums, a prototype of the plane was already flying and everybody who was anybody was brought down to the plant near Ben-Gurion Airport to marvel at what was certainly a very advanced piece of equipment, particularly with respect to its electronics (avionics) systems.

---

[25] On the particular point at issue the BOI's argument had neither formal legal basis nor sufficient parliamentary support, but the renewed public debate over the importance of fiscal prudence, even at a time of mass immigration, re-emphasized the central role of the 'non-printing' law, and may thus have prevented erosion of the law itself.

There were only two problems. One was financial: the USA, which had financed the project's early stages, was about to reduce its participation (by then $1.5 billion had already been jointly expended and at least another $2 billion was required, equivalent to 5–6 per cent of annual GDP). The other problem was one of potential marketing. The development of export markets would be barred by the USA to prevent competition with its own planes (the Lavi was to use US-built engines). Moreover, the Israeli Air Force was reluctant to pre-commit to buying a large number of planes within an increasingly stringent domestic budget constraint; the future open option of importing more US fighter planes out of a more flexible foreign-exchange budget seemed more attractive. The arguments for continuation of the project ranged from misperception of the sunk-cost argument, and the feared 'loss of the country's skilled manpower and technological edge', to the lack of an alternative 'national project'. Emotions and rational considerations were inextricably mixed, but in the end the very painful decision was made by a majority of ministers towards the end of 1987.[26]

Once the decision was made, the aircraft industry embarked on a very effective restructuring plan. It shed 25 per cent of its labour force in two years (some of whom went to work for aircraft industries in other countries) and became a leaner, but considerably more productive export-driven industry. Within two years previous output levels were regained and the share of

---

[26] Private information, conveyed to me by some public-spirited Air Force pilots with training in economics as early as 1985, suggested the disadvantage of a forced purchase of the Lavi from the cost-effectiveness and planning flexibility points of view. This helped me in preparing (in my capacity as Economic Adviser to the government) the economic case against continuation of the project. It had, from the beginning, seemed to be a white, albeit beautiful, public-sector elephant. Israel has a definite comparative advantage in the development and production of sophisticated avionics, but not in the mass production of its platform, a point that is not easy to convey to either ministers or the general public. There is no doubt that, given the powerful pro-Lavi bloc in the government—Peres, Shamir, and Arens (himself an aeronautics engineer and avid protagonist of the plane)—the decision to abandon the project would not have been made were it not for the new team at the General Staff of the Israeli Defence Forces, which took the 'alternative cost' implications of the new budgetary crunch seriously. The new Chief of Staff, appointed in 1987, was Dan Shomron. The main pushers for the decision, against the views of the aircraft industry and part of the Ministry of Defence, were the newly appointed commander of the Air Force, Avihu Bin Nun, and particularly the new Deputy Chief of Staff (and Shomron's successor) Ehud Barak, who holds a graduate degree in Operations Research.

exports increased from 60 to 80 per cent. No less important than this impressive restructuring effort was the signal to the rest of the economy that a new era of fiscal discipline had been ushered in, that the test of the market would henceforth be of paramount importance, and that the government would no longer automatically bail out ailing enterprises.

5.5 The Struggle over the Establishment of a Nominal Anchor: Credibility and Learning

The contest over policy in the aftermath of sharp stabilization, particularly when the latter comes at the end of a very prolonged period of high inflation, takes a special twist which would ordinarily not be present in the conventional inflation–unemployment or inflation–balance-of-payments trade-offs under brief spells of single- or double-digit inflation. A sharp stabilization may, for a time, reduce inflation dramatically, but it will not, in and of itself, eradicate the entrenched inflation mentality or the time-honoured norms of inflationary behaviour by all relevant agents, both public and private. Expectations of automatic nominal monetary, wage, and exchange-rate accommodation, as well as automatic bailing-out of failed enterprise, are a natural by-product of a sustained inflationary era (which, in Israel, lasted twelve years), and it is all too easy to become addicted to it. To this, one should add the false air of complacency that tends to accompany the first stage of seeming success in the dramatic reduction of inflation and the initial credibility signalled by the renewed build-up of foreign-exchange reserves. It seems that, immediately after the worst is over, the time appears ripe for a relaxation of the fiscal and monetary reins, especially if such a worthy objective as 'resumption of economic growth' can be invoked (see Section 5.2 and also Chapters 6 and 7 for the universality of this problem).

The most obvious bones of contention, apart from the need to hold a tight rein over the budget, were the real appreciation and the high real interest rates. There are really two separate credibility tests of the serious intentions of the policy makers. In the first of these—attaining credibility in the defence of fiscal restraint— the Bank of Israel and the Ministry of Finance (as well as the academic economists) have usually joined forces. But there is a different, though complementary, type of credibility game, which has to be played out even when fiscal balance is maintained, and that has to do with the defence of the nominal anchor.[27] In this test—notably maintenance of monetary restraint and adherence to stable nominal exchange rates—the Bank had to stand alone, often against the pressures of the Ministry of Finance, which, in turn, was coaxed by the Manufacturers' Association, representing the view of the exporters (with respect to the real appreciation), and the business sector more generally (with respect to the cost of borrowing).

While the choice of multiple nominal anchors was justified at the programme inception stage, there still remains the issue of choosing the key nominal variable to which monetary policy in its wider sense (namely including also exchange-rate policy) should be targeted. During sharp stabilization and immediately afterwards the advantages of the exchange rate over any monetary aggregate are almost too obvious to need mentioning again. The demand for money tends to be highly unstable and no monetary aggregate could be relied upon as an anchor. Moreover, the exchange rate has obvious signalling properties: it is quoted daily and directly affects the prices of a large part of the basket of goods in a small open economy. But it also has another important signalling advantage: it is a more visible and 'saleable' target *vis-à-vis* wage-setters in the economy, since the relative wage in foreign-exchange terms is a key factor in determining export competitiveness. This, of course, has another side to it. The problem of adhering to an absolute exchange-rate peg when inflation is still running at a positive, albeit low, rate is the potential loss of competitiveness resulting from real appreciation and the dangers of speculative attacks as the exchange rate is perceived to become unrealistic.

My own view has been that in a country with a highly unionized labour market and a long history of wage–price–exchange-rate and monetary accommodation (remember that the fixed peg had been given up in 1975) the only way to get nominal wage discipline is to continue, at least for a while, to work directly

[27] On the importance of drawing this distinction between the two credibility tests see also Kiguel and Liviatan (1990*a*). A more general analysis of the price-anchoring problem in an open economy is given in Bruno (1991).

through an exchange-rate peg, that is, act as if Israel were a member of the EMS (such membership, if politically feasible, would, of course, have made it easier to 'tie the government's hands'). In operational terms, this means adjusting the exchange rate at relatively rare intervals and at less than accommodation to past inflation, with a move to a more flexible exchange-rate regime (such as a crawl or a band), if needed, only later, once the stabilization lesson has been learned.[28] The likely cost of such policy stance and the learning process would be a period of real appreciation, relatively high real interest rates, and some unavoidable unemployment. What complicated the task was the fact that decisions on exchange rate level alignment had to be jointly managed by the Bank and the Ministry of Finance (at least until Israel moved to an increasingly flexible band at the beginning of 1989—see below). In the Israeli case the Ministry of Finance is, in general, less likely to want to adhere to a fixed peg, a stance of which the private sector was aware and which it exploited in the complicated game that ensued. Another complicating factor has been the fact that only a few of the academic economists supported the 'new' approach to exchange-rate policy, just as they had during the formation of the programme and in the early stages of its execution.

As we have seen, the slump that set in only two years after stabilization reflects the delayed emergence of the crisis in the real economy, hitherto hidden by the mirage of high inflation, the supply response to the profit squeeze, and particularly the real wage overshooting, which, in turn, was a major side-effect of the stabilization process itself. But it can also be viewed as a repeated credibility-formation game or as a learning process in which policy makers must signal their 'true type' to the private sector.[29]

Fig. 5.6 and Table 5.1 (cols. 2–4) show the patterns of movement of the exchange rate, prices (the figure gives the manufacturing wholesale price index), and nominal wages (hourly wage

[28] In contrast, in the case of Mexico, where the labour market is much more flexible, the early move to a pre-announced crawl made considerable sense (the experience of the two countries is compared in Ch. 7).

[29] Sample references to the relevant theoretical literature on credibility and reputation are Backus and Driffil (1985) and Rogoff (1985). For the context of the exchange-rate and wage-determination game see Horn and Persson (1988) and Cukierman, Kiguel, and Liviatan (1992).

(a) 1981–90

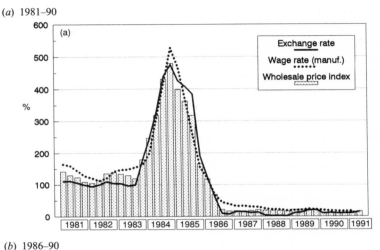

(b) 1986–90

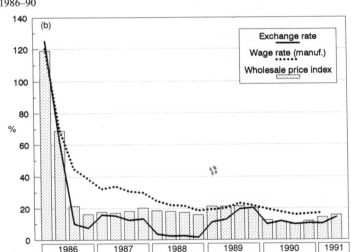

Source: CBS.
FIG. 5.6   Exchange rate, wage rate, and wholesale price index, 1981–1990

rate in manufacturing), each trailing the other in the monotonic
downward movement during disinflation. We note the very slow
but consistently downward monotonic convergence of nominal
wages towards a lower rate, converging with the inflation rate
and eventually overtaking it—the average annual rates of change

of nominal wages fell monotonically from 61.4 per cent in 1986 to 12.5 per cent by 1991. Some of this convergence, at least since 1989–90, has to do with the influx of immigration and a (slow) reform process going on in the labour market, of which more will be said in the next section.

The outcome was a partial reversal of the 1986–7 overshooting of real wages. As Table 5.1 (col. 10) shows, the cumulative drop in unit labour costs during the years 1988–91 only returned average labour costs to where they had been, on average, in 1985. Similarly, Fig. 5.7 shows the turnaround in the relative wholesale price levels some time around 1988–9. This partly reflects an easing up of exchange-rate controls followed by a change in the exchange-rate regime (see below), but it is no doubt also connected with the wage-moderation process described earlier. It can also be seen from Fig. 5.8, in which a convergence of non-tradable goods' prices to the price of tradable goods (more evidence of the stabilization of the real exchange rate after substantial real appreciation had taken place) closely follows the monotonic fall in wage inflation in the business sector.

By the first half of 1992 CPI inflation was down to an annual rate of 9 per cent, namely single digit for the first time since the

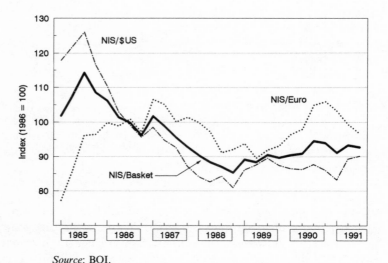

Source: BOI.

FIG. 5.7   Relative prices of industrial production, 1985–1991

Source: BOI.
Fig. 5.8   Traded and non-traded goods prices and wage inflation, 1986–1991

1960s. As Table 5.1 (col. 2) and Fig. 5.9 show, core inflation, defined as inflation net of controlled prices and housing prices (which were rising quite rapidly until the end of 1991 on account of demand for immigrant housing), was showing a consistent decline even earlier than that. Obviously rising unemployment and increasing wage moderation has a lot to do with this outcome. The slowness of the convergence process is reminiscent of the experience of traditionally inflation-prone countries like Italy and France after joining the EMS, for whom the convergence to the German inflation rate also took at least five years (see Giavazzi and Giovannini 1989).

A very similar slow convergence process, though one effected through a somewhat different mechanism, has characterized interest-rate behaviour. Fig. 5.10 shows a reduction of nominal interest rates (in terms of the interest rate on overdrafts) as well as a narrowing of the interest rate spread, both of which had been extremely high before and immediately after stabilization.[30] We note that after being very high in the second half of 1985, the rates came down and, as noted earlier, were then deliberately

---

[30] Because of the relative stability of the inflation rate after 1986, the fall in nominal rates also reflects a corresponding drop in real rates of interest.

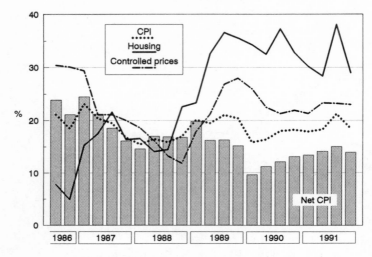

Source: BOI.
FIG. 5.9   Selected price indices, 1986–1991

increased in March 1987 during the first post-stabilization alignment of the exchange rate.

In view of the subsequent, very sluggish downward interest-
rate response to a substantial easing up of monetary restraint (by
a highly concentrated banking system, acting, at that point in
time, in cartel-like fashion), the cost of the preceding step on the
monetary brakes seemed excessive in hindsight. The kink in the
interest-rate curve in the first half of 1989 reflects my direct intervention as a frustrated central banker. In Britain it is allegedly
enough for the Governor of the Bank to raise an eyebrow; in
Israel, this would merely be shrugged off by the bankers. Instead,
an open public threat to invoke direct legislation (made by me
during the normally festive Annual Bankers' Association lun-
cheon speech) proved credible. Both that single act of 'brute
force' and a series of far-reaching reforms in the financial markets (see next section) have since moved Israel's financial markets
and interest rates into a much more free-market, Western-style
mode of operation.

At what point in the climb down from high inflation can the
relatively extreme form of monetary and exchange-rate restraint
be relaxed? The clamour from the business community is cer-

(a) 1984–1991

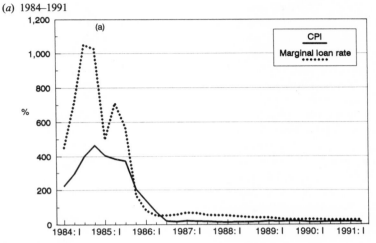

(b) 1986–1991

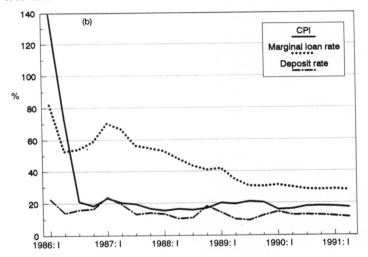

Source: BOI.
FIG. 5.10 Nominal interest rate and inflation, 1984–1991

tainly no guide (crying 'wolf' is commonplace anyway), but neither is there any scientific way of finding an answer in advance.
Some clues are provided by the extent of increase in unemployment and the gut assessment that the stabilization lesson may
finally have penetrated. A less benevolent interpretation of events
would view this analysis as an *ex post* rationalization of what
may have been a series of unpredictable events.

One event, which is of more than anecdotal significance, has to
do with the extended period from March 1987 to December
1988, in which no exchange-rate adjustment took place. Here,
traditional roles were reversed. Given wage and price developments in the preceding period and the emerging slump, the Bank
of Israel felt that an exchange-rate adjustment of around 6–7 per
cent was due some time in the first half of 1988. The Minister of
Finance (Nissim), on the other hand, dragged his feet, believing
that in the months preceding the impending general elections of
November 1988 a price hike would be unpopular. Since it takes
two to tango, that is, undertake a step-wise devaluation, the
adjustment had to be postponed until after the November elections. Rumours of an impending devaluation were followed by a
massive speculative outflow which forced a hurried 5 per cent
corrective devaluation in consultation with the newly appointed
Minister of Finance (by this time, Shimon Peres). Its forced timing, in the last week of December 1988, shortly before the closing
of the books, was received with great anger by the manufacturers
(and to some extent the banks), whose balance-sheet foreign-
exchange exposure makes for registration of net losses in the
amount of the devaluation. Many exporters, for that curious reason, prefer devaluations during the first half of the year, when
the enhanced export revenue dominates the cost–benefit calculation. Given the cumulative erosion of the real exchange rate an
additional correction was required anyway and it also showed in
the continued unrest in the foreign-exchange market *after* the
first adjustment. Thus an immediate additional 8 per cent devaluation followed in early January.

This rather traumatic experience with a relatively rigid
exchange-rate peg was instrumental in accelerating Israel's
change of regime, as a result of Bank prodding, to greater flexibility within a band. The 8 per cent adjustment was accompanied
with a move to a 3 per cent band, followed in the second half of

1989 by a much greater effective flexibility within a plus or minus 5 per cent band.[31] One incidental result of this shift was to give the central bank much wider control over exchange-rate policy from then on, turning it into a more integrative part of monetary policy formation.[32]

5.6 A Digression on the Role of Price Controls and their Removal[33]

Back in November 1984, Israel embarked on a tripartite package deal involving a wage–price freeze for a period of three months, in the wake of a price hike caused by a devaluation and a substantial cut in subsidies (which, in itself, reduced the budget deficit—see the preceding discussion). During this period the government maintained the right to adjust the exchange rate and the price of energy, so that an agreed correction of prices had to be made in the transition to the second package deal for February–March 1985. This, in turn, was followed by a third deal for the months April–June, leading up to the stabilization programme.

While these package deals could obviously not contain the inflationary process for long, they involved a learning process on synchronization and co-ordination from which doctrinal and administrative lessons could subsequently be applied in the design

[31] The move to a 5% and more effective band (namely a 'cleaner' float) followed another speculative wave. The 'speculators' (many of them exporters) wanted and expected a step adjustment (also taking the appropriate net asset exposure) and in fact burnt their fingers when the exchange rate unexpectedly appreciated on the day of alignment of the mid-rate. This particular episode taught the players in the foreign-exchange market a very important lesson, thereby turning it into a more flexible arena.

[32] In terms of the division of policy responsibilities, this represents a shift of control from the Finance Ministry to the Bank, a shift of whose implications the Ministry of Finance may not have been fully aware at the time. This process continued when another change in the regime was introduced in Dec. 1991 by my successor Jacob Frenkel. At that time the Bank and the Ministry jointly announced a preset daily change in the mid-rate of the band (corresponding to an annual cumulative 9% devaluation for 1992).

[33] This section borrows substantially from a draft of a retrospective paper written by David Brodett, who had designed and successfully led the introduction and gradual removal of price controls, and simultaneously served as member of the programme follow-up committee. I am grateful to David Brodett for allowing me to use parts of his paper here.

of the price-control system that accompanied the launching of the July 1985 programme. The first and most important lesson pointed to the need for a fully co-ordinated freeze on all nominal prices, including the exchange rate and other prices (as well as wages) that are directly affected by government, along with an attempted freeze on private-sector prices and wages. Not only is this a necessary condition for the avoidance of ratchet effects in the transition, it is the only way in which the programme could be implemented with minimum surveillance costs.

Price lists were widely published, and the general public constituted the most important price 'controllers' (the number of government employees directly involved in monitoring was usually around 100 and at no time exceeded 200).[34] Detailed legal procedures were carefully prepared whereby violators could be indicted speedily. Such procedure can only work, and for a limited period, if the freeze is imposed on *absolute* price levels, so as to avoid unnecessary 'noise' in the system, and if an agreed procedure is established by the parties to the deal for the inevitable exceptions that have to be made every now and then. Here this was based on appeals by the price-setters to a professional price committee, accountable to the tripartite co-ordinating body.

A crucial element is the assessment of 'entry' prices, prepared secretly while the plan was being worked out. Since considerable evidence had been accumulated on price determination from the preceding package deal episodes, estimates could be prepared on likely price increases arising from the up-front subsidy cuts and exchange-rate adjustments, using input–output calculations (these were made contingent on basic parameters such as the exchange rate, subsidy cuts, expected nominal wage increases, etc., which remained to be determined on 2 July). On top of these estimates a certain safety margin ('padding') was allowed, so as to enable producers to absorb unforeseen cost increases and, as experience has shown, even enable price reductions in response to the initial demand crunch.

[34] A helpful feature in a relatively small economy is the ability to monitor price changes through a relatively small number (a few hundred) of distribution channels and trading agents. However, in 1984 the share of supermarkets and the like in retail trade was still only 24%. In the course of the next four years their share increased to 35–40%, which, at least in part, resulted from the public credibility (in terms of pricing and quality) that these channels earned during the price-control period.

When the July programme was launched, maximum prices were announced for a group of 400 commodities and services. For all other groups of goods and services an allowed differential maximum rate of change was announced, based on the market-price vector on the eve of the first package deal (4 November 1984), inflated by the differential cumulative impact of the various basic parameters through the input–output system. Full disclosure of prices, denominated in shekels, was made mandatory (in view of exchange-rate stability, this latter requirement became redundant)—a major departure from the high-inflation period, when the tendency was to avoid displaying prices or else use the dollar as a unit of account. Longer-term contracts, previously denominated in dollars (such as housing rentals), were frozen in shekels at the rate of exchange of $US1/NIS1.5 established at the beginning of the programme.[35]

During the crucial first three months no departure at all from the price levels was allowed, even though some obvious anomalies must have been frozen at the initial price-setting stage. This extreme stance, at the cost of some distortion (though the actual number of appeals was extremely small),[36] is justified in view of the importance of signalling the 'right' initial expectation to the public, which, after all, measures stabilization by the price of individual goods. After the total three-month freeze and the more general attempt to 'weather the storms' of the month of October, it was agreed to continue with the controlling procedure. At this time, after three months, credibility dictated allowing for some essential price corrections, such as in the case of adjustment to the international price hike of sugar (see n. 36) and some obvious mistakes inherited from the launching stage. In all, during the second three-month period (October–December), thirty-five permits for 'justified' price increases were granted.[37] The corrections

[35] To this day, housing is the only market in Israel in which the dollar still serves as the unit of account, even though it makes no economic sense (the dollar has moved in ways that bear no relationship to the Israeli housing market).

[36] The first test came in Aug. 1985, when international sugar prices increased by 30–40%, which would have justified a domestic price increase of sugar and all the direct and indirect sugar-using products in the economy. It was decided to sell sugar from government buffer stocks at the old price, so as not to upset the price level during this entry stage.

[37] The control and decontrol policy, including its timing, was co-ordinated at the follow-up committee level. The joint monitoring by Emanuel Sharon as head

made were small, and given the small number (in relation to tens of thousands of goods and services), the effect on the perceived price stability was negligible.

One of the key ground rules established from the beginning was the limited time-span of the controls, initially six to nine months, and later gradually extended to thirty months although, from a technical point of view, a much shorter period would have sufficed. These extensions came at the request of the Histadruth in a bid to maintain these controls as a safety net as well as a means of justifying to its constituent members various wage concessions it had made. But to establish credibility an attempt was made not to stop any international price changes from affecting internal prices. Both upward and downward adjustments[38] were made, whose frequency gradually increased, while attempts were made to keep the changes small and, to the extent possible, to pair upward with downward adjustments.

In January 1986, six months from the onset of the programme and after relatively low inflation rates in November and December, the time was deemed ripe for a gradual removal of the control mechanism. Gradualism was chosen over a 'big bang' to prevent the deep-rooted inflationary norms of behaviour, at such juncture, from generating higher inflationary expectations than justified by the 'fundamentals'. Since by that stage there did not seem to be any remaining obvious distortions in relative prices, a gradual removal of controls, as low monthly inflation precedents were being set, seemed to provide an additional nominal anchor to the system (even though the main problem, as we have seen, was the wage–exchange-rate nexus). The share of goods and services under control was reduced from close to 90 per cent[39] during the initial programme period (after having been

of the two committees and of David Brodett, the price controller, as member of the follow-up committee, were of great practical importance.

[38] One piece of luck was the fall in oil prices which greatly helped in establishing the principle that prices can also go down. Import price competition, in a period when import licensing was still widely prevalent (having been reintroduced in the 1970s), was also affected by threatening to deregulate in a few cases of 'unjustified' price increases, e.g. books.

[39] The only goods not kept under control were fruits and vegetables, whose very large seasonal fluctuations often played havoc with individual monthly indices. For example, during Aug.–Dec. 1985 their price increased by 260%(!), in annual terms, while the general CPI (inclusive of fruits and vegetables) increased by only 38% in annual terms. A smaller gap continued into 1986 and it was only

25 per cent before 1985) to 55 per cent by April 1986, and from then on it sank gradually to return to the pre-programme share of 25 per cent by January 1988.

The evident success in the application of price controls in the Israeli case raises interesting, more general, theoretical issues as to when such direct intervention in the price mechanism can be justified and what method of decontrol (fast or gradual) should be used. A paper by Helpman (1987) justifies price controls within a monopolistic competition environment. Ball and Romer (1987) provide one of several relevant papers on price signalling and co-ordination. Zeira (1989) discusses the informational role of price controls during disinflation, also rationalizing the gradual removal of controls, and Persson and van Wijnbergen (1988) show how price controls may help to establish credibility.

Finally, it is worth repeating a comment made earlier on in our discussion of the stabilization programme. Price controls could not be the centre-piece of a programme because in themselves they would be a weak reed on which to base expectations of price stability (*vide* the experience of Argentina and Brazil during 1986–90). Also, the use of price controls as an auxiliary device hinges on the premiss that their distortive short-run effects are dominated by the extra welfare gains that a credible large reduction in inflation, aided by controls, could achieve. The smaller the disinflation and the larger the initial price distortions, the less likely is the argument to be true. The subject will come up again when we discuss Eastern Europe (Chapter 7).

5.7 *Structural Adjustment and the Reform Process*

The near balancing of the budget from 1985 onwards put a stop to the increase in net debt and provided the opportunity to free the financial and capital markets from the clutches of extreme government control. Naturally, the sheltered convenience of a government-monopolized capital market (in terms of easy access at preferential terms) or the ability to allocate credit through

in Jan. 1987 that a reverse trend set in. The quarter of the consumption basket maintained under control both before and after the programme included some basic foodstuffs and the price of public utilities—power, water, public transport, and some other public services.

extra-budgetary channels (and thus often sheltered from the scrutiny of parliamentary committees) is not a privilege that a Finance Ministry will easily relinquish. Nor was the government in Israel constrained by the kind of collective financial reform process that a typical member country of the EEC was forced to adopt in recent years. Unlike an extreme high-inflation or hyper-inflation crisis, where the politics of crisis management (or the need to obtain foreign aid) might lead one to adopt a 'big bang' stabilization solution, the urge to reform a distorted market structure hinges mainly on the internal pressures of the economists (led, in this case, by the Bank of Israel), occasionally helped by relevant parts of the business sector, and often obstructed by those in the business community (or in government) who stand to gain from the preservation of the status quo.

In the course of 1985–91 the greatest progress was made in those areas, primarily financial markets (including foreign-exchange decontrol), where the central bank's legal or coercive powers were the strongest. Financial markets indeed gradually shifted from extreme segmentation and quantitative restrictions, which showed up in huge interest-rate differentials (between domestic and foreign, directed and non-directed, short- and long-term credit), to a much more flexible, almost fully deregulated, system by 1991.

Before 1985, 70 per cent of all outstanding credit in the economy was government-directed (in terms of quantity, price, and destination) in one form or another. That included direct credit to exporters through the Bank of Israel, a distortive system introduced in the 1970s as a substitute for direct export subsidies. It was completely abolished in 1990, as were a number of other direct channels of government credit. By 1991, 70 per cent of all outstanding credit in the economy was completely free and only 3 per cent remained directed, while the remaining 27 per cent consisted of credit from government-approved deposits, most of them inherited from the past and phasing out gradually. Quantitative restrictions on direct and indirect foreign borrowing through the banks were virtually abolished, while far-reaching relaxation has taken place in the ability of Israeli firms to invest abroad.[40] The sharp changes in monetary policy and the process

[40] For a detailed description of the deregulation process, by the senior official in charge at the BOI, see Klein (1991).

of financial liberalization left several sectors in the economy in financial straits, especially those segments (primarily agriculture) that had previously been beneficiaries of the subsidized and directed credit schemes.

The real interest burden on a sector is the product of the interest rate and the ratio of credit to output. Throughout the high inflation period the ratio remained fairly stable in most sectors, except for agriculture, where it rose steeply. Excessive investments in the 1970s were, as we have seen, financed by cheap long-term credit (at highly negative real interest rates) rather than from own accumulated profits, which were often squandered on alternative uses. The government had already stopped handing out unindexed loans in the beginning of the 1980s; with the 1985 stabilization public long-term lending was virtually stopped. While the growth in net real capital stock in agriculture, for example, had come to a halt already in the early 1980s, the existing debt had to be increasingly recycled in the form of short-term debt at high real interest rates—a familiar 1970s phenomenon reminiscent of the Third World's debt problem. The financial leverage ratio of total outstanding debt to net capital stock in agriculture rose in the 1970s from around 20 to 50 per cent, increasing to 90 per cent by 1987.[41]

In agriculture the first major financial crisis occurred in the moshav (co-operative) movement, followed by the two biggest kibbutz (collective) movements. Both these types of organization had been characterized by highly diffuse mutual responsibility for individual, that is, kibbutz, borrowing. In the (co-operative) moshav movement, centralized credit and bookkeeping arrangements relieved the individual farming unit of the burden of strict accountability. In the kibbutz movement this 'soft-budget constraint' typified the relationship of individual collectives to the central organs of the whole movement, which obtained their funds from the government or the banks (the latter had naturally learned that the government would take responsibility on the day of reckoning). Internal mutual-reliance systems helped delay the crisis, but also gradually magnified the size of the cumulative

---

[41] See Kislev *et al.* (1989). The more general discussion here is from Bruno and Meridor (1991).

debt to 10 per cent of GNP (their share in GNP is only half of that).[42]

In both cases the government agreed to participate in a debt-rescheduling and relief scheme worked out jointly with the banks and the borrowers. The moshav movement's debt amounted to $1 billion, of which 40 per cent was to be written off by the banks and various other financing agencies and the rest to be rescheduled, primarily by the government. The above solution was upheld by the Parliament Finance Committee, under pressure from the borrowers. It had been only partly implemented by the time corrective legislation was introduced in 1992 which will entail a substantially higher cost to the banks (and thus to the budget). The kibbutz debt-relief programme involved a $1 billion write-off, two-thirds of which was borne by the banks and one-third by the government. In addition, $1.5 billion was to be rescheduled through government floating of bonds. The remaining $1.5 billion was taken up by the kibbutz movement, which has also undertaken very severe internal restructuring measures. Part of the programme, which is being more or less fully implemented, involves a radical change in the mutual-reliance system and a shift to individual kibbutz financial planning and accountability, with a link to a commercial bank that enforces the control of future credit allotments.

While kibbutzim constituted the biggest problem in terms of size of bad debt, some restructuring and debt-rescheduling schemes, under severe conditionality, have also taken place in the manufacturing sector. The most notable one is that of the Histadruth-owned industrial conglomerate Koor, which was based on a collectivization of losses and profits across enterprises, and whose past investment policy had often been dictated by the desire to establish a 'presence' in an area of the economy, rather than by pure profitability considerations. After the stabilization programme Koor tried to weather the internal storm by deepening its foreign indebtedness, but the crisis finally came to a head when the banks, both at home and abroad, refused to continue

---

[42] Only 30% of the increased debt between 1984 and 1988 can be ascribed to 'above-normal' interest rates. The rest came from the need to refinance old investment (much of which had to be written off), as well as collective consumption uses (such as improved housing at a time when finance was easy to come by). It should be noted that kibbutz activity by then derived only 45% of its income from agriculture, the rest coming from manufacturing and services.

lending without a major restructuring effort. Here, too, the government participated in the recovery programme, but very modestly. The Koor conglomerate has since become much smaller, in terms of the number of remaining enterprises (many of which have been sold off or liquidated), but it has also become considerably more productive. It reduced its 1985 work-force of 34,000 by over 10,000 while increasing productivity by 20 per cent over the period 1986–9. By 1991, it could show positive operational profits.

We now return to the process of financial deregulation. The opening-up of the economy to capital movements was greatly facilitated by the change in exchange-rate regime and the simultaneous development of the foreign-exchange market, with suitable new financial instruments that were introduced at the same time. The new regime stood up to the test of some minor speculative attacks. A further opening-up of the market in both directions, including granting permission to foreign citizens to trade in Israel government bonds and in domestic currency, took place towards the end of 1991. During the same period a major shift took place in the mix and application of monetary instruments. From extreme reliance on the use of reserve (liquidity) ratios, which are cumbersome and require government approval, Israel moved almost exclusively to periodic (monthly, weekly, and daily) money market auctions and open-market operations on short-term government debt.

One central aspect that distinguishes the financial reform from the sharp stabilization phase is the gradualist strategy that was chosen in this case (though partly with pre-announced targets). While a 'big bang' strategy for financial opening-up could be claimed to be more effective (and less prone to reversal), gradualism had the advantage, in the Israeli case, of being low-key, thus not attracting excessive political heat, and also enabling some check on unwanted or unexpected side-effects. As mentioned before, all these developments (in both monetary and exchange-rate policy implementation) also had the fortuitous result of giving an increasing measure of independence to the central bank. It is also worth pointing out that, with the increasing deregulation of financial markets, banking supervision by the Controller of the Banks (at the Bank of Israel) had to be considerably tightened in several respects. This is an important *sine qua non* of financial deregulation that is often taken too lightly (*vide* the 1990–1 upheavals in the US banking system).

In other areas of structural reform the power of the Bank of Israel is confined to its advisory role, so that results depend on the degree of persuasion (or lack thereof) and thus on the more diffuse parallelogram of forces involving all or most of the players mentioned in Chapter 4. Some progress was made with the support of the Finance Minister (and occasional obstruction by some of his officials) in deregulating capital markets. One issue had to do with the gradual liberalization steps in the mandatory investment of bank savings plans and pension funds in tradable (and hitherto non-tradable) government indexed bonds. Another measure undertaken was the free entry of the private sector into the indexed bond issue market, which had previously been monopolized by the government.[43] A gradual loosening was also taking place in the labour market, partly by agreement between the Finance Ministry and the Histadruth on the relaxation of wage–price and wage–wage linkages, and partly as a result of market forces, namely the increasing labour-market slack.[44]

Trade liberalization is one major area of structural reform in which Israel had made considerable progress since the 1960s.[45] During the crisis years this trend suffered a set-back as import licensing was reintroduced and non-tariff barriers proliferated.[46] Its associate membership in the Common Market (from 1975) and a free trade agreement with the USA (from 1985) exposed Israel to imports from these countries but left considerable protection against 'third parties'—mainly in trade with South East Asia, South America, and Eastern Europe. After a serious struggle between the Ministry of Commerce and Industry (represent-

---

[43] For an analysis of the objectives and preliminary results of the capital-market reform up to 1989 (when it slowed down) see Ben-Bassat (1990).

[44] The trouble with endogenous, market-forced, liberalization processes is that they may often have more distortive side-effects than one would get under explicit legislation or social compact. For example, minimum wage restrictions by profession or type of work (e.g. overtime pay) will apply in the organized part of the market (as in manufacturing, which is tradable) and discriminate in favour of the production of goods and services which are typically less unionized (e.g. services which are on the whole non-tradable).

[45] For a comparative cross-country study by the IBRD see Michaely *et al.* (1990). The Israeli study within the same project was conducted by Baruh and Halevi (1990).

[46] For a quantitative assessment of these trade barriers see Pelzman (1988).

ing the potentially vulnerable manufacturers) and the Ministry of Finance, in which the Bank of Israel was also quite active, a decision was finally made in 1991 to lift quantitative restrictions on a long list of imports from these regions and replace them by tariffs (of varying rates); this was to be done in pre-announced, annual stages, over a period of five to seven years. Israel's earlier experience with pre-committed gradual trade liberalization without reversal has been good, but it remains to be seen whether, and to what extent, the options for discretion left along the way are not abused.

Finally, an area in which least progress has been made is the privatization of state-owned enterprise. While the size of this sector in Israel's case is much smaller than it is sometimes made out to be (affecting about 5 per cent of the labour force), and some companies, such as the Israel Chemicals Complex, are run efficiently, it should none the less have been a more integral part of the structural reform process. The main obstacle to privatization had been political. Certain ministers can nominate appointees of their choice to boards of directors of government companies within their sphere of influence, and can veto candidates sponsored by political opponents.[47]

Another privatization issue, with whose analysis the Bank was more directly associated, is the sale of substantial commercial bank equity which became government property in the wake of the major bank-share crisis during the high-inflation period (1983). The micro-economic (and legal) implications of the 1983 Bank Share Arrangement for the management of the commercial banks in question, as well as the shape of their ownership structure, occupied much time and energy. While the legal and institutional foundations were fully laid down, progress in the sale of the government's equity has been sluggish, mainly because foreign investors have been slow to come in, and the domestic capital base too small for a speedier process. A much more determined effort should none the less have been made by the government to get domestic financial institutions (pension funds

---

[47] An attempt to overcome this hurdle was made by setting up a small ministerial committee (the Minister of Finance, the Minister of Justice, and headed, as an exceptional circumstance, by Prime Minister Shamir) with extraordinary fiat powers. But it is not clear how much had been accomplished by this committee by the time of the June 1992 elections.

and insurance companies) involved in the holding of equity both in privatized public-sector companies and in the sale of banks.

Starting at the end of 1989 the economy exhibited strong recovery in activity (see Fig. 5.1). The main push came from the demand side, namely the housing and consumption needs of new immigrants. Given the various components of structural reform described here, there has also been a considerable improvement on the supply side, showing in a substantial increase in productivity (exhibited already during the slump years, 1988–9) and in the fact that until the beginning of 1992, at least, resumed growth in activity had taken place without any increase in internal or external instability. At the same time, however, the test of a sustainable growth process still lay ahead. Physical investment in plant and equipment grew substantially, but its rate was still far from the estimated needs of future capacity.

A combination of a sluggish increase in profits and a high level of economic and political uncertainty were still the most important inhibiting factors. Economic uncertainty can be reduced by an improvement in pre-announced macro-economic policy rules such as a pre-committed fiscal policy over the medium term, which was in fact done by the end of 1991. On the other hand, in the first half of 1992 Israel was heading for early elections, brought about by the renewed beginning of the peace process. The long-term prospects looked good, given the added labour force from immigration and possible progress in the peace talks, but short-term uncertainties at the time were on the increase and the flow of immigrants tapered off with the mounting employment problems that new immigrants were facing.

The agenda faced by the new Labour government starting in July 1992 was dominated by the peace process but also required a renewed hard look at ways to speed up structural reform in the real economy. Further deregulation and dismantling of bureaucratic procedures, particularly in the area of private investment, was needed, in addition to a change of priorities on infrastructure investments by the government. Sustained growth combined with large-scale immigrant absorption also entails large capital inflows to supplement domestic savings for which loan guarantees were finally obtained.[48]

[48] For an assessment of investment-financing requirements and a general policy evaluation of the longer-term immigration absorption problem see the BOI Programme that was prepared in 1990 and published in 1991.

Successful absorption of the large influx of immigrants from the former Soviet Union (amounting to a 10 per cent increase in Israel's population by the end of 1991) is of crucial importance for Israel's long-term growth prospects. It has hastened the need for completion of the structural reform process. The interesting topic of immigration and its long-term absorption, however, lies outside the realm of our present study, which is confined to the 1970s and 1980s crisis and its resolution.

The developments described in this chapter have pointed to substantial success on the stabilization front and considerable, though insufficient, progress also on structural transformation. The most general lesson of this particular episode, already indicated at the beginning of this chapter, is the realization that stabilization from high inflation, even if conceived and implemented in a 'big bang' opening move, is itself quite a prolonged process in which the mental and institutional roots of the crisis have to be eradicated. If asked what, in hindsight, should have been done differently at the stabilization stage I would mention both the excessive pre-committed wage increases and the sluggish downward adjustment of interest rates. Even though a radical change of course in macro-economic adjustment policy seemed the most pressing need in Israel's case, I would also vote, in retrospect, for a tighter political commitment on structural reform, right from the start, when the government takes its big decisions and the social compacts get signed. It was less crucial in Israel than it turned out to be in some of the other experiences that we shall look at, but it might none the less have facilitated the subsequent reform process. We shall return to this issue as well as to other lessons from Israel's experience after broadening our scope of country experiences.

6

Latin American Comparisons:
Failures, Successes, Heterogeneity

6.1 Introduction

When Israel moved into its high-inflation epoch it was said to have taken on 'Latin American' features. Extreme inflation, at least after World War II, was usually considered a Latin American syndrome. As indicated in Chapter 1, the first manifestation of chronic inflation as a separate species indeed appeared in Latin America in the 1950s and 1960s, but rarely did inflation rise above 100 per cent.[1] The 1970s ushered in the new phenomenon of high inflation, which for a time affected only the two most problematic cases, Chile and Argentina. These two countries also showed growth rates that were below the MIC average already before the 1970s decade set in (see Table 1.6). Even Brazil's inflation during the 1970s, though it resembled Israel's step-wise profile (see Fig. 1.2 and Table 1.4), did not reach the 100 per cent threshold before the beginning of the 1980s. At the time the inflation–growth trade-off may not have seemed so bad, as Brazil managed to accelerate its GDP growth rate from an annual average of 6.1 per cent in the 1960s to 8.6 per cent in the 1970s.

The Latin American subcontinent as a whole maintained a relatively high growth rate (of 5.6 per cent annually) throughout the 1970s, in the aftermath of the first oil shock, apparently overcoming the worsening commodity terms of trade by tapping the temporary benefits of a large supply (at a seemingly low price) of capital inflows which the very same oil shock had set in motion. With the exception of Chile, which suffered the biggest terms of trade shock and launched its first and major stabilization in the 1970s, all other countries discussed here were hit by the worst external shock only at the time of the 1982 debt crisis.

[1] This happened in Argentina and Uruguay; see Ch. 1 and Pazos (1972).

The 1980s were for most of Latin America a 'lost decade' of very low growth (negative per capita) and very high inflation, with some variance among countries, especially in respect of macro-economic response and inflation rates. The second half of the 1980s has also seen increasingly successful attempts at adjustment and structural reform in many of the crisis countries. By the beginning of the 1990s, protracted crisis (as in the case of Brazil) has become the exception rather than the rule. An increasing number of economies have substantially shifted their trade policies towards greater openness, and market-oriented and fiscal reforms are becoming quite widespread, as the role of the public sector is undergoing dramatic change.[2]

In this chapter we attempt to concentrate on specific lessons that emerge from some of the more extreme Latin American episodes, as well as underlining or colouring some of our earlier conclusions from the case of Israel. Our emphasis is on similarities and richness of general issues in these country experiences and less on a detailed or comprehensive analysis of each and every country. For the purpose of our study this implies concentration on some cases more than on others.[3]

In the next three sections we take up some of the early lessons of the 'orthodox' Chilean stabilization experience, which affected some of the later policy choices in other Latin American economies and in Israel. Even though pronounced a failure at the time of its major second crisis in the early 1980s, Chile's extensive structural reform finally paid off; by 1991 Chile was at the most advanced stage in the process of return to sustainable growth. After discussing, in Section 6.6, the common and diverse elements in the structural reforms of the 1970s in Chile and Argentina (and to some extent Uruguay) we take up, in Section 6.7, Argentina's failed attempt to stabilize along 'heterodox' lines in 1985. A brief

---

[2] The latter development may in no small measure be connected with the perceived failure of the 'centrally planned' economies in Eastern and Central Europe, to which we turn in the next chapter.

[3] The literature on the various countries' experiences is abundant, and many references will be given as we proceed. For an overview of the recent reform process in Latin America as a whole see Meller (1992). Since we deal mainly with extremes here, it is also important to point out that within Latin America there were several countries with more moderate crises and a few countries that managed to avoid a major crisis altogether. We return to this subject in Ch. 8.

comparative discussion of Bolivia's contemporaneous orthodox stabilization from hyperinflation is also included in that section.

Brazil adds another dimension to the sample of countries: it had the most impressive growth record and, even in the common crisis years, successfully effected a substantial external resource transfer. Yet its inflationary process went out of control in 1986, after the failed Cruzado Plan. Brazil joined Argentina in several cycles of open hyperinflation during 1987–90, but its underlying internal fragility, compared with Argentina, appears to have been more monetary than fiscal. This comparison between the two countries is the subject of Section 6.8.

By 1991 Argentina may finally have achieved success in reforming its public-sector finances; its convertibility and quasi currency-board programme, reviewed briefly in Section 6.9, led to a sharp, and possibly sustainable, reduction in inflation. Finally we take up the case of Mexico (Section 6.10), possibly the most successful 'heterodox' stabilization, coupled with far-reaching structural reform, to date. The array of countries and episodes to be surveyed here will enrich our understanding of the factors that lead countries into a lengthy high-inflation and growth crisis as well as of the various components of the recovery process.

6.2 Chile: From Democracy to a Socialist Experiment[4]

During the 1950s and 1960s Chile's economy was already characterized by chronic inflation, relatively low-to-moderate growth, and frequent balance-of-payments crises. Like most Latin American economies, its development strategy had always been inward-looking. However, it had a very stable democratic political system—unusual in the Latin American setting.[5] The conservative and centre-right coalition that ruled Chile until 1964 had emphasized inflation stabilization, assuming that macro-stability would automatically generate growth as well as 'trickle-down' redistribution. This coalition was replaced with Frei's Christian Democratic

---

[4] For detailed analyses of Chile's crisis and reform on which our discussion draws see Bitar (1986), Corbo (1985), Edwards and Cox Edwards (1987), Larrain and Meller (1991), and Meller (1990).

[5] In Bollen's ranking for 1960 (see Table 1.6) it scores a maximum index of 1, as do several European countries, paralleled in Latin America only by Uruguay (the USA scores 0.95).

administration (1964–70), which, with an absolute majority, put major emphasis on structural changes such as land reform and Chilean participation in the hitherto foreign-dominated (mainly US) ownership of the country's large copper mines. The latter produced the bulk of Chilean exports. Basic structural reforms were slowly implemented so as not to rock macro-economic stability. Purchase of 51 per cent of the mines was carried out through bargaining, social expenditures towards enhancement of low- and middle-income groups were increased, and 100 per cent backward COLA indexation on wages was introduced.[6]

Average GDP growth during 1965–70 was almost 4 per cent; average inflation was a moderate 26 per cent, with a fiscal deficit of 2 per cent; unemployment was 5.6 per cent and real wage growth was at a high annual rate of close to 10 per cent(!), amidst a large increase in the number of strikes. As in the Israeli case, in the latter part of this period (1968–70) the same average indicators were, by and large, worse than in the earlier period 1965–7, namely a slow-down in economic activity and a gradual rise in inflation. Interestingly, this was also a period in which the foreign-exchange constraint was not effective (cf. the Israeli case): an all-time high real copper price boosted total exports to over $1 billion and foreign-exchange reserves quadrupled to $400 million (five months' worth of imports) within two years 1968–70. Perception of a growing unutilized pie, pent-up expectations, and a 'trap'-like worsening income and wealth distribution[7] set the stage for a democratically elected socialist take-over by a left-wing and centre-left coalition (*Unidad Popular*) headed by Salvador Allende in 1970, which brought Chile to hyperinflation within three years.

[6] Larrain and Meller (1991), on whose account this part of our discussion rests, note a substantial increase in political and social activity in the 1960s. Both the number of registered voters and the percentage of actual voters doubled over the decade (to 3.5 million and 30%, respectively) as did membership in the various unions (blue-collar, white-collar, and peasants) to over half a million, or about 20% of the labour force, by 1970.

[7] An interesting, and not entirely unfounded, structuralist theory of a vicious circle became very popular in Chile and elsewhere in Latin America: unequal income distribution generates a monopolistic productive system which reinforces income inequality. At the same time, the highly protected production structure gets more and more oriented towards the consumption demand of the wealthy at the expense of production of basic wage goods. Concentration of economic strength and political power go hand in hand to spring a 'trap' that can be escaped only by effecting a radical change in ownership patterns.

TABLE 6.1 *Macro-economic indicators for Chile, 1965–1991*

	Fiscal deficit/GNP (%)	CPI inflation	GDP growth rate	Gross fixed investment (growth rate)	Unemployment rate (%)	Real wage index (1969= 100)	Terms of trade[a] (1987= 100)	Current account deficit ($ bn.)
Democracy								
Import substitution, 1965–70	2.1	23	4.3	6.0	5.3	98	306	—
Allende socialism, 1971–3	16.1	150	0.5	4.6	-9.8	98	271	0.3
Military government								
Reform 1974–6	5.1	358	3.1	14.2	-7.8	69	140	0.2
1977–8	1.3	59	9.0	13.6	16.7	82	122	0.8
Tablita, 1979–81	-2.1	30	7.3	12.2	17.8	100	111	2.9
Debt crisis, 1982–3	3.1	12	-7.8	22.2	-26.6	102	110	1.7
Recovery, 1984–5	3.7	27	4.4	17.8	11.8	91	102	1.7
Normalization,[b] 1986–90	-2.2	19	6.2	11.1	11.8	95	132	0.7

[a] End-of-period figures (source: IBRD, *World Tables 1992*).
[b] Chile returned to democracy in Dec. 1989.

Sources: 1965–83: based on Corbo, de Melo, and Tybout (1986), and Corbo (1985); 1984–91: based on Edwards and Cox Edwards (1987), Meller (1990), and official data.

It was a clear case of an almost complete socialist take-over. The political objective was to transfer power from the dominant capitalist group to the workers and peasants. The economic means were a redistribution of asset ownership by nationalization of the copper mines, other basic resources (coal, nitrates, and iron), industrial enterprises, and banks. On the macro-policy level, a strategy of increasing nominal wages coupled with price controls and a fixed exchange rate was meant to increase real wages and boost demand and production for basic goods. Reactivation of the economy would further be helped by increased public expenditures, while monetary policy would play a passive role. High international reserves were to provide an escape valve by enabling increased imports, in an environment of price stability. The macro-policy stance was based on a structuralist theory of inflation whereby the ownership reform, the elimination of monopolistic profit margins, and the existence of price controls would allow growth without further inflation.

The share of public ownership did indeed change dramatically, from around 14 per cent in 1965 to 39 per cent by 1973 (see Larrain and Meller 1991), reaching 85 per cent in mining and in the financial sector. The emerging management problems read well as an introduction to the problems of East European transition (see Chapter 7). But the more relevant issue for the present discussion is the evolution of the macro-economy from a resounding initial boom (GDP growth of 8 per cent) with low inflation (22 per cent) in 1971, coupled with a 22 per cent increase in real wages and a drop in unemployment to less than 4 per cent, to the inevitable decline and collapse in 1972–3.

In the two years 1972–3 GDP fell cumulatively by 4.4 per cent, the price level shot up by 2,400 per cent, unemployment increased to 4.8 per cent, and real wages fell by 39 per cent. Exports (mainly of copper) were still going strong, rising in 1973 by 31 per cent (to $1.3 billion) over their depressed 1971 level; thus, imports (including food) could serve as an escape valve when domestic shortages appeared. Imports increased by 43 per cent (to $1.4 billion) over the same two-year period, leaving only a relatively small current-account deficit. The average performance of the basic indicators in the Allende period, 1971–3, appears in Table 6.1.

The announcement, at the end of 1972, of impending rationing contributed to the shortages and accelerating inflation and, in retrospect, it is hard to understand how the government was still able to secure 43 per cent of the vote in the parliamentary elections of March 1973 (distribution of food prior to the election apparently helped, as did a large dose of rhetoric). At the economic source of the crisis lay a large increase in the public-sector deficit, from 3.5 per cent in 1970 to an average of 16 per cent in 1971–3, resulting from a combined rise in expenditures and fall in taxes (including revenues from the copper mines) and financed by borrowing from the banking system, that is, monetization. This was coupled with extremely distorted commodity, trade, and labour-market regimes.[8] Finally, the US government contributed to Allende's downfall by withdrawing aid, placing an embargo on exports to Chile, and financing Allende's political opponents.[9]

6.3 The Military Government and the Lessons of Pure Orthodoxy[10]

A drastic change in policy occurred when the military took over in September 1973. The new strategy combined a tough orthodox stabilization package with a set of far-reaching structural reforms. Prices on the domestic market were deregulated and subsidies eliminated. This was helped by privatizing over 500 enterprises that had been seized or nationalized during the Allende regime. Most non-tariff restrictions on trade were eliminated up-front and, over a five-year period, starting in 1974, the average tariff on manufacturing goods was brought down from 151 per cent (with a standard deviation of 60) to 51 (and 16) in 1976, gradually reaching a uniform 10 per cent tariff by 1979.[11] To reduce the budget deficit, a substantial tax reform was implemented in 1974 together with drastic cuts in government spending and the introduction of strict cost–benefit practices in the public sector. Privatization helped finance the fiscal gap.

[8] Corbo (1985) mentions that at the end of the Allende regime more than 3,000 prices were set by the government regulatory committee (DIRINCO), and the ratio between the highest and lowest effective exchange rate was 52:1. The labour market was characterized by very low mobility resulting from large severance payments and an increasing rate of employment in the public sector.

[9] See Cardoso and Helwege (1991).

[10] This part of the discussion relies mainly on Corbo (1985).

[11] Data based on Edwards and Cox Edwards (1987: ch. 5).

Relatively high copper prices in 1974 and a rollover of 30 per cent of the outstanding debt service for 1973–4 eased the adjustment to the oil shock. However, in late 1974 and early 1975 Chile suffered the biggest terms-of-trade shock in Latin America when copper prices plummeted by 50 per cent while oil prices stayed at four times their 1973 value.[12] This brought about a large devaluation and further stressed the need for the austerity programme. By 1976–7 the budget was balanced and more or less remained that way (with a surplus in some subperiods) in the fifteen years thereafter (see Table 6.1 and Fig. 6.1).

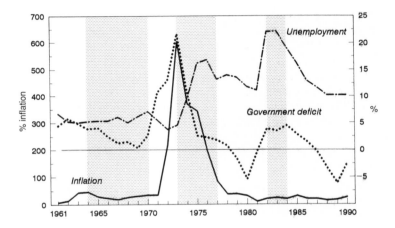

Source: Table 6.1.

Fɪɢ 6.1   Inflation, unemployment, and the government deficit, Chile, 1961–1990

The cost of the sharp policy turnaround is revealed in the very large—10 percentage points—rise in unemployment and the simultaneous sharp drop in the real wage by between 20 and 30 per cent of the pre-reform level. The real wage erosion, which was apparently unintended, had to do with the very slow disinflation (inflation, the budget deficit, and the unemployment rate are plotted in Fig. 6.1). This stands in sharp contrast to the quick reduction of inflation after an equivalent drop in the

---

[12] As Table 6.1 shows, the terms of trade fell by 60% from 1970 to 1978.

government deficit in the Israeli programme of 1985 (see Chapter 5). In 1978, five years after the inception of the sharp fiscal cut, Chile's inflation was still running at close to 40 per cent in annual terms, while unemployment stayed at 14 per cent (only to go up further in the subsequent stage).

The slow reduction in the inflation rate provides one major lesson to be learned from pure 'orthodox' stabilization in the context of persistent inflation.[13] Since the budget had been balanced for some time, neither the need for seigniorage nor lack of credibility would seem to provide an explanation of inflationary persistence. Rather, it was a problem of nominal price (wage, exchange-rate, and money) synchronization of the kind that a coordinated disinflation of all nominal magnitudes could give once the most important source of inflationary pressures, namely the budget, had been put in place. Ten years later the lessons of this episode helped in the adoption of a 'heterodox' alternative. The correct lesson, one unfortunately not generally applied in the Latin American case, was to *add* elements to the orthodox component, rather than replace it with price freezes. Another, more generally shared problem remaining in the aftermath of Chile's stabilization was the persistence of a very high real interest rate (of the order of 50–60 per cent in 1976–7), due to financial distortions in the enterprise and banking sectors, to which we will return below.

6.4 From Tablita to Confidence Crisis

The persistence of inflation motivated a policy shift that led to what turned out to be the second major macro-policy error (repeated in Argentina and Uruguay, at around the same time, and three years later in Israel). In February 1978 an active crawling peg (*tablita*) was established as the major stabilizing device. This was a pre-announced decreasing rate of crawl, below the previous month's inflation rate, gradually leading up to a fixed rate in June 1979, when inflation was still running at 2.5 per cent a month. The rationale behind the active downward crawl rested on the openness of the economy and on the Law of One Price

[13] We note from Table 6.1 that even during 1965–70, with a very small budget deficit, inflation in Chile averaged an annual rate of 23%.

(i.e. the assumption of PPP in international trade), forcing the prices of tradables and expectations of inflation downwards. Convergence was assumed to be fast. Integration of Chile's capital markets, which was taking place around the same time, under the assumption of interest-rate parity, was supposed to lower domestic interest rates by reducing the expected rate of devaluation.[14]

The main villain of the piece in the Chilean case was formal *ex post* wage indexation, which had been in place since 1974 and, by the end of 1979, was locked in at 100 per cent indexation by law. Prices of many non-tradables (housing rentals, mortgages, tuition fees) were likewise indexed to *ex post* inflation. Here we have another illustration of the importance of synchronization, and 'severing the memory of the past' in the process of rapid disinflation.[15] The lack of synchronization between wages, prices, and the exchange rate in the Chilean disinflation throughout the period 1976–80 can be seen clearly in Fig. 6.2. Over a period of five to six years (1975–81) the relative price of tradables to non-tradables fell by about one half, while Chile suffered another drop in its terms trade (see Table 6.1). A corresponding rise in the real wage, expressed in terms of tradables, took place between the beginning of 1978, when the *tablita* was announced, and the end of 1981 (estimates are from Corbo 1985). This episode provides a critical test of the importance of synchronization, as against a simplistic monetarist approach, since the fiscal balance had clearly been in place in the case of Chile. The same could not be said of the corresponding Argentinian episode (see Section 6.6) or of the subsequent application of a similar policy in Israel, since in both these cases fiscal balance had not been secured before the *tablita* was announced.

There is another problem that was overlooked in Chile (here the timing and the misperception are similar to those of Israel in 1977–8). The lifting of controls on capital movements enabled Chile to finance the increased demand for non-tradable goods

---

[14] The theoretical rationale, based on interest-rate parity as applied to the case of Chile, was provided by Mckinnon (1991), while a more formal approach, applied to the case of Argentina, was given by Rodriguez (1982, first version appeared in June 1979).

[15] Incomes policy and co-ordination can be important in the process of disinflation even when there is no formal indexation, since informal indexation is likely to develop in its absence.

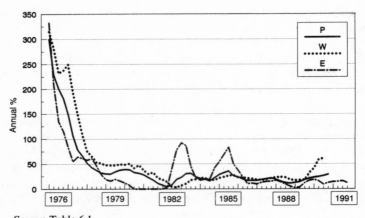

Source: Table 6.1.

Fɪɢ 6.2   CPI inflation, wages, and the exchange rate, Chile, 1976–1991

which, in turn, was motivated by the fall in their relative price. The active crawl further enhanced capital flows because it increased the spread between domestic and foreign interest rates. The only way to reduce that spread would have been either to start from a higher initial rate of devaluation (at a prohibitive domestic inflationary cost) or to tax capital imports, an instrument to which Israel resorted after a similar episode in 1978–9.[16] Over the period 1977–9 capital inflows into Chile totalled almost $5 billion, comprising a substantial portfolio change in domestically held assets and causing a sharp reduction in interest rates. It also deepened the 'trap' by postponing the inevitable balance-of-payments crisis, as in the meantime the current-account deficit was rising precipitously to reach over $5 billion in 1981, while foreign-exchange reserves continued to increase.

In addition to the earlier problem of the timing and choice of the *tablita* policy, the lack of timely response to the external events of 1981 was to blame for the depth of the ensuing crisis. During 1981 international interest rates rose steeply and the world price of copper fell by 10 per cent (implying a cut of $300 million in export revenues). The recession was mistakenly per-

[16] The proposal and its rationalization are given in Liviatan (1979). A capital import tax was introduced in Chile much more recently, in 1991, when renewed capital inflow caused an exchange-rate appreciation.

ceived as being short-lived and the structural reforms that had been made, as well as Chile's good standing with the international banks, strengthened the belief in an automatic capital account adjustment mechanism which would preclude the need to intervene. Thus the drop in the supply of external private capital came as a great surprise.

In the meantime, the attempt by the central bank to sterilize the extra capital inflow reversed the trend of the domestic interest rate, while inflation had dropped unexpectedly (to 10 per cent in 1981). By the end of 1981 the capital inflow came to a halt, partly as a result of difficulties that the international banks were beginning to face in other Latin American countries (see below). The increase in interest rates was accompanied by an increase in expected devaluation, and a financial crisis, Chile-style, occurred in the second half of 1981. Several financial institutions had to be bailed out by the central bank and exchange-rate collapse could no longer be avoided.

The next two years marked a serious confidence crisis. The exchange rate was first devalued and then floated, there was a run on the banks and a further financial crisis, leading the government (in 1983) to take over the two largest commercial banks. As Table 6.1 shows, the years 1982–3 saw a deep recession, with GDP dropping by 16 per cent, investment dropping even more sharply, and unemployment rising to 22 per cent with the effective unemployment rate rising as high as 32 per cent.[17] Finally, Chile was in a debt crisis, having almost tripled its external debt during 1979–83. Knowledgeable observers could, by 1984, pronounce the Chilean attempt at structural reform (along with those of Argentina and Uruguay, see below) an almost complete failure.[18]

---

[17] The usual unemployment figures relate only to open unemployment. They do not include workers in the Minimum Employment Programme, introduced by the government in 1975. These accounted for another 5% of the labour force in 1976–82, a ratio that doubled to 10% by 1983.

[18] This was the opinion of several key observers at the time—see Corbo (1985); Corbo, de Melo, and Tybout (1986); and Edwards and Cox Edwards (1987). While not knowledgeable myself, but as a member of the advisory board for the World Bank Study on which the first two papers were based, I must admit to having been convinced by the evidence. Given the depth of the crisis, Chile and Argentina did not appear to differ much at this particular juncture.

6.5 Recovery and Normalization: Reaping the Benefits of Reform

Now for the next and final surprise of the Chilean experiment. The policy change and the *tablita* proved, *ex post*, to be a major macro-policy mistake, and so did the lack of immediate response to the external shock of 1981. But the previous achievements of fiscal and structural reform had not been in vain. Let us recall that by 1981 Chile had an open, free-market economy (only twenty-five firms of the initial 500 remained in government hands), a homogeneous 10 per cent tariff, free domestic interest rates, and a reasonably open capital market. A distorted sales tax had been replaced by a uniform 20 per cent value added tax, employment in the public sector had been substantially reduced, and fiscal surpluses reigned during 1979–81 (see Fig. 6.1 and Table 6.1). Hence, by that time only the private sector was a large external borrower (in contrast, as we shall see, to the case of Argentina). Finally, the labour market had become much more flexible; there were no unions, no collective bargaining power, and non-wage labour costs had been reduced.

In short, the structure had been radically transformed and was, in principle, ripe for normalization; it was the short-term macro-policy and the response to the change in the external capital market environment that were to blame for the deep crisis that none the less occurred. It took a major adjustment programme, backed by substantial IMF, World Bank, and inter-American bank loans, as well as additional money from the commercial banks, to set Chile back on track (see 1984–5 in Table 6.1). The main avenue was a sharp correction in the current-account deficit, which had reached 123 per cent of exports in 1981 and was gradually reduced to 15 per cent by 1987, while external financial flows bridged the gap.[19]

In addition to a sharp reduction in domestic absorption (which, in itself, reduced import requirements by 50 per cent over 1982–5), a series of substantial discrete devaluations took place in 1982, 1984, and 1985, interspersed with (and followed by) a

---

[19] Using post-devaluation corrected figures the analogous percentages of GDP are 25.5% in 1981 and 3.4% in 1987 (see Meller 1990: table 3.8). The total external financing, mostly through multilateral institutions, over the five-year period 1983–7 is estimated at almost $8 billion (Meller 1990: table 3.8).

return to a crawling peg, all of which doubled the real exchange rate between 1981 and 1986 (thus correcting the previous erosion), as inflation remained substantially below the rate of devaluation and above the rate of wage inflation (see Fig. 6.2 between 1982 and 1986). The macro-preconditions for all this were provided by a combination of fiscal and monetary discipline with wage de-indexation, plus a sharp real wage erosion, which was helped by massive unemployment.[20] However, it also resulted in a substantial switch of production to tradable goods, primarily in the export sector, including the development of non-traditional exports.

At this point it is interesting to contrast the sharp Chilean adjustment of the external accounts, while maintaining relatively low inflation, with the much greater difficulty faced by Israel in changing *relative* prices, both before and after the 1985 stabilization, on account of a much more rigid labour market. Even though Chile, like Israel, exhibited substantial inflationary inertia until around 1982, its subsequent dynamics of exchange-rate, wage, and price inflation looked entirely different from Israel's around the same time,[21] and showed a flexibility which was much more conducive to the resumption of growth. There is, of course, also another side to the coin—the social costs as reflected in protracted high unemployment (three times the Israeli rate) and a more or less permanently low real wage which, in Chile, by 1990 had barely caught up with its level ten and twenty years earlier.

There is one structural issue in which Chile encountered difficulties that were at least as great as Israel's, and that is the financial fragility exposed by the liberalization of 1981 and the subsequent crisis. Persistently high real interest rates during

---

[20] The real wage erosion between 1982–3 and 1984–5, according to the official index, was 11% (see Table 6.1), but is estimated by Meller (1990), on the basis of a large, privately collected sample of firms, to have been substantially higher (around 17%).

[21] This also has an interesting corollary in the specification of inflationary dynamics and its econometric representation. Upon inspection, each of the nominal variables (P, W, E, M) had the same unit-root property in the rates of change of variables in Chile as it had in Israel, with one basic difference—applying the Augmented Dickey-Fuller Test I could not establish the existence of co-integration among these variables in the case of Chile (nor for Mexico—see below). This also seems to make sense when considering 'eye-econometrics'—Fig. 6.2 (Chile) looks generally much 'choppier', namely much less synchronized, than Fig. 5.6 (Israel).

1976–81 affected the solvency of firms and of the major banks with which these firms were closely interlocked. The large increase in stock prices and in real estate, following the boom, further compounded the degree of financial entanglement. The 1982 bust, recession, and steep devaluation implied a ballooning of bad debts in the business and banking systems. Total collapse could only be avoided by massive bailing-out and rescue operations by the central bank, amounting to large quasi-fiscal subsidies totalling, on average, about 4.5 per cent of GDP during 1982–7. One outcome of that episode was the need to revamp the financial monitoring and regulation system. The other, reminiscent of Israel's 1983 bank-share crisis, was the creation, through debt-equity swaps, of an area of ambiguous private/public ownership of banking-sector assets and the need for a prolonged reprivatization effort.

Finally, it is worth mentioning an additional financial intermediation reform element which was important in helping develop Chile's capital market. A far-reaching social security reform since 1981 transformed most of the state-administered pay-as-you-go pension funds into a system of privately run and capitalized pension funds, financed by a mandatory 10 per cent tax on wages paid by the government into the funds. While this generated an extra fiscal deficit (some 3–4 per cent of GDP, to be eliminated gradually) which had to be covered from other cuts in expenditure, it also turned the pension funds into a source of funding in the capital market, including the purchase of equity in privatized state-owned enterprise.

As Table 6.1 indicates, during the five-year period 1986–90 Chile enjoyed substantial growth (over 6 per cent per annum), reduced its unemployment rate, kept inflation below 20 per cent (an independent central bank is likely to bring it down further), and reduced its current-account deficit to low, manageable levels, easily financed by new long-term capital inflows.[22] On top of this the economic transition has been successfully sustained as Chile has reverted to a democratic electoral system. The observers of 1984 thus proved wrong, but the costs, and the policy lessons for subsequent reform processes, remain. In all likelihood Chile of

[22] As the figures in Table 6.1 show, sometimes luck also helps—the terms of trade during this period turned around in Chile's favour, increasing by 30% during 1985–90.

the 1990s is in better general shape than Chile of the 1960s; within our selected group of countries it has travelled the longest distance from its initial crisis phase. Finally, we recall that each phase of Chile's development during these twenty years carries a specific important general lesson of its own. First, the Allende period (1971–3) shows how a reckless socialist take-over, coupled with poor macro-economic policies, can transform a democracy into a repressive military regime. Second, the initial reform period (1974–7) under the military regime provided the socially costly lessons of sharp orthodox stabilization. Third, the *tablita* phase (1978–81) gives a pure test of the synchronization issue. Fourth, the ensuing confidence crisis (1982–3) illustrates the vagaries of financial openness when it is coupled with internal financial fragility (to which we will return in the context of Eastern Europe). The fifth and last lesson from the most recent recovery since 1986 again illustrates the importance of labour-market flexibility in effecting a structural transformation and transition to growth in an open economy: the choice is one between going about it forcibly, as in the Chilean case, or by consensus, along the lines of the Swedish (or Israeli) model. But it appears that in either case there is no escape from paying the price of substantial unemployment in the transition.

6.6 How Different was Argentina from Chile in the 1970s?

Chile was not alone in its attempted reforms of the 1970s. It shared many similarities with at least two neighbouring countries, Argentina and Uruguay. All three countries had, since the 1930s, pursued inward-looking, import-substitution-led growth (unlike Israel, which had a predominantly pro-export bias) and, like many other MICs, had substantial government intervention and heavily controlled financial systems. In all three countries the military seized power (Chile in 1973, Uruguay in 1974, and Argentina in 1976) after a period of severe macro-economic crisis—high fiscal and balance-of-payments deficits and runaway inflation—on top of serious micro-economic price distortions.[23]

---

[23] This discussion partly borrows from the results of a World Bank Study of the Southern Cone reform process, conducted in 1983–4. The study also included Uruguay, which is only briefly mentioned here (as its inflation stayed within the

Annual inflation rates were approaching 1,000 per cent in Chile (September 1973) and 2,300 per cent in Argentina (March 1976). During the preceding crisis the budget deficits had reached 16 and 12 per cent, respectively, of GDP, and foreign-exchange reserves had disappeared. In Argentina, as in Chile, strong populist redistributive tendencies of the Peronist regime explain the size of the deficit.[24]

Uruguay differs from Argentina and Chile in having had a much smaller macro-economic imbalance when the military took over. Inflation was slightly less than 100 per cent in 1973; the government deficit averaged only 3 per cent of GDP; there was no immediate crisis of central bank reserves. But the economy was characterized by gross micro-economic distortions and it had been virtually stagnant for twenty years. We shall not discuss Uruguay separately here, but it is a convenient reference country to bear in mind: while it went through reform processes and made some macro-policy mistakes that resembled those of its neighbours, the overriding difference, at least compared to Argentina, is Uruguay's more prudent fiscal policy. But it also suffered persistently higher unemployment and showed a much bigger real wage erosion than those of the other two countries.

In all three countries the military governments combined orthodox stabilization policies with substantial structural reforms in the commodity, labour, and financial markets, with different sequencing and intensity. As shown in the preceding discussion, Chile eliminated its budget deficit and all price controls and non-tariff barriers to trade, but implemented the liberalization of the capital account more gradually, keeping controls on short-term capital flows until late 1981. Uruguay, on the other hand, removed all controls on capital flows already in 1974 and moved to full convertibility in 1977.[25] Uruguay also removed many commodity-price controls, but during 1974–80 moved much more

two-digit class), but in many ways underwent a similar reform process. The main references are Corbo, de Melo, and Tybout (1986), already mentioned in our discussion of Chile, and a Symposium published in *World Development*, 13/8: 863–6 (see 'Overview' by Corbo and de Melo and the introduction to part I by the present author).

[24] For a description of the 1973–6 populist episode in Argentina see Sturzenegger (1991).

[25] In many ways Uruguay provided the conduit for capital flight from Argentina.

slowly on trade liberalization. Argentina (temporarily) eliminated price controls, but also removed most restrictions on short-term capital flows before the liberalization of the current account and the reduction of tariffs. This reverse ordering of reform between the capital and current accounts eventually aggravated matters in Argentina (and, on the financial side, also in Uruguay) during the debt crisis, quite apart from the persistent fiscal deficits which determined the negative outcomes in Argentina.[26]

All three countries faced a simultaneous external terms-of-trade shock—the rise in oil prices and the fall in the dollar price of a major export (beef in Argentina and Uruguay; wool in Uruguay; copper in Chile).[27] While they all included large real devaluations in their stabilization packages (followed by a passive exchange-rate crawl), Chile's monetary and fiscal squeeze had much more severe recessionary effects (see Tables 6.1 and 6.2 for the differences between Chile and Argentina in GDP, investment growth, and unemployment). While the stabilization stage temporarily removed the balance-of-payments constraint, domestic inflation came down only gradually, though much further in Chile (it was still an annual 50 per cent by the end of 1977) than in Argentina (about 200 per cent around the same time). Uruguay's inflation stayed moderately high at 50 per cent in 1978.

As in Chile, the persistence of inflation caused Argentina and Uruguay to shift to the exchange rate as an anti-inflation device through a pre-announced *tablita* in 1978. The theoretical rationale was the one already described in the Chilean case, based on a free trade PPP assumption and interest-rate parity. In both countries, as in Chile, this experiment ended in a sharp real appreciation and a major foreign-exchange crisis, though in Argentina the fiscal deficit and the completely open capital account aggravated the results. As early as 1976–8 Argentina already suffered from capital flight (of close to $5 billion), after an initial capital inflow at the start of the *tablita*, but this paled in comparison with the estimated $30 billion of capital flight in 1979–83, which almost neutralized the vast increase in the gross external debt ($31

---

[26] We return to these issues of sequencing in Ch. 8.

[27] As Table 6.2 shows, Argentina's terms of trade fell by close to 40% over the period 1973–8, less than Chile's (55% over the same period), while in Uruguay (not shown here) the drop was close to Chile's.

TABLE 6.2 *Macro-economic indicators for Argentina, 1965–1991*

	Fiscal deficit/GNP (%)	CPI inflation	GDP growth rate	Gross fixed investment (growth rate)	Unemployment rate (%)	Real wage (1976= 100)	Terms of trade[a] (1987= 100)	Current account deficit ($ bn.)
Democracy								
Import substitution, 1965–73	3.0	24	4.2	6.6	5.7	125	204	—
Populism, 1973–5	12.0	78	2.9	0.1	2.4	154	149	—
Military government								
Reform, 1976–8	7.7	246	0.8	4.9	3.4	100	128	-1.8
Tablita, 1979–80	7.9	128	3.7	4.0	2.2	118	122	1.7
Debt crisis, 1981–3	17.8	189	-3.0	-15.1	4.7	111	118	3.2
Democracy								
Transition, 1984–5	7.7	518	-1.4	-15.2	4.6	146	118	1.6
Austral, 1986–7	6.4	210	3.9	17.4	5.0	124	100	3.5
Runaway inflation, 1988–90	7.6[b]	663	-3.5	-15.7	7.4	104	110	0.4
Convertibility,[c] 1991	2.2	17[d]	5.0	17.6	5.3	—	—	3.0

[a] End-of-period figures (source: IBRD, *World Tables 1992*).

[b] Figure for 1990 was 3.3%.

[c] Preliminary estimates.

[d] Mar.–Dec. 1991 in annual terms.

Sources: 1965–83: based on Corbo, de Melo, and Tybout (1986); 1984–91: based on Machinea and Fanelli (1988), Heymann (1991), and official data.

billion, mostly public) that Argentina incurred in the same period.

In all three cases the large exchange-rate adjustment led to severe banking crises, to the abandonment of the *tablita* policy, and to a deep recession. The apparent similarity of the results may explain the observation, made in 1984, that the Southern Cone reform attempts of the preceding decade had failed. In fact, as subsequent developments have amply shown, Argentina and Chile were at that point in time very differently placed on the adjustment and structural reform ladder. Argentina, unlike Chile, remained burdened with severe fiscal deficits and half-baked, inconsistent reforms. Its return to democracy in 1984 liberalized the country politically, but made the economic adjustment that much more difficult, because no internal consensus over economic priorities could be reached.

6.7 Argentina and Bolivia in 1985: Why was the Austral Plan Short-Lived?

By 1985 the four countries with the highest price inflations since World War II were Argentina, Bolivia, Israel, and Brazil (see Fig. 1.2). The first three launched major stabilization programmes in 1985; the fourth, Brazil, did so in 1986. We proceed to discuss some aspects, relevant to our previous discussion, of the three Latin American experiences in the order in which stabilization programmes were introduced, starting with Argentina.[28]

Argentina's response to the 1981–3 debt crisis had left it with an unfortunate combination of a 10 per cent cumulative drop in GDP and substantially accelerated inflation (reaching over 600 per cent in annual terms in the fourth quarter of 1983), fuelled both by a high budget deficit and by an attempt to correct relative prices (the exchange-rate and public-sector prices). Government expenditure on servicing the external debt increased sharply, not only because of the real devaluation but because

---

[28] The Austral Plan and its aftermath are analysed in Machinea and Fanelli (1988), Canavese and Di Tella (1988), and Heymann (1991). Our discussion here will draw on these papers and on other complementary material.

Argentina opted to convert a large portion of the private debt into public debt.[29]

At the same time both the inflationary (Olivera–Tanzi) fiscal lag effect and the drop in economic activity depressed tax revenue. Public- and private-sector financial difficulties placed an additional burden on the budget deficit, which increased to 16 per cent of GDP at the end of 1983 (Fig. 6.3) and was primarily financed through compulsory loans and the introduction of interest-bearing reserve requirements of the commercial banks.

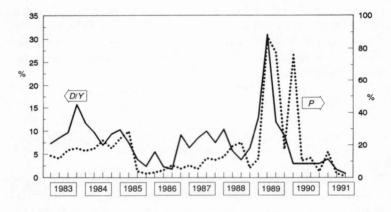

Source: Table 6.2.

Fig. 6.3 Government deficit/GDP and monthly rate of inflation, Argentina, 1983–1991

Taking over from the military government at this juncture Alfonsin's constitutional government faced the dual ordeal of coping with mounting external debt arrears and responding to demands of a population that had just achieved political liberty (the 'transitional democracy' syndrome). As elsewhere, gradualist attempts at inflation reduction brought about accelerated inflation, while the budget deficit was temporarily reduced. At the same time no agreement could be reached either with private creditors or with the IMF on the basis of the existing fiscal plans.

The Austral Plan was announced in June 1985, after a few

[29] Between 1980 and 1984 the external debt of the public sector almost tripled, from $14 to 36 billion, while that of the private sector fell from $13 to 11 billion (see Machinea and Fanelli 1988: table 3.5).

months of 'softening-up' by exchange-rate and public-sector price increases. It was in many ways based on the same conception as Israel's plan (started two weeks later)[30]—an attempt to combine an 'orthodox' attack on the fundamentals (primarily the elimination of the budget deficit and its monetary financing) with a wage, price, and exchange-rate freeze (after an up-front devaluation) aimed at affecting both the underlying driving forces of inflation and agents' expectations of the change in inflation, thereby minimizing the costs of adjustment.[31] All prices, except those in flexible markets, were frozen at their pre-programme levels. A new currency was introduced, the austral, and the exchange rate was pegged to the dollar (at only 0.8 australs per dollar, instead of 1, presumably to allow for a correction afterwards). Wages were set by decree at a level that gave compensation for the previous month's inflation (22 per cent).

The envisaged reduction of the deficit from 12 per cent of GDP in the first half of 1985 to 2.5 per cent in the second half was supposed to come from an increase in public utility rates, a cut in public expenditures (though massive lay-offs were to be avoided), an increase in taxes on foreign trade, a rescheduling of direct taxes (based on new legislation yet to be approved by Congress), and by reversing the fiscal lag (the by now familiar Olivera–Tanzi effect). In addition, a decline in the quasi-fiscal deficit (coming from the operating losses of the central bank) was expected with the envisaged drop in nominal interest rates.

[30] The similarity in content between the two programmes, which were launched at almost the same time, raises the interesting question as to how independent the thought processes leading to these programmes had been. I have no clear answer to this question. Obviously, economists in both countries had studied the experiences of extreme inflations and their resolution both those of the 1920s in Europe as well as the more recent one in Chile. Latin America in general, and Argentina in particular, had a tradition of using direct intervention in the price mechanism (misleadingly called the 'heterodox shock' approach), in a way that is doomed to failure. But the idea of combining the two 'prongs' of the budget and the nominal synchronization within one comprehensive programme (including a currency reform) was new. The details of the proposed Israeli stabilization programme (in the version that included a currency conversion to the 'sela'—see Ch. 4) had been conveyed orally to a member of the Argentinian team at the end of 1984, but I am not sure whether this played a role in the design of the Austral Plan, which also included an important innovation in the form of the interest-rate 'conversion table' (see below). At any rate, the Israeli team was not aware of the existence of the Austral Plan until after its announcement, in mid-June 1985, when the Israeli programme had already assumed its final form.

[31] For details see Machinea and Fanelli (1988).

The novel and quite ingenious element of the programme was the way the implied interest-rate component of the monetary reform was implemented. The new currency, the austral, was initially declared equivalent to 1,000 old pesos and was to be revalued daily against the peso so as to effect a quick conversion. Peso-denominated contracts with maturity dates after the date of implementation (14 June) were depreciated against the austral (and thus also against the dollar, according to a well-specified conversion table) by an amount equivalent to the pre-plan inflation rate. The idea was to avoid a sharp increase in real interest rates and the wealth redistribution that would otherwise accrue to creditors (from the debtors) with the drop in inflation, since existing nominal contracts had embodied the expected pre-plan inflation rate. The regulated interest rate was simultaneously dropped from a monthly 28 per cent level (the pre-programme inflation was running at 25 per cent monthly) to 4 per cent a month. Finally, a new agreement was signed with the IMF, which had approved the programme, and a settlement was also reached with the private external creditor banks concerning the 1984–5 financial plan (involving the credit arrears) so as to provide the required external financing.

We have described the Austral Plan at some length although it was only moderately successful and the subsequent disinflation was of rather short duration. The plan certainly encountered some inherent structural weaknesses, primarily in addressing the particular political environment for which it was designed, compared to its Israeli analogue. Nevertheless I believe this programme, unlike its Brazilian (1986) or Argentinian successors (before the successful 1991 convertibility programme was introduced) was basically well designed. It also involved some innovative elements, especially the interest-rate conversion, which, in the Israeli case, had been poorly tackled. Moreover, it had been designed and carried out by a thoughtful and knowledgeable team of experts.[32]

The results of the programme's implementation are well known. It was extremely well received, both in Argentina and abroad, and had substantial initial success in bringing down

[32] The team included Mario Brodersohn, Alfred Canitrot, and José Luis Machinea (the third later served as central bank Governor). The idea of the interest rate conversion table was formulated by Daniel Heymann.

inflation and repatriating flight capital. The fiscal deficit did indeed come down to 2.4 per cent by the fourth quarter of 1985 and inflation sank to 1.4 per cent a month. But the fiscal correction proved to be transitory (associated primarily with the Olivera–Tanzi effect of the price freeze); by the fourth quarter of 1986 it was already close to 10 per cent, with inflation staying low for a while but inevitably creeping up too (see Fig. 6.3).

Apart from the fiscal problem, to which we shall return, it can be argued that the Austral Plan had two other weaknesses, relative to its Israeli counterpart. In Israel, the co-operation of the federation of trade unions (Histadruth) was crucial in achieving the initial synchronization of wage and price freezes. In Argentina the trade unions were controlled by the Peronist opposition and sought to block the implementation of the programme. By April 1986 price controls were relaxed, unions were allowed to negotiate wages, and a crawling peg on the exchange-rate and public-sector prices was reintroduced. The other component, an assured foreign-exchange safety cushion, was certainly inherently weaker quantitatively in the case of Argentina because of the accumulated credit arrears and its poor past record as a debtor. Yet it is generally agreed by all observers, including the Austral Planners themselves, that the primary weakness (and for another four years) was the fiscal deficit and its finance. In Argentina the budget also seems to explain the inflationary profile better than in other countries, with the exception of Bolivia (see below).[33]

For a time, as inflation receded and the demand for money showed a one-time increase, the government could collect large seigniorage revenues.[34] This helped the growth of foreign-

---

[33] Argentina's high inflation profile and protracted high budget deficits (see Table 6.2 and Figs. 1.2 and 6.3) suggest that its inflationary process was much less stable and more directly deficit-determined than those of Israel, Chile, Mexico, or Brazil (until 1985). In a comment on Canavese and Di Tella (1988) Carlos Rodríguez shows that Argentina's rate of inflation between 1965 and 1986 can be well explained by a simple regression of the inflation rate on two or three annual lagged public-sector deficits (as percentages of GDP). Including a dummy variable for 1985 (testing for the contention that the structure of the inflationary process changed in 1985) did not add anything, as it was statistically insignificant. I ran the regression for quarterly data over the period 1983: I to 1991: III and obtained basically the same result. The one- and three-lagged quarterly deficits come out highly significant ($R^2 = 0.53$). A dummy for the third quarter of 1985 is negative but not significant.

[34] Seigniorage revenue was estimated by Heymann (1991) at 9% in the third quarter of 1985, subsequently dropping to a 3–4% steady rate.

exchange reserves held in the central bank, but domestic debt also increased as the bank had to raise its interest-bearing reserve requirements to prevent an excess increase in the money supply. High interest rates paid on bank reserves and rediscounts of bad loans, reflecting financial fragility, increased the deficit. In time, as inflation rose again, money demand fell, and the external sources of finance could not be replenished, resort to short-term domestic debt finance under high interest rates again intensified the vicious circle of a high deficit and high inflation.

Underlying the structural components of the fiscal deficit in Argentina's case were inherent weaknesses inherited from the previous military government, which grew worse with the transition to democracy. The unifying factor was the lack of a clear legal and enforcement mechanism by which parliament in a normal democracy pre-commits and consistently resolves—before the fiscal year starts—the political and social conflict over the allocation of expenditures and the sharing of taxes between different interest groups in society. The budget was approved late in the year and vested-interest groups could bargain with a weak central government on a one-to-one basis at any point in time, rather than be subjected to a comprehensive solution of the bargaining game.[35] A particular problem was the regulation of the division of tax proceeds between the central government and the provinces, which was done on an *ad hoc* basis. New legislation on that issue was introduced only in 1988.

Another element of fiscal weakness was a notoriously poor record in effecting tax compliance. Thus, even though on paper the value added tax was 18 per cent and the marginal income tax was 45 per cent on the highest income-tax bracket, the joint revenue of these taxes in Argentina amounted to no more than 4–5 per cent of the total, the reason being both tax evasion and special negotiated exemptions.[36] We can summarize this part of the

[35] For a description of the problem in the case of Argentina see Heymann (1991). For a theoretical analysis of the inflationary resolution of a conflict over shares of the budget pie, when there are externalities of this kind, see Aizenman (1992). The attempt to get extra slices of a disappearing budget, or cause its inflation, even after it is approved by parliament, is a familiar problem in other parliamentary democracies (Israel is no exception), but there is a difference between its being considered an exception or the major 'rule'.

[36] Teitel, in a discussion of Heymann (1991), cites an average figure of 26% of total tax revenue coming from income and capital for the middle-income economies in 1986, among which Argentina was the lowest, at 4.9%. This

discussion by stating that although the Austral Plan did succeed in reducing inflation for a few years, it did not provide a sufficiently concerted pull out of the bad equilibrium 'trap' in which Argentina had been caught for a long time. In some sense, the ensuing developments deepened the crisis.

Before returning to the post-1987 evolution of inflation in Argentina let us digress briefly to the case of Bolivia, which started its major stabilization programme shortly after Argentina. As mentioned in Chapter 1, both Bolivia and the Bolivian hyperinflation episode differ in many ways from the other Latin American economies discussed here. It had one of the lowest inflation records in Latin America right until 1980 (see Table 1.5) and its hyperinflation outburst, lasting seventeen months until September 1985 (during which period the price level increased over 600-fold) was of the 1920s kind, associated directly with a relatively speedy fiscal crisis, in almost textbook fashion.[37] However, Bolivia is an important success story to bear in mind as far as rapid disinflation is concerned.

Hyperinflation was preceded by a combined rise in borrowing rates and credit rationing imposed on Bolivia by the debt crisis, and a serious internal political crisis involving frequent changes in government and military coups. A series of failures to control inflation by direct controls, the loss, through inflation, of the primary export tax base (from companies producing tin and natural gas), and resort to the printing press account for the outburst of hyperinflation. The remarkable fact is that after a period of political unrest, amidst failures to control inflation, a democratic election, won by the centre and centre-right parties, and lost by the left (including the power base of the trade unions), brought about a new stable government with Estenssero sworn in as President and several prominent businessmen in key cabinet posts. The new government immediately adopted a sharp orthodox stabilization programme (fiscal balance with IMF-supported financial restructuring) and inflation was brought down almost at once to less than 20 per cent a year, where it stayed at least until 1991 (see Fig. 6.4). Here we have an example of a 'transitional

was even lower than Bolivia with 6.5%. Brazil had 18, Chile 12, and Mexico 24%. Israel was one of the highest in that group, with 37%. The average for the industrial-market economies in 1986 was 40%.

[37] For references see Sachs (1987) and Morales (1988, 1991).

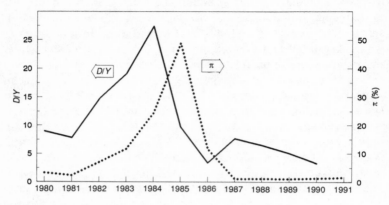

Note: Annual averages.
Source: *IFS* and Morales (1988, 1991).
Fɪɢ 6.4 Government deficit/GDP and monthly rate of inflation, Bolivia, 1980–1990

democracy' (Bolivia moved from 0.25 in 1975 to 0.83 in 1985, on the Gastil index given in Table 1.6) which achieved stabilization without going through the prolonged and arduous process experienced by Chile and Argentina. Something in the different economic and social structure of Bolivia must explain this but we do not know exactly what. One should also bear in mind the fact that Bolivia's growth record since stabilization has been quite poor.

6.8 Price Controls without Fundamentals: Brazil and Argentina in 1986–1990

Adding Brazil to the discussion introduces new elements, although there are also similarities with aspects already discussed earlier. Being by far the biggest economy in Latin America (a population of 150 million compared to Argentina's 32 million and Mexico's 86 million) Brazil also had the fastest growth rate both in the 'Golden Age' of growth and through the 1970s (see Table 1.5). It suffered a growth standstill only starting in the early 1980s. Since it had a large internal market and thus a relatively 'closed' economy in terms of its size, inward-looking policies were not as distortive as they were in the smaller economies of Chile or Argentina. Yet Brazil also managed to carry out an export diversification strategy through a crawling-peg exchange-rate policy and active export promotion helped by various subsidy schemes.

Brazil weathered the first oil shock by combining an enhanced import substitution policy with increased external borrowing, which helped to keep high rates of investment and growth but at the same time also turned Brazil into the world's largest single debtor with an increasing debt-service burden.[38] In 1981 real product declined for the first time as an austerity programme was undertaken. Afterwards Brazil differed from its neighbours in managing an impressive shift from domestic uses to export recovery, which substantially improved its foreign-exchange balance and also enabled a modest resumption of growth in GDP per capita by 1984, although for the decade of the 1980s as a whole GDP per capita fell by 6 per cent. So much for real output and the external balance. It is on the domestic imbalance and inflation front that Brazil's performance worsened to the point of turning it into the most problematic high-inflation and, since 1986, hyperinflation case.

During the 1970s and until 1985 Brazil's inflation profile looks remarkably like Israel's (see Fig. 6.5), and for similar reasons, although not with the same mix. A smaller fiscal deficit (of 5–6 per cent of GDP) but very similar wage indexation (with shortening adjustment periods), exchange-rate adjustment, and monetary accommodation patterns made for accelerating (yet still stable) inflation rates reaching around 200 per cent per annum in 1984–5 (less than Israel's at the time).

The year 1985 marks a clear turning-point in Brazil's inflation profile, which, after the abortive Cruzado Plan of 1986, quickly moved into the hyperinflation range. Over the period 1985–90 as a whole the average inflation rate in Brazil was similar to that of Argentina (and even higher—see Table 1.5), as has been the 'choppy' profile of inflation for the two countries (cf. Figs. 6.4 and 6.5).[39] What made 1985 a watershed for Brazil, even though

---

[38] We rely here on papers by Modiano (1988) and Cardoso (1991).

[39] Both Argentina's and Brazil's inflation profiles raise the question of what constitutes a 'hyper' rather than just 'very high' inflation. Using Cagan's threshold, both countries had only four and five months, respectively, with a monthly

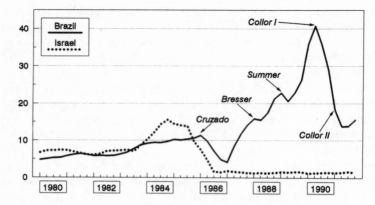

Note: Quarter over corresponding quarter of preceding year.
Source: IFS.

FIG 6.5   Brazil's (and Israel's) average monthly CPI inflation rate, 1980–1991

the external adjustment had been well managed? A political answer to the query may be the fact that in that year, and for the first time after twenty-one years of military government, Brazil had a democratically elected President and the beginning of a sequence of governments that lacked the consensus that is needed to undertake the required domestic austerity measures.

If one looks for a more specific economic answer there seem to be two alternative or complementary explanations. One line of argument, pursued in an interesting paper by Kiguel and Liviatan (1991), considers the similarity of the two countries' inflation profiles and the recourse in both countries to a series of income-policy packages in which wage and price controls were introduced for brief periods of time, without the accompanying correction of fundamentals. In Brazil, the series of steps started with the Cruzado Plan of April 1986, where only one of the two

inflation rate above 50% (see Table 1.4). Using the lower threshold (a 25% monthly rate) would lengthen the period to around a year and a half in both countries. However, note that, counter to what one might surmise, an econometric test on the data of both countries (see Welch 1991) rejects the existence of rational inflation and real internal debt bubbles (which would have testified to intertemporal government insolvency and a potential real debt and inflation explosion).

'prongs' was in place for a while;[40] this helped the party in government win an election but immediately afterwards evaporated and led to two similar plans with successively mounting peak inflation rates (the Bresser and Summer programmes in June 1987 and January 1989, respectively). Argentina had a similar succession of five plans of temporary price controls and rising peak inflation (see Fig. 6.4).

Kiguel and Liviatan attribute these explosive inflationary cycles, after the failure of the Austral and Cruzado plans, to the expectations and norms of behaviour of economic agents, given the repeated use of price controls without the supporting fundamentals. When there is no credibility in the government's resolve to undertake the tough policies that are required (and controls are considered as temporary palliatives), firms, according to Kiguel and Liviatan's interpretation, know that once inflation exceeds a certain rate (not known in advance) a freeze is likely to be introduced. Firms therefore attempt to enter the freeze in a favourable price position and 'overshoot'. This tendency will intensify as inflation accelerates and exchange rate and money are accommodating. Once the freeze is in place, firms will rest on their 'cushion' for a while, which explains why inflation fell so quickly after the freeze. Time passes, and a new cycle starts.

While the similarity of policies and the inflationary profile in Argentina and Brazil give substantial credence to this interpretation for the period 1986–9, subsequent developments in both countries look less consistent with this theory. But the subsequent programmes were not of similar nature either. There is also a question as to whether such an explanation can account for the behaviour of inflation averages over the longer period. We have already noted the fact that Argentina's inflation can, by and large, be directly linked to the size of budget deficits and the importance of seigniorage at crucial points in time. No such explanation seems to work in the Brazilian case, and what makes the enigma particularly puzzling is the fact that while Argentina's

---

[40] The Cruzado Plan was originally modelled by its designers after the Israeli and Austral plans and considerable preliminary thought went into it (see Arida and Lara-Resende 1985; Modiano 1988). However, the link between the original design and its implementation was tenuous, to say the least. At any rate, the period of reduced inflation after this plan was minimal—only six months (see Fig. 6.5), compared with a much longer period (almost two years) following the Austral Plan.

average inflation rate stayed approximately the same between the two periods 1980–5 and 1985–91 (and dropped dramatically at the end of the period) Brazil's quadrupled (from 148 to 624 per cent; see Table 1.5). But there is no evidence that fiscal deficits in Brazil were very much larger in the latter period, nor were they, barring measurement problems, considerably smaller than Argentina's. Moreover, seigniorage revenue in Brazil was always relatively low, at 2–3 per cent.[41]

A more likely explanation of Brazil's internal difficulties seems to lie in the way the fiscal deficit was short-term debt-financed (in highly liquid form) and in the accommodating way in which monetary and financial policy was conducted during these years. Detailed reading of the gyrations of policy decisions and their frequent changes over this period obscures the picture, but the basic fact is that money seems to have been very expansionary in Brazil (with the exception of a brief period under the Collor I Plan in 1990, see below) and real interest rates relatively low. Using the overnight rate for both countries, the real rate of interest in Brazil was usually no more than 2 per cent on an annual basis and often negative, as in 1990 and 1991 (1984, 1986, and 1989 are exceptions with 7, 8, and 12 per cent, respectively), while the figure for Argentina was close to 15 per cent and often higher during most years.[42]

While Brazil successfully withstood the pressure on its external balance, real depreciation and rising real interest rates exerted pressure on its budget deficit; this deficit could no longer be financed by external borrowing, and since 1984 it had to be financed by internal borrowing from public and financial institutions. To an increasing extent this debt could be automatically resold to the central bank at supported prices (i.e. too low real interest rates), which became the main source of growth of the money supply, broadly defined. The rules under which the Bank of Brazil operated did not allow it to let the price of bonds fall and the real rates of interest to rise, and as a result the central bank increased its share in the total bonded government debt (which reached close to 90 per cent by 1990).

---

[41] See estimates in Kiguel and Liviatan (1991).
[42] Data for 1981–8 appear in Kiguel and Liviatan (1991: tables 6.5 and 6.6). For later years estimates were calculated from respective central bank statistics.

In a conference comment in January 1990, Persio Arida, who had been one of the designers of the Cruzado Plan, said:[43]

Achieving fiscal equilibrium will not suffice. To the extent to which the money supply is to work as the nominal anchor of stabilization, it becomes crucial to cut the deposit facilities of the treasury in public financial institutions, to suppress multiple compulsory requirements in favour of a single rate, to separate out short-run monetary control bonds from long-run indexing bonds financing treasury deficits, etc. Policy debates in Brazil have given much more emphasis to fiscal than to monetary policy control.[44]

The Collor administration, inaugurated in March 1990, indeed introduced a programme (with IMF blessing), now called Collor I, aimed at an abrupt reduction of inflation by monetary means. Two-thirds of the stock of financial assets in the economy (M2 plus government bonds held by the public) was blocked for a period of eighteen months, subject to some size restrictions on the amount that could immediately be converted into a new currency (the cruzeiro). Nominal interest payments on the domestic debt were reduced and a once-and-for-all capital levy was imposed. Floating interest-rate securities were converted into 6 per cent bearing indexed bonds upon being blocked, so as to reduce the fiscal cost of tight money which was also affected by an increase in reserve requirements.

The sharp monetary squeeze had an immediate effect on inflation but it did not last long as the pressure on the government to relax the reins quickly eroded the programme (during March the monthly overnight real rate jumped from −2.4 to 3.2 and then turned negative again). Forty per cent of the blocked deposits were released between March and May 1990 (ostensibly to meet firm tax and payroll obligations) and were shifted into more liquid financial assets, with a very large rise in the money base reflecting a loss of confidence in the new programme. Monetary policy then went through a number of stop-go cycles leading to another new stabilization programme in January 1991

---

[43] The comment (or, rather, footnote to a comment) was made in a discussion of the case of Brazil in the conference volume edited by Bruno *et al.* (1991).

[44] A systematic attempt to explain Brazil's more recent inflation as a monetary policy problem, rather than a pure fiscal or 'shocks and accommodation' story, is given by Meltzer (1991). Added support to that thesis is given in a paper by Aurenheimer (1992).

(Collor II), including a renewed wage–price freeze with new restrictions on the financial system. It also included the abolition of the overnight market in government securities and of backward-indexation on financial assets (indexation of wages had been abolished earlier). Brazilian inflation between January and May 1991 was down to 8 per cent a month, compared to about 15 per cent in the second half of 1990. However, it accelerated back to a monthly rate of 20 per cent in the second half of that year. On an end-of-year basis (see Fig. 6.5), inflation looked like 'settling' on a monthly rate of 15 per cent (close to 500 per cent on an annual basis). Was this to become a new steady state?

6.9 Argentina's 1991 Convertibility Plan: Has the Turning-Point Finally Come?

By mid-1989, as we have seen, Argentina had reached its highest rate of price increase ever (the July 1989 rate was 197 per cent— see Table 1.4 and Fig. 1.2). Upon assuming office the Menem administration first effected a major correction in relative prices (the exchange-rate and public-sector prices) but also passed through Congress two major fiscal reform bills to eliminate subsidies and exemptions from VAT, raise corporate taxes, and impose various restrictions on public-sector employment and wage payments. Drastic measures were also taken to curb expenditure, reform administration, and tighten control over the public-enterprise sector.

This was followed at the end of the year by unification of the foreign-exchange market under a freely floating system to protect the central bank reserves from capital flight, a large depreciation took place, and there was a run on banks. Shortly afterwards a compulsory conversion was announced of austral-denominated debt into long-term dollar-denominated government bonds (BONEX), so as to regain monetary control in a stormy environment. The further depreciation of the austral, together with an increase in public-sector prices in the first quarter of 1990, caused another inflation spike, but by then the fiscal reform had taken hold (see Fig. 6.3) and inflation receded substantially. On the external side, the new administration[45] implemented a substantial

---

[45] The first programme—the BB plan—was named after the multinational firm of Bunge Born that provided a senior executive who became the first Minister of

import liberalization programme. The import tariff structure was simplified and tariffs were reduced (to 22 per cent on finished goods, 13 per cent on production inputs, 5 per cent on primary products, and zero on capital goods). Export taxes were slashed and so were non-tariff barriers.

The reform process under the new administration culminated with the Convertibility Act of April 1991, which is directed at the stabilization of the price level by anchoring the system on a fixed foreign-exchange parity with convertibility. The law stipulates 100 per cent foreign-exchange and gold backing for the currency, in a currency-board fashion. Indexation has been abolished, while contracts can be denominated and legally enforced in foreign currencies. Wages can only be increased, under collective bargaining, once productivity has increased. Also added and implemented in practice were harsher measures (substantial fines and temporary closures of businesses) to tighten tax compliance of large taxpayers. Finally, the government embarked on a substantive privatization programme which by 1991 had resulted in a reduction of close to 40,000 employees in state-owned enterprises.

As a result of all of these measures both the deficit and the central bank quasi-deficit were more or less eliminated and inflation came down to monthly rates of 1 per cent in the third quarter of 1991. At the same time output in 1991 was up and unemployment fell (see Table 6.2). At the time of writing it is probably too early to declare victory,[46] but this time Argentina appeared to be on a more sustainable stabilization and structural reform path.

the Economy, a rather unusual beginning. At a later stage, however, Domingo Cavallo was appointed Minister of the Economy and Rocque Fernández became Governor of a much strengthened central bank. Both were highly respected and influential economists in their own right, but what is no less important, especially when recalling the weak political support under the Austral Plan (including that of Alfonsin), they now had the full backing of a new President, Menem, who, in contrast to his populist election slogans, turned out to be very conservative and very determined in leading the economy, and the public sector in particular, into substantive and painful structural reforms.

[46] Among the familiar problems encountered are the fixity of the exchange rate, the inevitable real appreciation, and the problem of export competitiveness. As expected, trade liberalization has caused a sizeable increase in imports, showing in a substantial increase in the current account deficit in 1991 (see Table 1.2). But even if the exchange rate cannot be held fixed and inflationary tendencies may not yet have been eradicated, the structural measures that Argentina had undertaken seem to go much deeper than before.

Argentina's tortuous way to reform raises the natural question if and why this stage could not have been reached earlier. Was it the choice of a different strategy, a more determined political leadership, or a more receptive social environment that brought success this time around? The answer probably combines a mixture of elements. The Austral Plan failed not because it was the wrong programme but because there was no political and social consensus at the time, either in Congress or among the political rank and file, or the population at large; nor did the constitutional foundations exist for a fundamental fiscal reform. What followed was a series of stop-go attempts to rectify the gradual worsening economic situation, but, more than anything else, a painful and protracted collective learning process. It is doubtful, considering the experiences of various countries that we have encountered so far, and given the complexity of Argentina's situation, whether any short cuts are possible in this process. Also, there seems to be a limit to what countries are willing to learn from other countries' mistakes—and even that comes only with a long time-lag. We shall return to this issue below.

6.10 Mexico's Successful Heterodox Stabilization and Reform[47]

Mexico adds another important dimension to our discussion as it had been a relatively fast-growing and relatively stable economy in the 1950s and 1960s. Even though it developed some internal problems in the course of the 1970s, its high inflation erupted only in the early 1980s and marked the beginning of the debt crisis. However, within a period of six to eight years Mexico managed to engineer a turnaround, applying, in two stages, a heterodox stabilization programme and a series of structural reforms which have made it one of the best success stories in our sample of countries. Mexico's political system has throughout been characterized by a relatively autocratic[48] single party (PRI)

---

[47] For references to the Mexican crisis and reform see Gil Diaz and Tercero (1988), Beristain and Trigueros (1990), Ortiz (1991), Bazdresch and Levy (1991), and Aspe (1992).

[48] We recall the index of 0.5 in the Gastil scale (Table 1.5) for both 1976 and 1985. In the 1990s, with the economic opening-up and structural reform, Mexico may be beginning to move gradually towards a more democratic political system.

rule, where each President serves a six-year term at the end of which he appoints his successor. Correspondingly, economic strategies can also be identified with particular presidential tenures.

Even though the main story begins later, it is of some interest, especially for comparison with other countries in our sample, to start with the 1970–6 reign of President Echeverria, when developments were marked by a considerable increase in public expenditure on health, education, and agricultural development, and a corresponding emergence of a deficit in the government budget—Mexico's mini-version of a populist phase—whose timing, interestingly enough, coincided with similar events in Israel and elsewhere.[49]

Mexico underwent a political crisis in 1970 which was preceded by student-led protests in 1968. The government's political legitimacy was at risk and there was apprehension that left-wing tendencies in neighbouring Latin American countries threatened to 'invade' Mexico. A long period of rapid growth (average GDP growth throughout the preceding twenty-five years had been close to 7 per cent), with relative price stability (at 3.5 per cent average annual inflation), and a comfortable foreign-exchange position (foreign debt stood at 16 per cent of GNP in 1970) made it politically easy to opt for an increase in public expenditures in favour of redistribution. The syndrome resembles the Israeli episode of the late 1960s, and in Mexico economists[50] who could not be considered 'leftist' pressed the government in that direction, citing the problems of poverty and maldistribution of income and wealth.

The first commodity and oil shock in 1973 contributed to inflationary pressures in Mexico through import prices. At the same time it also made available a new source of private capital flows. Between 1972 and 1975 the current account more than quadrupled, from $1 to 4.4 billion,[51] the foreign debt increased

---

[49] The discussion here borrows from Bazdresch and Levy (1991). The social unrest of the late 1960s seems to have been a world-wide phenomenon.

[50] Bazdresch and Levy (1991) mention well-known economists such as Solis, Urquidi, and 'even' Ortiz Mena, an ex-Governor of the central bank, who advocated an increase in public expenditures to meet social needs. See also Aspe and Beristain (1984).

[51] These figures are almost identical to those of Israel which, however, has a considerably smaller (and a much more open) economy: one-eighth in terms of population, approximately one-half in terms of GNP.

rapidly, inflation edged up to 24 per cent in 1974, while the budget deficit continued to increase (see Fig. 6.6), with an increase in public expenditures.[52]

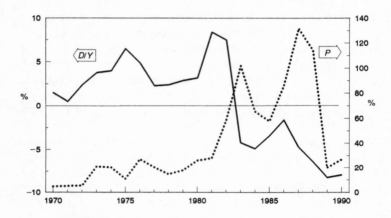

Source: Table 6.3.

Fig. 6.6   The deficit and annual inflation, Mexico, 1970–1990

In September 1976 a major (59 per cent) devaluation took place and an orthodox, IMF-supported package started the next President's (Lopez Portillo) term of office. While some tax reforms (VAT and adjustments in the personal income tax) took place, structural reforms could be postponed as the oil bonanza started Mexico on its public-sector spending spree, and eventually a renewed increase in inflation, as the second oil shock affected import prices (see Table 6.3 and Fig. 6.7). Table 6.4 gives the breakdown of the increase in expenditures and revenues for the whole period 1973–82, showing how total government expenditure increased by 10 percentage points of GDP, financed primarily by oil revenues, but also by a further increase in the deficit. With an exchange-rate crawl that did not keep up with inflation (see Fig. 6.7), real appreciation helped to inflate the current-account deficit to $16 billion in 1981 and the foreign debt more than doubled again from 1978 to 1981, to reach $74 billion.

[52] The private sector resisted attempts to raise taxes.

TABLE 6.3 *Macro-economic indicators for Mexico, 1965–1991*

	Primary deficit/Y (%)	Operational deficit/Y (%)[a]	CPI (%)	GDP growth (%)	Investment growth (%)	Real wage index (1978=100)	Terms of trade[b] (1987=100)	Current account deficit ($bn.)
Growth, 1965–72	0.9	2.3	5[c]	6.7	8.0	78	166	0.8
Oil shocks								
1973–6	4.8	7.5	20	6.1	8.0	96	144	3.2
1977–80	2.7	5.9	22	7.3	5.9	99	137	5.0
Debt crisis, 1981–2	8.0	11.8	60	3.7	-0.2	91	142	11.1
Fiscal adjustment								
1983–6	-3.5	4.2	76	-0.5	-7.7	73	90	-2.3
1987	-4.7	-1.8	159	1.7	-0.1	69	100	-4.0
PACTO								
1988	-8.1	3.5	52	1.4	5.8	66	92	2.4
1989	-8.3	1.6	20	3.1	6.5	70	98	4.0
Back to growth								
1990	-8.1	-1.2	30	3.9	13.4	72	110	6.4
1991	-5.4	-3.3	23	3.6	8.5	75	—	13.3

[a] Adjusted for inflation only until 1986.
[b] End-of-period figures (source: IBRD, *World Tables 1992*).
[c] 1969–72.

Sources: Gil Diaz and Tercero (1988), Bazdresch and Levy (1991), Aspe (1992), and Banco de Mexico.

TABLE 6.4   *Changes in public-sector expenditures and revenues, Mexico,*
1965–1986ª (% of GDP)

	1965 (level)	1965–73 (increment)	1973–82 (increment)	1982–6 (increment)	1986 (level)	1990 est. (level)
Total expenditures	**19.8**	**5.9**	**16.2**	**–8.2**	**33.8**	**31.8**
Current spending	15.0	2.2	9.7	–4.3	22.6	21.0
Capital spending	3.7	3.0	3.9	–4.8	5.8	4.8
Interest payments	1.1	0.7	2.6	1.0	5.4	6.0
Total revenues	**18.0**	**2.4**	**10.5**	**0.7**	**31.6**	**33.3**
Internal revenues	16.2	3.0	1.7	3.3	24.2	28.1[b]
External (oil) revenues	1.8	–0.6	8.8	–2.6	7.4	5.2
Miscellaneous	–0.8	0.3	0.6	0.6	2.0	—
Total deficit	**1.0**	**3.8**	**6.3**	**–8.3**	**4.2**	**1.5**

[a] The budget data for 1965–86 have been consistently corrected for inflation; the data for 1990 may not be fully consistent.
[b] Worked out as a residual (including miscellaneous items).

Sources: 1965–86: based on Gil Diaz and Tercero (1988); 1990: estimates based on Banco de Mexico, *The Mexican Economy in 1991*.

The end of Portillo's presidency was marked by the end of the oil-price boom, and a large increase in foreign debt (of short duration and variable interest rates) precisely at the time when interest rates began their increase and massive capital flight took place by the private sector. A huge devaluation took place (see Fig. 6.7), import controls were imposed, and an all-time high government deficit and 100 per cent inflation led to another stabilization package in 1982, while Mexico had to repudiate its external debt in what was its worst crisis ever.

The next President, de la Madrid, started with a tough IMF-supported orthodox stabilization programme which produced a shift from an operational deficit to a surplus within a year (see Fig. 6.6 and Table 6.3). A simultaneous import liberalization and privatization programme was also launched. The 1985 earthquake and the fall in the price of oil in 1986, which temporarily increased the deficit, necessitated another large devaluation, renewed the upsurge of inflation, and brought about a collapse of the stock market.

By the end of 1987 both the primary and the operational balance of the budget as well as the external current account showed a surplus (see Table 6.3) yet inflation was still running high. This

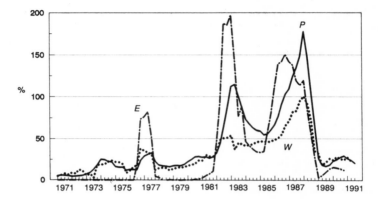

Source: Table 6.3.

Fig. 6.7 Annual rate of change of CPI, wages, and the exchange rate, Mexico, 1970–1991

gives another clear illustration of a case of inflationary dynamics in the short run, under inertia, not necessarily following the time path of the fundamentals. It was only at this point that the second 'prong' of a heterodox programme was introduced. In December 1987 Mexico signed a tripartite pact (*Pacto de Solidaridad*), modelled after the Israeli 1985 programme, between representatives of the workers (and peasants), the business sector, and the government.[53] Having largely corrected fundamentals in the preceding years, the need for additional fiscal correction was small, and the *Pacto* mainly signalled a synchronized freeze of the exchange rate, money, and wages (price controls were minimal, compared to the Israeli case).

Inflation came down immediately and hovered around the

[53] The Mexican team, of the highest professional calibre, was headed by Pedro Aspe as Minister of Finance, Miguel Mancera as Governor of the Bank of Mexico, and several other ministers with Ph.D.s from top US universities. It was fully supported first by President de la Madrid and, after 1988, by his successor Salinas, himself an accomplished economist with a Ph.D. The team had prepared its strategy with meticulous care, learning from the failures and successes of its predecessors, by sending a mission of senior economists to study the stabilizations of Argentina, Brazil, and Israel in great detail *in situ* and prepare a written report. Having acted as host to this group at the BOI in 1987, I was immensely impressed by the way the Mexican plan was being prepared and also had the good fortune to watch it in action in two brief visits to Mexico, in 1988, right after the *Pacto* was signed, and in 1990, shortly after the debt settlement.

'magical' 20 per cent annual rate. Real interest rates stayed high
for a while (at 30 per cent per annum), but substantially below
the initial Israeli levels. Figs. 6.8 and 6.9 underline the differences
between the Israeli and Mexican plans as regards the behaviour
of the two important factor prices—real wages and the real interest rates. The most important difference, in real wages, stems
from a much more flexible labour market in Mexico. This also
explains why Mexico could opt for a crawling peg (pre-
announced depreciation by a peso a day) within a year. The combination of lower real wages and a smaller increase in real
interest rates may, at least in part, explain why Mexico, unlike
Israel, did not have to go through a deep recession after the second stage of stabilization in 1988.

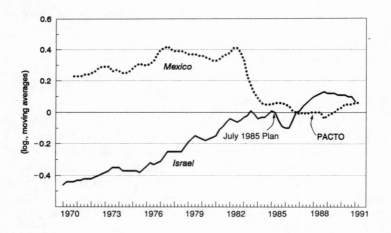

Source: Mexico: Table 6.3; Israel: BOI.

FIG. 6.8   Real wage in manufacturing, Israel and Mexico, 1970–1990

Success on the stabilization front was supplemented by active
structural reform: a further substantive import liberalization and
massive privatization of state-owned enterprises. By the end of
1990, 80 per cent of the 1,155 state-owned enterprises that had
existed in 1982 had been sold, merged, or liquidated (see Aspe
1992). Finally, the debt renegotiation of 1990 put Mexico back
on track as far as its external finances were concerned, as

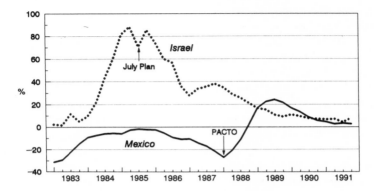

Note: Annual terms, *ex post* rates, quarterly moving averages.
Source: IFS.
Fig. 6.9   Real short-term borrowing rates, Mexico and Israel, 1983–1991

revealed in a marked improvement in various financial market indicators.

Summing up this discussion it is quite clear that, while Mexico's debt crisis and the crisis in its real economy were very deep, it also managed to take the bull by the horns early on, before inflation could run into the prolonged Israeli or Brazilian high inflation syndrome. The fruitful combination of an excellent team of policy makers with a well-balanced reform strategy, actively supported by the highest level of government, and also aided by the consensus of important economic agents,[54] can work wonders within a short span of time.

In ending this survey of Latin American crisis, stabilization, and reform experiences, we briefly point again to the specific additional lessons that each of the countries has taught us, some of which are also relevant to our next chapter on Eastern Europe. Chile, which we addressed in greatest detail, has taught us the lessons of a socialist take-over, the hazards of orthodox stabilization in the presence of inflationary inertia, and the importance of price synchronization. Chile's most recent experience illustrates

[54] There is no escaping the fact that an authoritarian regime can more easily carry out such swift reforms, but Mexico's past history has shown that consensus plays an important role even in a less than full-fledged democracy.

the necessary components of market and relative price flexibility in the transition to growth. Bolivia seemed to provide an exception to the rule that 'transitional democracies' necessarily take a long time to overcome an inflation crisis (sustainable growth, however, has yet to come). In contrast to the pure inflationary explosion and orthodoxy of the Bolivian case, Argentina exemplified the arduous road through a series of temporary stabilizations, until the key building-block of a successful stabilization, the fiscal balance, was set on more permanent micro-foundations. As we shall see, this is, in a way, a precursor to a problem that more and more reforms encounter in Eastern and Central Europe—macro-fiscal adjustment in a distorted structure gets eroded in the absence of the micro-building-blocks of a profound fiscal reform. An analogous problem, in the financial and monetary area, is encountered with respect to the micro-underpinnings of monetary control. Problems of enterprise financial fragility, a weak banking system, and automatic repercussions to the budget as a result of real devaluations and excessive foreign-exchange exposure, or unexpected increases in real interest rates, were common to several crises both in Latin America and in Israel. Failures of stabilization in Brazil, whose growth crisis has been the most marked, have taught us the importance of distinguishing between monetary and fiscal control.

Returning to our last country case: in addition to the importance of dealing separately with inflationary inertia, Mexico has broadened our perception of the effectiveness of simultaneous implementation of stabilization and structural reform measures (the opening-up as well as the privatization effort). In many respects we will find some of these common elements, though on a very different scale, when discussing the case of Eastern Europe.

Finally, let us recall that the major growth and inflation crisis in the Latin American subcontinent erupted with the debt shock of 1981–2, itself the delayed product of earlier 'liberal' borrowing by governments[55] (or over-liberal lending of the recycled petrodollars by the international banks). Now that capital on a large scale is flowing back into Latin America, amidst an ongo-

---

[55] Chile, let us remember, was an exception in that most of the borrowing was done by the private sector. However, when the chips were down the private banks were, at least in part, bailed out by the government.

ing reform process, will governments have learned the lessons of the 1980s and immunize themselves and their economies from the likely effects of future reverse outflows?[56]

[56] For discussion of the real appreciation and the sources and implications of renewed capital inflow in Latin America see Calvo, Leiderman, and Reinhart (1992)

7

Stabilization and Reform in Eastern Europe

7.1 Introduction

The transformation of Eastern and Central Europe presents an unprecedented challenge for policy makers in these countries as well as for the international community involved in financing and monitoring their economic programmes. It is also an unusual challenge for the economics profession, mainly because there is hardly any past experience from which lessons could be learned for this transition process.[1]

The customary classification places the East European countries in the group of middle-income countries. Their relative income levels (with suitable correction for relative prices), their past growth rates, their levels of education and health, all put them in this category. Their political and economic crises came in the wake of increasing maladjustment of the whole Soviet bloc to the changing world growth and trade environment. The outward

Most of this chapter is based on an IMF discussion paper (Bruno 1992) which was written at the request of Massimo Russo, Director of the European Department, IMF, during my stay as Visiting Scholar at the Research Department of the Fund in Dec. 1991–Jan. 1992. A draft of that paper was used as the background document for a Staff Seminar held in Paris in Feb. 1992, in which the chief negotiators from the five East European countries that were running Fund-supported programmes at the time participated: Hungary, Poland, Czechoslovakia, Bulgaria, and Romania. The motivation for that paper may explain the policy-evaluation emphasis in this chapter. Even though Yugoslavia was not part of the same 1989 political upheaval (its later dismemberment puts it in a different category anyway), a brief discussion of its 1989–90 stabilization programme is included here mainly for historical and comparative purposes. At the time of writing (summer of 1992) it was premature to incorporate an analysis of the reform process in the former Soviet Union, which is only included in some of the historical background tables.

[1] Hungary started its reform process at an earlier stage, and some of the lessons from its experience are of considerable importance. However, the scope of and speed at which the reform in the other countries was initiated has no precedent in a command-type economy.

manifestation of this maladjustment can be seen in the sharp deceleration in the growth rate observed in all these countries since the mid-1970s (Table 7.1). It turned into a negative or very low growth rate in the 1980s, an order of deceleration reminiscent of some of the MICs included in our earlier discussion (for summary reference, compare Table 1.5).[2] In some respects, the adjustment and structural reform problem of Eastern Europe would seem to belong to the class of reforms in MICs such as Brazil, Mexico, or Israel, which had enjoyed long periods of growth and relative price stability in the past but underwent severe structural crises in the 1970s and 1980s, which were either exacerbated or caused by poor response to external shocks such as the oil and debt crises. Some of the same shocks (e.g. energy and raw material prices) are only now having a delayed effect in Eastern and Central Europe. The difference, however, is not only one of timing or of degree. An entire political and economic edifice has collapsed. Far-reaching political reform was followed by adoption of economic reforms whose objective is similar to that of some other MICs, but the distance between the initial point, at which the reform impinges, and the desired goal is substantially larger in a systemic sense.

Since most of the countries in question were subject to a highly controlled (and distorted) internal pricing system well into the 1980s, aggregate measures of price inflation in these countries do not convey any information about internal imbalances in the earlier period (for measures of external imbalances see Section 7.3). Table 7.2 gives such measures starting in 1986, showing inflation acceleration in respective countries as the price-liberalization process set in, first in Poland in 1989, and later in the other East European countries in 1990–1. The breaking apart of the USSR and the price liberalization process there does not really show up until 1992.

Apart from a brief mention of Yugoslavia the discussion in

---

[2] It is, of course, a moot question whether the attempt to measure GNP and its growth in these countries can be related to more conventionally measured GNP figures. Just as it can be claimed that the very sharp drop in growth after 1989 may be exaggerated (much of the output, it is claimed, could not be sold in free world markets anyway), the high growth rates up to the 1970s may well be exaggerated as well. The order of magnitude of the slow-down within each country, however, is so large that even under different sets of relative prices a substantial slow-down in the growth of standards of living must have taken place.

TABLE 7.1 *East European and Soviet GNP growth, 1971–1991 (% annual growth rate)*

	Hungary	Poland	Czechoslovakia	Bulgaria	Romania	GDR	Eastern Europe[a]	USSR	Yugoslavia
1971–5	5.6	11.9	6.1	8.6	11.3	4.9	7.9	5.1	5.8[a]
1976–80	1.7	0.4	2.2	2.8	7.2	3.6	3.5	3.9	5.6[a]
1981–5	−0.9	−1.6	−0.0	3.6	4.4	1.1	2.1	2.8	0.6[a]
1986–9	0.2	2.9[b]	3.3	1.7	1.7	3.8	2.4	1.9	0.0
1989	−1	0	3	−5	−8	2	−1	1	−2
1990	−4	−12	−1	−11	−7	−16	−9[c]	−2	−8
1991	−11	−7	−16	−23	−13	−31	−16[c]	−10	−29
1992 (prov.)	−5	3	−5	−3	−5	—	—	−16	—

[a] Net material product.
[b] IBRD estimate is 1.0.
[c] Unweighted average of first six countries, including the GDR.

Sources: 1971–89: Vienna Institute for Comparative Economic Studies, *COMECON 1990*; 1990–92: IMF estimates for GDR; GDR: Deutsches Institut für Wirtschaftsforschung (see Dornbusch and Wolf 1992).

TABLE 7.2 *East European and Soviet CPI inflation, 1986–1991(% annual rate)*

	Hungary	Poland	CSFR	Bulgaria	Romania	USSR	Yugoslavia
1986–8	10	33	0	1	2	—	131
1989	20	700	1	4	1	—	2,700
1990	30	517[a]	11	26	5	6	584[b]
1991	37	70	59	460	161	89	270
1992[c]	21	45	14	49	181	1,180	—

[a] Inflation over the year was 249%.
[b] Inflation over the year was 119%.
[c] Estimate based on first half of the year.

Sources: IMF and IBRD.

this chapter is confined mainly to the lessons that can be learned from the aftermath of stabilization and price-reform programmes adopted in five East European countries: Hungary, Poland, Czechoslovakia, Bulgaria, and Romania, in the course of 1990 and 1991. By this stage the beginnings of some institutional reforms were already evident, such as the breaking-up of the monobank into separate central bank and commercial banking systems. Yet privatization was only in its early legislation stage.

How similar are the aims of reform to those recently observed elsewhere? One point of similarity is the attempt to reform and adapt the economic structure for integration into the world economy. This involves an opening-up process from a completely controlled and distorted set of *relative* prices to relative world prices (as far as tradable goods are concerned). The other point of similarity is the macro-economic stabilization objective, having to do with the price *level*, as well as internal and external balances. This, in turn, implies the elimination of high or hyperinflation, which either already existed at the point of departure or was bound to erupt once prices were decontrolled because of the initial repressed inflation situation (due to open-budget deficits or soft-budget constraints, monetary overhang, etc.). Thus far the objectives, and even the means, are quite similar to those in other reforms; consider, for example, the Mexican simultaneous stabilization and opening-up reform discussed in the previous chapter.

The main novelty in Eastern Europe lies in the revolutionary change in institutions and in the required norms of economic behaviour—in the financial system (such as the break-up of a monobank system), in the fiscal structure, in the establishment of private property rights, and in mass privatization. One could clearly point to large segments of non-centrally planned economies that have either soft-budget norms of behaviour and/or a financially repressed business sector, and/or highly subsidized state enterprises. However, they differ from their Eastern Europe analogues in that their underlying structure is none the less largely market-oriented and private property rights are reasonably well defined.[3] While there is a lot to learn from the reforms applied to distorted subsystems in the other economies, it makes a world of difference if almost the whole economy is a single, centrally controlled, non-market, publicly owned and financed system, with virtually no other normative internal reference point, and where a market economy has to be created literally from scratch. This dictated an even more comprehensive approach to the reform process than ever adopted before and raised tough problems of sequencing and timing.

The need for a simultaneous approach to macro-economic stabilization, price reform, and property rights reform was recognized in the IMF's approach to these programmes at the inception stage.[4] While the programmes have been largely 'heterodox' in their approach to the stabilization of the price level, they differed from their predecessors (e.g. Israel and Mexico) in several respects, especially in the way in which wages were controlled. But the programmes were much more far-reaching and ambitious in their attempt to move at great speed from the initial production equilibrium of the old system to the desired new market-based productive structure.

[3] Chile is the only exception, having gone through a relatively extreme socialist episode in the Allende period (see Ch. 6), but it was too short and not far-fetched enough to resemble anything like the countries discussed here.

[4] See 'The Role of the Fund in Assisting Eastern European Countries', internal IMF memorandum Feb. 1991. The comparative details of the various programmes are given in Table 7.3. It is important to point out from the outset that, unlike many of the cases with which the IMF has been confronted in the past, Fund programmes in East European economies have typically been self-imposed, drastic adjustment programmes, to which the Fund has given its blessing rather than having been the primary initiator. Even in these cases, however, the Fund missions have played an important role in the conception and the details.

TABLE 7.3 *Eastern Europe: Comparison of fund programmes*

	Hungary	Poland	Czechoslovakia	Bulgaria	Romania
1. Date	20 Feb. 1991	5 Feb. 1990	7 Jan. 1991	15 Mar. 1991	11 Apr. 1991
2. Duration	36 months	13 months	14 months	12 months	12 months
3. Exchange system	15% devaluation in Jan., then managed	Initial sizeable devaluations, then fixed	35% devaluation in Oct. 1990, 15% devaluation and unification with tourist rate in Dec. 1990, then fixed	Floating inter-bank	Official rate-fixed Floating inter-bank Convergence of official and inter-bank
4. Wages	Tax-based incomes policy	Tax-based incomes policy	Tax-based incomes policy	Real wage cut by 35%; implemented by ceilings on wage bills	Tax-based incomes policy
5. Interest rates	With the abolition of interest-rate ceilings will be market based	Establish positive real interest rates	Increase before programme and flexible management thereafter	Very large increase before programme; flexible adjustment thereafter	Complete liberalization CDs with flexible rates
6. Privatization	Continue in 1991	Continue in 1991	Start in 1991	Start in 1991	Start in 1991
7. Two-tier banking system[a]	1987	1990	1990	1989	1990

[a] The establishment of a two-tier banking system served to end direct central bank involvement in commercial banking.

As we shall see, the initial results as regards stabilization have, by and large, been impressive, even though the initial price shock in all countries was larger than expected, leading to some persistent inflation in most economies. Likewise, the balance-of-payments improvements may in some cases be transitory rather than permanent. The main surprise from the point of view of both policy makers and the Fund initial forecasts was the estimated speed of response of the productive system to the new price and incentive signals. The collapse of the CMEA, which, in a sense, was an exogenous event from the point of view of each country separately, had disastrous consequences on output in almost all countries, but this was probably not the whole story. While a private, small enterprise sector was developing quite rapidly, both demand and supply factors played their respective roles in reducing the output of the large state-owned enterprise (SOE) sector more sharply than expected. Some of the contradiction may have to do with the nature of the stabilization, but the more problematic issues are the slow speed of structural adjustment and the sluggishness of the privatization effort in virtually all cases. We distinguish between the stabilization of the price and exchange-rate *levels*, which can be achieved fairly rapidly, and the responses of production structure, investment, and ownership patterns to sharp changes in *relative* prices, all of which tend to be extremely slow processes. Market failure may indeed persist for a long time, naturally raising vexing issues of sequencing and the need for, or extent of, residual government involvement in the transition stage.

While this chapter addresses issues common to the region, one should not ignore differences in performance, some of which originate from the considerable diversity in the conditions that the various countries faced at the start of the present reform process. Such diversity is found both in structure (centralization versus market) and in the degree of macro-economic imbalance at the point of departure. After a brief discussion of Yugoslavia (Section 7.2) we start (Section 7.3) with a survey of the initial conditions in the Group of Five, and proceed to give an outline of the Polish programme—the first of the 'big bang' variety, followed a year later by three other countries in the same group.[5]

[5] A more detailed discussion of developments in each country can be found in individual country surveys published by the OECD and in IMF working papers.

The rest of this chapter deals with a series of pertinent issues emerging from the early East European stabilization and reform experience. The price overshooting and the output collapse, and their relation to the choice of policies, are taken up in Sections 7.4 and 7.5, respectively. Section 7.6 discusses the fiscal balance and especially its sustainability in view of the inevitable erosion of the state-enterprise tax base while pressures continue to be exerted for additional social expenditures (replacing the old subsidies). In Section 7.7 we address the problems of financial reform, bad loan portfolios, inter-enterprise credit arrears, and the need for a major clean-up and capitalization of the weak commercial banking sector. Section 7.8 raises the question of interim production, trade, and financial regimes for the state-enterprise sector during the ambiguous ownership and control period. Section 7.9 discusses the choice of exchange-rate, monetary, and incomes policies to maintain relative stability during the transition period. The chapter ends with a few concluding remarks.

7.2 Yugoslavia's Inflation in the 1980s and the 1989–1990 Reform Effort

Most of this chapter is devoted to an analysis of the stabilization and economic reform process that has been taking place in the wake of the political upheaval in centrally planned, CMEA-linked Eastern Europe. Yugoslavia did not belong to this group since it had broken off politically from the Soviet bloc and had already replaced its central planning with a system of self-management in the early 1960s. Moreover, its internal political break-up and military confrontations after 1991 put an end to its economic unity and reform process. Brief reference to the Yugoslav economy up to that point is none the less justified, for comparative purposes, since some of the internal structural and financial control problems it encountered in the 1980s were in many ways precursors of similar problems faced later by other countries, even though central planning and ownership, in the strict sense of the word, was no longer of the same species. Also,

Papers on Hungary (Dervis and Condon 1992), Poland (Berg and Blanchard 1992), and Czechoslovakia (Dyba and Svejnar 1992) were also presented at a Feb. 1992 NBER conference on Transition in Eastern Europe, to be published in 1993.

the major stabilization and reform programme that Yugoslavia adopted on 18 December 1989, while attempting to follow the Israeli and Mexican heterodox approach, was in many ways similar to the much better-known Polish 'big bang' plan adopted only two weeks later (1 January 1990). The latter, in turn, became the model for the plans in at least three other countries (Czechoslovakia, Bulgaria, and Romania) a year later.

Without going into greater detail,[6] let us mention the fact that Yugoslavia shared with other MICs considered in this book a sharp acceleration of inflation in the late 1980s, in the wake of the debt crisis (Yugoslav inflation figures for the 1970s and 1980s appear in Table 1.4). On the one hand, the inflationary dynamics of exchange-rate shocks, coupled with monetary accommodation and formal wage indexation (adopted in 1987), resembled similar processes that we have already looked at in the context of Israel and Latin America.[7] What is of special interest here is the particular way in which the fiscal and external deficits fed into the fundamental imbalance without which high inflation cannot take off. Yugoslavia had no open fiscal deficit, yet it developed a very large quasi-deficit, concentrated in its central bank's balance sheet, coming from cross-subsidization of enterprises, commercial banks, and the central bank. This is reminiscent of other ex-communist economies, even though Yugoslavia appeared to have had separate commercial and central banking functions for much longer than the other countries of the region.

The story starts with massive losses incurred by (worker-managed) enterprises as a result of misinvestments made in the 1960s and 1970s, under distorted relative prices, and financed by relatively abundant and seemingly cheap (at that time) foreign credit. Another distortion was the enterprise income-tax system (based on gross income with no allowance for either wage costs or inflation) along with relatively high payroll taxes.[8] A major

---

[6] For an analysis of the Yugoslav inflation and 1989–90 stabilization see Bole and Gaspari (1991) and Rocha (1991). Coricelli and Rocha (1991) provide a detailed comparison of the Polish and Yugoslav 1989–90 programmes and their immediate aftermath.

[7] For a detailed econometric analysis of Yugoslav inflation, including unit-root tests, for the period 1977–89, see Rocha (1991).

[8] Inflation-adjusted accounting was introduced only in 1987. Enterprise losses are estimated by Rocha (1991) to have risen from 2–3% of GDP in 1981–6 to 6–7% in 1987–8, jumping to 15% of GDP in 1989.

source of the losses was real devaluation, which increased both the cost of imported inputs and the domestic cost of interest-rate payments on foreign credits, the bulk of which were held by the enterprise sector. To this we must add the rigidity of employment in a labour-managed enterprise regime at a time of sharply falling growth rates.

Enterprise losses in themselves, of course, need not cause inflation unless they are deficit-financed and monetized, directly or indirectly, through the public purse. In the Yugoslav case the deficit was 'buried' in the central bank. In addition to a large increase in inter-enterprise credit (a more general problem, to which we will return below),[9] virtually unlimited credit was supplied by the commercial banks, most of which were enterprise-controlled and at the same time paid negative real interest rates on deposits (this was changed only in 1989). The final link in the chain was provided by the Bank of Yugoslavia, which not only provided selective rediscounts for favoured sectors (cf. the Israeli and some of the Latin American precursors) but also 'nationalized' the cumulative enterprise and banking-sector debt by introducing a foreign-exchange insurance scheme, which involved payment of the actual foreign-exchange interest by the central bank against the granting of low (nominal) domestic interest credit to the banks (and thus to the enterprise sector). Thus, while seigniorage on base money creation in the Yugoslav inflation was relatively high (4–5 per cent in the second half of the 1980s, reaching 11 per cent by 1989), the bulk of it was channelled into covering enterprise losses.[10]

As the economic crisis deepened, Yugoslavia, like its predecessors, went through partial stabilization programmes such as the use of wage–price controls in 1985 and the imposition of wage and credit controls in 1988 without the required fiscal support, and failed. Lessons were learned both from these failures and from the preceding successes of Israel and Mexico. The comprehensive programme that was finally launched in December 1989

---

[9] Forced financing of bad by good enterprises within the same industrial conglomerate, of the kind observed in the Israeli Histadruth-owned enterprise sector, was also quite common in Yugoslavia.

[10] The process and the orders of magnitude appear in Rocha (1991) and in Bole and Gaspari (1991); the latter also use the Bruno–Fischer (1990) seigniorage framework to account for the step-wise rise in the inflation rate.

included a wide set of measures in the area of fiscal, monetary, trade, payments, and incomes policies, as well as a currency reform (four digits were struck off the old dinar) and the beginnings of structural reform in the enterprise and banking sectors.

The incomes policy (hetero-) part of the programme included, after an initial devaluation, a six-month freeze on the DM exchange rate, later extended to a year. There was a six-month freeze on nominal wages and on some key public-sector prices (comprising some 20 per cent of the CPI basket). Fiscal adjustment was planned to cover the 5 per cent of GDP required to finance the central bank deficit and enable banking and enterprise restructuring; 3.5 per cent was expected to come from increased taxation, and the rest (1.5) from the Olivera–Tanzi effect. As for monetary policy—controls were imposed on net domestic assets of the central bank, the discount rate was set, and interest rates were otherwise liberalized. In trade policy, quotas and licences were relaxed. A novel feature of this programme was the introduction of substantial convertibility of foreign exchange, over and above current-account convertibility; the main reason being the need for large-scale repatriation of workers' remittances from abroad. As part of the restructuring effort and to enforce the new financial regime, a bankruptcy rule was introduced whereby enterprises that failed to meet their obligations within sixty days would be declared bankrupt.

In the first half of 1990, the programme was a resounding success, at least in bringing inflation down from 60 per cent in December 1989 to virtually zero by May and June 1990. Substantial repatriation of foreign-exchange proceeds, by both workers and firms, resulted in a $3 billion increase in foreign-exchange reserves. Real tax revenue rose substantially in spite of the inevitable drop in output and economic activity and the sharp crunch on the enterprise sector. On the internal political front it even appeared for a time as if the initial credibility and success of the stabilization programme was a way of reuniting the country and easing internal tensions between republics, already brewing for quite some time.[11] In the second half of

---

[11] The major economic problem, apart from the purely ethnic or nationalist one, was the enormous income, wealth, and resource disparity between Slovenia (and Croatia) to the west, and the poorer republics to the east—Serbia, the

1990, however, tensions that were building up around the budget and on relaxation of monetary and wage discipline added to the renewed inter-republican political and nationalistic tensions and weakened the consensus on macro-policy without which no comprehensive reform programme can last. By 1991 the civil war dominated the scene, invalidating any economic analysis of Yugoslavia as a whole.

7.3 Poland and the East European Economies: Initial Conditions and Country Programmes

While almost all five countries in question had at some stage in the 1960s embarked on partial structural reform, all but one—Hungary—of these reforms ground to a halt. Hungary pursued a very gradual reform process, beset with many set-backs, over a period of twenty years. While the ultimate objective of that reform process had not been a market-based economy, Hungary emerged better prepared than the other countries on the institutional economic front for the dramatic political liberalizations of 1989–90. This shows up in the extent of earlier price and trade liberalizations,[12] and in an earlier start in the small-scale private ownership sector. Before 1989 Hungary also put in place a two-tier banking system, a tax reform, and a system of corporate law. Some private-sector developments prior to 1989 also characterized Poland, which always had a private agricultural sector. Also, in Poland the weakening of state control had started back in 1981 with two Solidarity-sponsored laws that gave a measure of autonomy and self-management to firms and stimulated the extension of a small private sector outside agriculture, mainly in trade, services, and construction (see Balcerowicz 1990). Poland's other institutional reforms, however, lagged behind those of Hungary. Both countries suffered from an initial external debt overhang (Table 7.4), and both showed practically no growth in

largest in terms of population, and Montenegro. The internal economic transfer problem was also central in the breaking-up process.

[12] By 1982 over 50% of consumer goods were free of control, the percentage gradually increasing to 80% by 1990 and over 90% in 1991. Trade liberalization proceeded more slowly. For the Hungarian economic reform process since 1968 see Boote and Somogyi (1991). For an account of the more recent economic developments see OECD (1991).

TABLE 7.4 *Five East European countries: Initial (pre-programme) conditions*

	Population[a] (millions, mid-1989)	GNP per capita[a] (1989 $US)	GNP growth[b] (average annual rate in % at constant prices) 1970s	GNP growth[b] 1980s	Administered prices (% of total)	State ownership	Money ownership (M2)/GNP 1990	External debt/GNP (1990, %)	External debt service ratio (1990)	Exports to CMEA[c] % of total exports	Exports to CMEA[c] % of GDP
Hungary	10.6	2,590	4.5	0.5	15	90%	0.4	65	57[d]	43	16
Poland[e]	37.9	1,790	5.5	−0.7	100 (excluding food prices)	70%	0.9	80	56	41	14
Czechoslovakia	15.6	3,450	4.6	1.4	100	Economy-wide	0.7	19	23	60	25
Bulgaria	9.0	2,320	7.0	2.0	100	Economy-wide, except for 15% of agriculture	1.3	50	116	69	34
Romania	23.2	2,290	9.3	1.8	80	Economy-wide	0.6	3	—	—	—

[a] WDR (1991); IMF staff estimate for Romanian GNP per capita. All of these data are highly sensitive to the choice of exchange rates.

[b] Vienna Institute for Comparative Economic Studies, *COMECON Data, 1990*; net material product.

[c] Estimates are highly tentative as they are very sensitive to distortions in intra-CMEA prices, and exchange rates. Data for exports are based on estimated world market prices (considerably above the official traded prices); however, the GDP data are based on actual official prices. For Romania export data are only available at official prices, which would tend to underestimate the weight of CMEA trade; on this basis, CMEA exports were 39% of total exports and equivalent to 6% of GDP.

[d] % of merchandise exports.

[e] M2/GDP and exports to CMEA in percentage of total exports are 1989 figures.

the 1980s. Unlike Hungary, Poland's imbalance prior to 1989 was also felt on the internal front, owing to its large 'monetary overhang', which the partial price liberalizations and ensuing hyperinflation of 1989 helped to eliminate, or at least reduce substantially, before its January 1990 programme.

In the absence of an explicit measure of the monetary overhang, the estimate of the money/GNP ratio (line 6 of Table 7.4) gives a rough indicator. An order of magnitude of 0.4 or thereabouts could be considered the norm, a higher ratio points to the extent of possible overhang, which was large in Poland (in 1989, and probably even larger before that) and Bulgaria, smaller in Czechoslovakia and Romania, and by this measure there was none in Hungary.

It is interesting to note that in the twenty years after the Spring of 1968, Czechoslovakia reverted to a most orthodox centrally planned economy (see Table 7.4) and was thus, in a structural sense, much less prepared for the sharp change. Yet it enjoyed the most favourable initial internal and external macroeconomic balance. It had only a small monetary overhang and an extremely low external debt-to-GNP ratio on the eve of the January 1991 reform. In an interesting recount of the various countries' developments in the pre-communist era (Solimano 1991), Czechoslovakia stands out as having had a very prudent macro-economic tradition. As Table 7.5 shows, Czechoslovakia also had the most developed industrial structure by the time the communists took over. The major subsequent development in that respect took place in Slovakia, with the relevant repercussions for the structural reform and inter-republican political and social problems that turned into a crisis in 1992.

Table 7.5 ranks countries by the share of agriculture in 1938 (which is also the ranking in terms of the falling share of industry), starting with Czechoslovakia.[13] With the exception of Hungary, all countries show dramatic shifts in inter-sectoral shares over the fifty-year period. The last country in that ranking, Bulgaria, stands out in having had the most extensive

---

[13] Solimano (1991), from whose paper the 1938 data are taken, also provides the share of manufacturing in trade in 1938. In this respect, too, Czechoslovakia stands out as the only country that was exporting manufactures on a large scale—72% of exports, compared with only 13% in Hungary, 6% in Poland, and only 1–2% in the other three countries.

TABLE 7.5 *Structure of GDP by economic sector in Eastern Europe: 1938^a and 1988 (%)*

	Agriculture		Industry		Construction and services	
	1938	1988	1938	1988	1938	1988
Czechoslovakia	23	6	53	57	24	37
Hungary	37	14	36	36	27	50
Poland	39	13	32	52	29	35
Romania	53	13	28	61	19	26
Yugoslavia	54	13	22	49	24	38
Bulgaria	63	11	18	58	19	31

[a] In 1938: share of national income.

Sources: 1938: Solimano (1991); 1988: IBRD, *World Tables 1992*.

industrial development in relation to its starting-point, with some 60 per cent of GDP (and similarly for the labour force) in industry, compared to less than 20 per cent in the 1930s. Much of Bulgaria's manufacturing was export-confined to the USSR (see col. 9 in Table 7.4). In the years after 1985 Bulgaria incurred a sizeable external debt as its foreign finances faltered; by the time the reform started it faced a severe foreign-exchange constraint as well as a substantial monetary overhang. Romania, which had no external debt at all and was less dependent on CMEA trade, was none the less plagued by very severe internal economic, social, and political problems on top of specific supply problems in the oil market.

We now turn to an account of the programmes adopted in these countries during 1990–1, starting with the background to Poland's programme of January 1990, one of the most radical attempts made to transform a country at great speed into a market economy. It followed a prolonged period of chronic inflation and failed attempts to use a gradual reform strategy in the 1980s. The Polish inflation, which averaged about 35 per cent in 1981–8, resembled the shocks and monetary accommodation process observed elsewhere. As in some of its predecessors (Israel, Yugoslavia) the shocks came from exchange-rate devaluations and catch-up adjustments in controlled prices, which reached a climax in 1989.[14] As in Yugoslavia, sizeable hidden interest-rate subsidies in Poland were channelled to the enterprise sector from the banks (hence, indirectly, from the central bank). Attempts to tighten credit during 1987–9 were frustrated by increasing inter-enterprise credits, which reached 155 per cent of bank credit at the end of 1989.[15] With negative real interest rates on household deposits, there was large-scale currency substitution into foreign-exchange holdings. In the first half of 1989 the fiscal position substantially worsened as tax revenues declined and expenditures increased, in familiar fashion, on public-sector wages and subsidies.

When a new Solidarity-led government took office in September 1989 it tried to improve the worsening macro-economic situation through various partial fiscal, monetary, and wage-restraining measures.[16] However, diverging inflation dynamics took place, caused by the liberalization of food and energy prices and a sequence of exchange-rate adjustments (bringing the rate close to the parallel exchange market which had gradually assumed official status), plus more extensive wage indexation (with shortening periodicity of adjustment). The price increase in October 1991 was 55 per cent (after 40 and 34 per cent, respectively, in August and September), to be surpassed again only by the price increase during the first month of the January programme (80 per cent—see discussion in the next section).

The comprehensive stabilization programme launched on 1 January 1990, in many ways resembled its Yugoslav 'heterodox' predecessor, involving the two 'prongs' of stabilization that were discussed in the contexts of Israel and Mexico. The programme was launched by the new Finance Minister, Leszek Balcerowicz, an academic economist, helped by a team in which Jeffrey Sachs of Harvard University played a major role, and in collaboration with the IMF mission. The fundamentals involved a sharp fiscal

---

[14] For an econometric estimate of the relevant quarterly inflation equation see Commander and Coricelli (1991).

[15] Coricelli and Rocha (1991).

[16] An incoming new coalition government reacting to an inflation crisis by a set of partial policies before a comprehensive programme is finally adopted is reminiscent of the Sept. 1984 developments in Israel. However, the monthly rates of inflation in Poland were already much higher and the time that elapsed before the comprehensive programme was finally adopted was much shorter—three months rather than nine.

cut, a monetary squeeze, and an exchange-rate devaluation of 46 per cent, which considerably overshot the parallel market exchange rate. The exchange rate was pegged to a level of 9,500 zlotys per US dollar,[17] after unification of the two markets and a declared current account convertibility of the zloty. An external stabilization fund of $1 billion provided by foreign banks, and a tight internal credit policy, were intended to defend the exchange rate. Fiscal tightening came from a sharp cut in subsidies (of about 8 per cent of GDP) and an increase in tax rates on turnover and on the assets of the enterprise sector. Wage ceilings were enforced by a sharp progressive tax penalty.

The stabilization package was accompanied by far-reaching liberalization of the price system—only 5 per cent of the consumer basket remained under central control—notably energy prices, which were raised 400 per cent. External trade was liberalized almost completely. Additional structural measures included amendments to the banking law to strengthen the independence of the central bank, and an announced programme of privatization and restructuring of SOEs, with new rules for bankruptcy proceedings to be triggered by failure to pay the new asset tax. We defer discussion of the post-January 1990 developments until after mention of other subsequent countries' programmes.

Exactly a year later, at the beginning of 1991, three other countries—Czechoslovakia, Bulgaria, and Romania—adopted programmes that essentially resembled the Polish programme of 1990: the main breakaway from the past consisted of an almost complete price liberalization and a substantial elimination of price subsidies, with the aim of achieving fiscal balance coupled with the establishment of strict monetary targets and wage

---

[17] This was a compromise rate adopted by Finance Minister Balcerowicz. It was substantially lower than the rate demanded by some participants in the debate, such as the Ministry for Foreign Trade, but higher than seemed necessary on objective grounds. Having participated in an informal preview of the programme in Warsaw in Dec. 1989, to which some foreign experts were invited, my own opinion (stated in a letter to Minister Balcerowicz), was that the high rate in the parallel market reflected the demand for foreign exchange for asset holding (in the absence of alternative savings hedges against high inflation) and that for competitive purposes as well as for prevention of excessive cost pressures a considerably lower rate should have been chosen. This 'disequilibrium' market undervaluation of the currency is well known to tourists, who are surprised to find that, at the going rate, they can obtain goods and services at one tenth (or less) the price they would pay in the West. The same syndrome reappeared in Russia in 1992. See further discussion of the issue in Section 7.4.

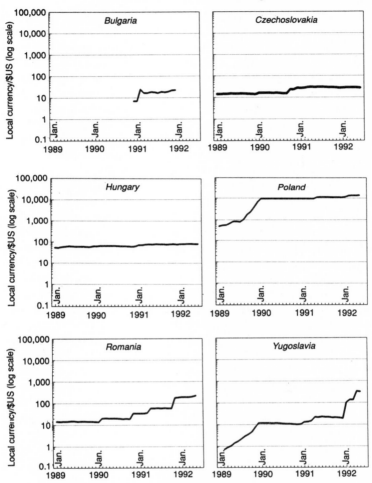

Note: Local currency per $US, log scale, end-of-period figures.

Source: National authorities and IMF staff estimates.

Fig. 7.1   Eastern Europe exchange rates, 1989–1992

ceilings. With respect to the exchange rate, Czechoslovakia, like Poland in 1990, adopted a peg as a nominal anchor (after several devaluations in the preceding months, which almost doubled the exchange rate). Bulgaria and Romania, for lack of foreign-exchange reserves, floated and let the inter-bank market determine a considerably depreciated exchange rate, thereby tripling the previous official rate (see Fig. 7.1). The two countries did, however, differ in the phasing of the exchange-rate reform, which was more gradual in the case of Romania. In all three countries the programme included substantial trade liberalization with current-account convertibility and various other measures and institutional changes pertaining to structural adjustment and privatization.

Given its different starting-point, Hungary adopted a gradualist programme in January 1991, involving a much smaller devaluation (15 per cent), a further liberalization of prices (up to 90 per cent of the consumer basket, having previously moved gradually from less than 50 per cent in 1985), and restrictive fiscal, monetary, and incomes policy. This programme, which had been preceded by other, less ambitious programmes, also included a substantial further liberalization of imports and another set of structural adjustment and privatization measures.[18]

The programmes for the first four countries (excluding Hungary) were obviously conceived as 'big bang' moves. Their guiding principle was that the price and trade systems, with few exceptions, had to be liberalized all at once, under the umbrella of fiscal, monetary, and incomes restraint. At the same time new financial institutions were being put in place and the productive systems were slated for rapid privatization, so as to minimize the uncertainties of operation under public ownership and controls.

In all countries the initial price-liberalization stage was expected to involve a substantial price-level shock, to be followed a few months later by relative price stability. The actual results are discussed in Section 7.4. The prior assessment of output response is discussed in relation to actual outcomes in Section 7.5.

7.4 Stabilization: Was the Initial Price Shock Necessary?

In all cases except Hungary, the initial price shock proved substantially more severe than expected, while inflation within six

[18] The average tariff dropped from 18% in 1985, through 16% in 1986–9, to 13% in 1991. The share of imports liberalized rose from zero to 16% (1989), 37% (1990), to reach 72% in 1991; see Dervis and Condon (1992).

months of the programme launch came down to less than 2–3 per cent a month in Poland, Czechoslovakia, and Hungary. In the other two countries inflation edged up, after a temporary drop, to an average monthly rate of 4–5 per cent in Bulgaria and 10 per cent in Romania (see averages in Table 7.6 and monthly data in Fig. 7.2). Of the first three countries, however, by the end of 1991 only Czechoslovakia and Hungary were running rates of inflation below the 20 per cent annual mark,[19] or a monthly rate of less than 1.5 per cent, while Poland's rate has been at least twice as high (some 3–3.5 per cent a month, or 40 per cent per annum). Of all five East European countries, the Czechoslovak stabilization was virtually a textbook case—the initial price shock was followed by relative price stability (see Fig. 7.2).

Differences in initial conditions no doubt played an important role. Poland, as mentioned earlier, started its programme in the midst of a hyperinflation caused by a series of earlier price hikes which may or may not have eliminated the monetary overhang by January 1990.[20] At any rate, a price shock of 45 per cent was forecast for January 1990, but was actually an 80 per cent increase *ex post* (for January and February together the respective figures are 67 *ex ante* versus 122 per cent *ex post*). During the whole of 1990 inflation was expected to be less than 100 per cent but was actually about 250 per cent, showing that even the residual inflation, after the initial shock, turned out to be higher than planned. Czechoslovakia, which started from a stable price level and apparently a considerably smaller monetary overhang, planned a price increase of only 25 per cent, and *ex post* had a price-level shock of 40 per cent in the first quarter of 1991, a smaller relative discrepancy than Poland's. Moreover, the residual inflation during the first year was only 10 per cent higher than expected, after allowing for the first quarter's shock. Both Bulgaria and Romania set off from a much worse initial position

[19] This is a convenient reference point as it corresponds to recent rates of inflation in the previously successful stabilizers from high inflation: Bolivia, Chile, Israel, and Mexico.

[20] Lipton and Sachs (1990) argue that the *stock* disequilibrium caused by the monetary overhang had already been eliminated by 1989, leaving only the (fiscal) *flow* disequilibrium as an inflationary driving force before the programme was launched. Given the relatively high M2/GDP ratio for 1990 (see Table 7.4) and the large subsequent price shock, it is not clear whether this can provide the whole explanation.

Table 7.6 *Eastern Europe: Selected indicators, 1990–1991*

	GDP[a] (% change)	Consumer prices (year end % change)	Nominal wage (year end % change)	Broad money (year end % change)	Budget balance[b] account (% of GDP)	Convertible current account (% of GDP)	Convertible current account ($USbn.)	Total exports[c] ($USbn.)
Hungary 1990 Actual	-4	33	27	29	-0.1	0.4	0.1	8.9
1991 Programme	-3	31	32	23	-1.5	-3.6	-1.2	12.6
1991 Actual	-8(-8)	32	35	29	-4.1	1.0	0.3	9.6
Poland 1989 Actual	—	640	472	236	-7.4	-2.7	-1.8	8.1
1990 Programme	-5	94[d]	—	87	-0.1	—	-3.0	—
1990 Actual	-12	249	160	122	3.5	1.3	0.7	15.0
1991 Programme	3	36	—[d]	43	-0.6	-2.7	-2.7	—
1991 Actual	-8(-4)	60	54	49	-7.2	-2.9	-2.2	13.2
Czechoslovakia 1990 Actual	—	18	8	1	-0.3	-2.4	-1.1	11.6
1991 Programme	-5	30	17	6	0.8	-7.1	-2.5	12.6
1991 Actual	-16(-9)	54	14	27	-2.1	0.7	0.2	10.9
Bulgaria 1990 Actual	-12	64	32	12	-9.2	-16.1	-1.2	5.7
1991 Programme	-11	234	146	24	0.1	—	-2.0	6.6
1991 Actual	-23(-16)	339	142	25	-3.7	-11.8	-0.9	3.7
Romania 1990 Actual	-7	5[d]	11[d]	17	-0.5	-8.0	-1.7	5.8
1991 Programme	—	104	—	15	-1.5	—	-1.7	5.4
1991 Actual	-12(-10)	223	124	66	-3.0	-6.6	-1.3	3.5

[a] Figure in parentheses provides an estimate of the fall in GDP due to the fall in exports; percentage point contribution of the change in total exports to the percentage change in GDP.

[b] For Poland: general government balance. For Czechoslovakia: central and local governments, and extra-budgetary funds, excluding take-over of export credits, and transfers to the banks and foreign trade organizations on account of devaluation profits and losses. For Bulgaria: based on actual external debt-service payments; for 1991, after external debt rescheduling and debt deferral.

[c] Including transactions in non-convertible currencies.

[d] For Poland: year average only available for programme; on this basis 1990 and 1991 programmes: 240% and 68% respectively; compared to actual of 382% in 1990 and estimated 76% in 1991. For Romania: year average figures.

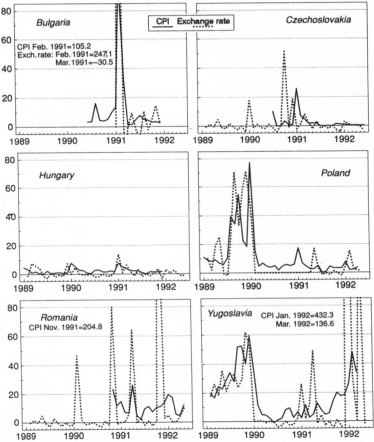

FIG. 7.2 CPI inflation and exchange rates, Eastern Europe, 1989–1992

and made a number of additional price corrections during the year, and it would be premature to pass judgement on the success of the initial move as far as price stabilization is concerned, particularly in the case of Romania. The sharp foreign-exchange shortage in these two countries, which necessitated a different exchange-rate regime at the start and a considerably larger initial exchange-rate hike, may also account for their worse subsequent inflation profile. Hungary, as in other aspects, is an outlier: its initial price shock was small (10 per cent, as expected), and its residual inflation also hit the target (see Table 7.6).

Three questions arise in the face of these initial price developments, after taking due consideration of the fact that price comparisons between a post-liberalization system and a distorted and
rationed pre-liberalization stage impart a considerable upward
bias to the data.[21] Why was the price shock in most cases so
much higher than expected? What are the implications of the
initial shock for the subsequent inflation profile (the implications
for the real system will be discussed later)? Was an initial price
shock as large as Poland's, say, necessary?

Possible answers to the first question (sources of the higher-
than-expected price-level shock) are: existence of a larger unab-
sorbed monetary overhang, underprediction of the effects of a
large initial devaluation, and monopolistic behaviour on the part
of state enterprises such as would follow from the anticipated
imposition of price controls, etc. In Bulgaria, and partly in
Poland, the initial monetary overhang may have played a sizeable
role, while in the other countries (including most of the effect in
Poland) the price shock seems to be associated with one of, or a
combination of, the other factors, such as the price response to
the exchange-rate devaluation. For example, it is known from
inflationary experience elsewhere that the exchange rate, in the
absence of another reliable measuring rod, often serves as the
indicator to which pricing agents attach themselves even when
their product is not tradable.[22]

This leads us to the second question: what is the relationship
of the initial shock to the consequent inflation profile? If the
answer to the first question is confined to an existing monetary
overhang, it would follow that a higher initial price jump would
spare the system additional inflationary adjustments later on and
thus there would be a positive trade-off between the initial shock
and the ensuing price stability. If this is not the case, and if there
is also a tendency for other nominal magnitudes in the system
(money and credit, wages) to 'catch up' with their initial
'planned' positions relative to the price level, then an initial price-
level discrepancy will also lead, through inertia, to higher-than-

---

[21] An interesting question is whether different initial conditions in the various
countries might have led to different *relative* biases in these price-shock estimates.

[22] In Israel this is called the 'dentist effect' because dentists allegedly raise their
fees by the same rate at which the price of their material inputs rises even though
these inputs comprise only a small portion of the cost of treatment.

expected inflation profiles. This may have been the case in Poland and Bulgaria, but probably not, or less so, in Czechoslovakia. In the second half of 1990 money, credit, and wage ceilings were adjusted upwards in Poland, and a similar correction was made in the second half of 1991 in Czechoslovakia and Bulgaria. In Poland the difference between the actual wage and the wage ceiling in the earlier phase could, according to the rules of the game, be made up later, and enterprise managers availed themselves of this option, paying substantial additional taxes while doing so.

Hence the third question: was there an option of a smaller planned, or a smaller actual, price-level shock at the beginning in Poland, for example (or, for that matter, in Bulgaria or Romania)? In technical terms the answer is yes, in principle. Compare these programmes to one successful 'heterodox' predecessor: Israel in July 1985 (see Chapter 5). With the substantial elimination of subsidies Israel limited its initial price shock to 27 per cent by opting for an attenuated devaluation (relative to what the fundamentals seemed to dictate) and introduced temporary price controls which were then gradually removed. It obviously had no monetary overhang and its relative price levels were certainly not as distorted as those of the East European economies. Yet it may be argued that Poland could have chosen a smaller up-front devaluation[23] and/or left price controls at a higher initial price vector for three months, say, and only then decontrolled completely, either all at once or gradually. On the other hand, one might argue that with distortions as big as they were, and the new government's initial high credibility, it might have been preferable to 'chop off the dog's tail all at once'. It is interesting to note that Czechoslovakia did keep some controls on its initial price shock. This was done by stipulating maximum prices or trade margins on some key commodities, by requiring prior notification of price increases in some monopolistic sectors, and by moral suasion. In some cases, such as Czechoslovakia

---

[23] As already mentioned, in the Polish case, in the initial absence of alternative inflation-proof financial assets, the free-market exchange rate reflected a stock demand and far exceeded the relevant PPP exchange rate. This was the reason for choosing a smaller devaluation than initially planned. *Ex post* it may still have been too high—note that it took a year and a half of substantial inflation until the real appreciation of the exchange rate began to 'bite' from a competitive point of view.

and Bulgaria, certain price increases were delayed (energy, housing). The issue of the size of the desired initial price jump, as well as the fall in economic activity, to which we turn next, is really one of intertemporal economic and political trade-offs.

Do the initial benefits of a very big price bang[24] outweigh the eventual costs of higher inertial inflation and/or other social costs resulting from the price shock? As far as the twin issues of devaluation and price liberalization are concerned, Poland was probably right in choosing to abolish price controls straight away, but it could have devalued by less and thus reduced the initial shock. One result may have been the need to realign the exchange rate earlier than in mid-1991, but the cumulative price increase over the two-year period could none the less have been smaller. Czechoslovakia (and Hungary) seems to have chosen the right level. As for the other two countries, the question arises whether an economy can afford to opt for drastic relaxation of foreign-exchange restrictions when the foreign-exchange shortage is as acute as it was (and still is). One counter-argument is that the administration of such restrictions would be ineffective.

Ending on a positive note, and notwithstanding all the comments and quibbles made with the benefit of hindsight, the over-riding fact remains that in most cases far-reaching liberalization has been achieved together with a reasonable measure of macro-economic stability in spite of a highly distorted starting-point and immense potential economic and political risks. Finally, it is important to point out again, from a consumer-welfare perspective, that against the statistical measure of price increase one should weigh the dramatic qualitative change that has taken place in the market environment that is now facing consumers in these countries.

7.5 Was the Output Collapse Unavoidable?

There are several possible reasons for the large fall in output. Let us start with one channel, not necessarily the most important one, that is directly linked to the price shock. First, the anticipation of a sharp price increase stimulates hoarding, which is imme-

---

[24] It was the Polish authorities who opted for the toughest of three options suggested by the Fund mission at the time.

diately followed by a substantial reduction in demand. Next, when prices rise by more than planned while money, credit, and wages are kept within specified nominal bounds, the obvious result is a considerably larger-than-expected reduction in real money and credit as well as in real wages. This happened in Poland in 1990 and was repeated in the experience of the other three shock cases. How much of the output reduction, which was considerably larger than expected, can be directly linked to this price shock discrepancy? The results for the Polish programme of 1990 show a considerable reduction in measured output—around 12 per cent larger than anticipated.[25] Both the real wage squeeze and the real monetary squeeze certainly affected consumer demand and thus depressed output on the demand side. The credit squeeze can also operate on the firm supply side, if we consider the finance of working capital as a factor of production (see Calvo and Coricelli 1991). Another channel through which the credit squeeze operates is the real interest rate if nominal interest rates are initially set at a level that is too high relative to the *expected* inflation rate after the initial price-level shock. There is some evidence that the high initial real interest has, in fact, constrained firms more than the quantity of credit[26] (to which they could, and did, adjust, through inter-firm credit arrears). But how much of the output decline, even in 1990, could be ascribed to this factor alone remains an open question.

In addition to the impact of the CMEA collapse, to which we turn next, there was a general shock both in Poland and in some of the later programmes on the supply side that, for want of a better term, might be called a comprehensive 'management shock'. Enterprise managers who were used to operate in a completely different environment in which their 'market' was assured (the main problem was how to obtain inputs), and whose finance was accommodative, suddenly had to make their own decisions in a completely transformed environment of tremendous uncertainty. The first natural impulse is to adopt a 'wait and see' attitude, or to continue producing for inventory, as long as working

---

[25] There is some doubt as to the relevance of the –5% projected output drop. According to the participants in the planning stage this had been a very arbitrary estimate, not based directly on any of the plan's parameters.
[26] From an unpublished survey by the World Bank resident mission based on interviews in seventy-five state-owned enterprises, Sept. 1991.

capital lasts. There is evidence pointing to unfulfilled credit ceilings in the first few months of the Polish, Czechoslovak, and Bulgarian programmes, followed by a period in which credit ceilings were effective but wage ceilings were not reached. The latter was the case during much of 1991 in the Bulgarian and Romanian programmes where, as occurred previously in Czechoslovakia, the nominal interest rate was set at a level corresponding to the estimated post-shock rate of inflation rather than at a level that would assure a positive real rate of interest in the first month. However, it is important to remember that, unlike the Polish case, these three countries did not have to contend with an existing hyperinflation. Therefore, the fact that a more moderate interest-rate policy did not lead to an inflationary outburst is no proof that this policy should have been pursued in a hyperinflationary situation (such as Russia's).

It is also important to remember that a credit crunch and high real interest rates are universal problems in the immediate aftermath of sharp stabilizations (Bolivia, Mexico, Israel). It could also be argued that with *ex ante* uncertainty about the outcome of stabilization, a highly contractionary monetary policy is justified as providing support for the exchange rate and/or wage anchors. Of the two types of mistakes that can be made it is better to err on the side of an overly restrictive stance. However, once initial success is achieved, a gradual, though careful, relaxation is called for. A more pertinent problem is that of the high bank interest margins associated with a bad loan portfolio. This issue will be dealt with separately.

Table 7.6 gives rough internal IMF estimates of the part of the output drop in 1991 that could be ascribed potentially to the export drop owing to the CMEA collapse. This estimate was based on demand-side considerations, under the assumption of no short-run market substitutability (which was obviously not the case in Hungary or Czechoslovakia—see Section 7.10). It did not explicitly take into account the very sharp terms-of-trade effect of the CMEA collapse, which was a substantial exogenous supply shock to the economies in question, very much like the effect of the relative rise of energy and raw materials prices on the industrial countries in the 1970s and 1980s. It is interesting to point out that, with the exception of Hungary, the implied unaccounted-for drop in output in Table 7.6 seems to be correlated with the degree of prior dependence of the country on CMEA trade (see Table 7.4, cols. 10 and 11), which may be a proxy for the relative size of the potential terms-of-trade shock.[27]

The fact that the discrepancy in Poland in 1991 seems larger than warranted by CMEA dependence may have to do with the complementary component of an aggregate supply shock, namely, the degree of rigidity of real wages. In Poland the real product wage in 1991 did not continue to fall; rather, it increased by 15 per cent, thus exacerbating the effect of the terms of trade. The CMEA collapse caused most damage in Bulgaria, the bulk of whose exports had been to CMEA. Bulgaria, more than any other country, suffered from a lack of raw materials due to a severe foreign-currency constraint.[28] At any rate, the demand- and supply-side components of the output collapse must be subjected to more detailed country studies before one can assess how big a margin needs to be explained over and above the 1991 CMEA effects (see Borensztein, Demekas, and Ostry 1992).

In this connection there is the obvious policy evaluation question: was this unprecedented output drop avoidable? And if it was not, the question remains whether there was enough in the set of policies to facilitate a more flexible subsequent output rebound. Part of the answer lies in the realm of structural adjustment policies and privatization, to which we turn later. However, even before going into these issues there are the regional trade issues to consider. A substitute for CMEA in the form of a payments union or trade arrangement could certainly have helped. Given the financial and political problems afflicting the ex-USSR, it is not clear whether such an arrangement would have worked in 1991. Preserving some of the 'distorted' bilateral arrangements during the transition period might have softened the blow. One example is the revival of some trade between Bulgaria and Russia

---

[27] An estimate by Rodrik (1992) of the Soviet trade shock, which includes the effect of the terms of trade for Hungary, Poland, and Czechoslovakia, is remarkably close to the numbers in brackets in Table 7.6, so that they may include terms-of-trade effects after all. In any case, none of the estimates by IMF or Rodrik includes Keynesian multiplier effects or the effect of aggregate supply curve shifts under wage rigidity (see Bruno and Sachs 1985).

[28] This is a clear case in which the short-run marginal product of an additional infusion of foreign capital was very high. Given excess capacity in complementary factors of production, the marginal GDP product of foreign exchange equals the reciprocal ratio of raw materials to GDP.

under a clearing arrangement (applying a *disagio* on the Bulgarian export rate), which was finally carried out in August 1991, but could have been implemented earlier. The point is that, given the magnitude of the output shock and the long time-lag of response of the productive system to the new market signals, there is no escape from looking for ways to soften the blow to output and employment in the interim period even if they may seem 'distorted' from the long-run point of view, provided the long-term signals are clearly made. The alternative, though not the first-best one, is very probably government intervention in other forms—extending credit and granting subsidies to ailing enterprises in a particular region, or assigning larger budgetary allotments to unemployment relief.

On the question of the speed of trade liberalization, the wisdom of the 'cold turkey' solution can be questioned. A move to current-account convertibility can also be envisaged with a more gradual reduction of tariff barriers (see also Greene and Isard 1991; proposals by Tanzi 1991; Mckinnon 1991). There is a strong argument in favour of the elimination of import licensing and quotas in one go. However, there is no good inherent reason to move all at once to a zero, or a very low, tariff. The objection to a gradualist strategy is clear, since it is vulnerable to discretionary reversals by governments with low credibility. When credible, however, the advantage of gradualism lies in the attenuation of the immediate output and employment costs while retaining the right price signals for long-term investment. A commitment has to be made to a well-defined time path from a differentiated tariff structure towards a common low tariff within a short span of years (no more than five, say). There are examples in the history of trade liberalization of a successful move along a pre-announced gradualist path; consider, for example, the formation of the Common Market by a pre-committed gradual mutual removal of tariffs in the 1950s and 1960s,[29] as well as individual country cases such as Israel's trade liberalization in the 1960s.

Even when the gradual path is chosen the question remains whether there should be substantial differentiation of initial tariffs across goods. To avoid political pressures one may, for example, differentiate only by general category of good (raw materials,

[29] It has taken the Common Market quite a few years to phase out declining industries, e.g. in coal and steel.

investment, and consumption goods) rather than by individual commodity or producer. In the next section, in discussing the fiscal balance, we argue in favour of at least a flat across-the-board tariff, for purely fiscal reasons, until VAT is introduced. This in itself would not, of course, allow for a differentiated speed of adjustment across groups of goods.

A country that opts for an ambitious trade reform from the start may not want to backtrack later because of the cost in terms of loss of credibility. On the other hand, objections have been raised to the introduction of any customs duties or tariffs in some countries, either because of the complete openness of borders or for lack of the necessary administrative capabilities. Unfortunately, the latter argument would also hold against any taxation like VAT. The fact is that Poland eventually introduced a new higher tariff structure in the second half of 1991.

Even when the output downturn is reversed, past reform and structural change experience shows (elsewhere as well as in Eastern Europe) that there is substantial labour shedding and increasing unemployment while output rebounds. The sources of the output collapse are obviously very important subjects for further scrutiny. No less important is getting a better idea of the actual numbers. While the public sector's output collapses, the small-scale private sector, especially in trade and services, seems to have thrived. Given the small initial starting base, even very large increases at an early stage cannot affect the overall result unless the country starts off with a larger private sector to begin with. Poland may have been in this situation by 1992, when aggregate GDP started rising; at the time of writing one can only rely on partial evidence. There were also very different interpretations of the meaning of the unemployment numbers. While unemployment in Bulgaria was already around 10 per cent, it was argued that there could be no serious unemployment problem if one could not even find cleaning help willing to work at the minimum wage; at the same time other observers were claiming that serious unemployment problems were emerging among the young. These arguments are not necessarily contradictory, just as zero unemployment in Budapest or Prague can be entirely consistent with very serious unemployment in other heavily industrialized regions. It was also argued that one reason why a major employment reduction in the Bulgarian state sector was feasible with minimum social upheaval was the fact that many of these workers could return to family farms or work on their own privately owned plots. For a country with excessive industrialization (60 per cent of the labour force!), a shift to small-scale services, trade, and agriculture could be considered a move towards the correct long-run equilibrium composition of output. From a policy planning point of view, however, the most relevant issue is an assessment of the likelihood of immediate reversals in output and especially the employment down-turn, as it determines the economic, and especially the political, sustainability of the initial set of stabilization policies.

7.6 Was the Fiscal Balance Sustainable?

A key feature of the initial stabilization phase in all cases has been the balancing of the budget, primarily through a substantial permanent cut in government expenditure on subsidies to goods and services. As against that, a certain increase in expenditure on the social safety net was envisaged. Given the existing tax-revenue base, budget balance was assumed to be assured, as the figures for the respective programmes show (see col. 5 in Table 7.6). The budget balance always requires careful scrutiny to isolate transitory from permanent changes. While the initial budget outcome seems to have been satisfactory in most countries, later developments (usually starting in the second half of the first year) point to the emergence of serious problems for the second and third years of the programmes. Let us consider the various causes and implications of these developments, using the experience of Poland to start with.

At first glance, the Polish fiscal balance in 1990 was a resounding success. It switched from a deficit of 5–7 per cent of GDP in 1989 to a surplus of about 3 per cent. As Lane (1991a) shows in detail, it was initially expected that the budget would follow a U-shaped profile over the year, with a shortfall in revenue in the first part of the year and an approximate balance over the year as a whole. In fact, the balance followed an inverted U-shape, with an increasing surplus in the first two quarters of 1990 turning into a drop in the surplus in the third quarter and a deficit in the fourth quarter of 1990. The estimates for 1991 point to a deficit of 5.5 per cent for the year (compared to a planned approximate balance), possibly leading to an even larger deficit in 1992. The reasons for this outcome are important for future reference. As a result of the price shock there was an unexpected deep fall in real wages resulting in larger-than-expected profits and higher tax revenues. To this was added a tax on capital gains, on inventories, and on foreign-currency deposits. This element is an entirely fortuitous one-time effect which resulted from the lack of proper inflation accounting. The profit tax element fell substantially once real wages rebounded and profits were squeezed. It is the latter element that persisted into 1991 and is the more permanent effect of the liberalization process to which Mckinnon (1991) has drawn attention.

Czechoslovakia went through a very similar process: a temporary surplus in the first few months of 1991 and an increasing deficit towards the end of the year. Similar problems emerged in Bulgaria, which differed from its precursors by not having the initial capital gains of enterprises taxed away. Bulgaria showed a large increase in its deficit along with the output and import collapse. Romania's budget was close to balance. In the case of Hungary, a deficit of close to 4 per cent emerged in 1991 and a further increase was forecast for 1992, even though it already had the new VAT and PIT (personal income tax) in place.

As shown by Tanzi (1991), East European countries typically enjoyed a profit tax revenue of about 15–20 per cent of GDP, compared to a 3 per cent average for the OECD. Table 7.7 gives an average breakdown of general government revenues and expenditures for 1985, compared with the USSR and the EEC. While the cut in subsidies may account for 8–10 per cent of GDP saved on the expenditure side, additional safety net expenditures and unemployment benefits were introduced. These tend to expand as the process of structural change and labour shedding gathers momentum. As against that, the drop in profit taxes is likely to continue to exceed the net drop in expenditures.

A crucial problem in all the countries examined is the transition from a relatively egalitarian and generous social welfare network into a market system in which all the income- and wealth-distribution problems, risks of unemployment, and other objectionable social side-effects of capitalism suddenly emerge (see Kornai 1992). Social and political pressures develop, aimed at continuing the existing generous social security services or to correct for their erosion through sharp price-level increases. A large percentage of voters are pensioners; in Hungary, male employees retire at age 60, females at 55, and 25 per cent of the

TABLE 7.7 *Comparative structure of general government budget, 1985: Eastern Europe, USSR, and EEC (% of GDP/GNP)*

	5 East European countries[a]	USSR	EEC
Total revenue	**56**	**46**	**44**
Enterprise taxes	17	18	4
Personal income tax	4	4	9
Social security	11	4	13
Trade taxes	2	6	—
Expenditure taxes	16	12	11
Other	6	2	7
Total expenditures	**55**	**56**	**46**
Current goods and services	20	21	16
Investment goods	3	8[b]	3
Subsidies and transfers to enterprises	19	18	4
Transfers to households	12	8	15
Interest payments	1	—	5
Other	—	1	3

[a] Unweighted average.
[b] Includes some investment transfers to enterprises.
Source: Based on Kopits (1991: table 2).

population are pensioners; in Bulgaria they account for an estimated 35 per cent of the voters; the share of pensioners in Poland exceeds 40 per cent. In Czechoslovakia, pressure came from the higher-than-average unemployment rate in Slovakia (over 11 per cent by the end of 1991, and rising, compared with only 4 per cent in the Czech Republic, up from virtually zero only a year earlier). As against these elements there is also room for streamlining the social welfare framework, for example, privatization of some of the health services, charging for medication, which is presently very wasteful, progressively taxing child allowances (Hungary), etc.

One way or another, the net outcome is likely to be a permanent imbalance unless the output, sales, and profit base rebound quickly or new taxes are imposed. Past experience in the West shows that the introduction of VAT takes at least three years to take effect in a country with reasonably organized enterprise accounts. It is unlikely that this period can be effectively shortened. In the first year in which a VAT is introduced and existing taxes are replaced there tends to be a reduction in revenues anyway. There is thus urgent need to deploy temporary substitutes. For example, had trade liberalization been coupled from the beginning with a considerably larger tax on imports, even at a flat rate, this could, at least in part, temporarily have closed the gap.

In the absence of a tax alternative, the pressure to balance the budget usually leads to expenditure cuts where political opposition is weakest, but the long-term economic cost is highest, namely investment in infrastructure (roads, communications). This is the one area in which government intervention is usually essential and the positive externalities for the long-term growth of the private-enterprise sector may be highest. There may be differences in the urgency of the problem, but there is a minimum requirement in each of the countries, quite apart from the common need to cope with a heritage of environmental damage. This discussion leads to two important policy considerations. First, should the existence of a certain fiscal deficit be allowed in the interim period (until tax reform is fully in place)? Second, should infrastructure investment be treated as part of regular government expenditure?

The answers to both questions have to be considered in the particular context of each economy. The first and most important general point is that, given the time-phasing nature of the problem, one must embed the annual budget plan within a well-specified medium-term framework (of at least three years). One way, for example, is to endorse a pre-committed budget framework trajectory for each year with full budget balance to be regained within at most three years and the deficit in no year exceeding a certain percentage of GDP, say 4 or 5 per cent, as a safety margin. To minimize inflationary consequences, the finance of such deficit should not come from direct central bank money creation[30] but should be the responsibility of the Ministry of

---

[30] In theory, once there is positive real growth of GDP, money supply could be increased, assuming stable velocity, at the rate of real growth. However, this had best be left to the discretion of monetary policy and an independent central bank, and not be built in as a potential source of deficit finance. Otherwise political

Finance, which must finance it from foreign or domestic private-sector borrowing, depending on the country's initial internal and external debt situation. A clear signal of pre-commitment along these lines may help to avoid the harmful inflationary or crowding-out effects that a protracted deficit would otherwise entail.

Should infrastructure investment be treated differently? A textbook solution would be to distinguish between the total deficit and the concept of government (dis)saving. The latter is the more important concept for gauging the internal balance (although the former will still be important for financial planning). In such a case infrastructure investment could appear 'below the line' as part of a separate capital budget which need not be financed by taxes. The objection to a 'pure' solution of this kind comes from the potential abuse of such a procedure. Practically anything could be redefined as 'infrastructure investment', be it teachers' salaries, defence expenditures, or retraining the unemployed. The way out would be to use very strict definitions of what could legitimately be defined as direct government investment and limit the percentage of GDP allowed (say, to no more than an extra 3–5 per cent), and also take into consideration future revenue increments coming as a direct result of the investments to be made. Earmarking specific foreign lending (e.g. by international institutions) does, of course, ease matters. There are no universal rules for these kinds of considerations, and they must be geared to each economy's specific risks or past record. There remains the issue of the fiscal treatment of financial restructuring of enterprises or banks, and the proceeds of privatization. These are discussed in the next two sections.

7.7 What to Do with Bad Loan Portfolios and Enterprise Arrears?

In all the East European countries the former economic and financial regimes left a legacy of bad enterprise debts which have since mounted considerably and have been stacked in the portfolios of the commercial banking system. The credit crunch and

pressures on the central bank to accommodate any deficit may prove ruinous. Recent developments in several of the countries in question point to the prime importance of this caveat.

the collapse of the rouble-zone export market have exacerbated the problem, as has the mounting inter-enterprise debt. In the early stages of stabilization this problem was in most cases set aside. Unfortunately, such problems do not disappear while waiting; on the contrary, they grow worse, and may interfere with the process of stabilization and structural adjustment. On the one hand, the existence of a large bad loan portfolio in the bank balance sheets contributes to the persistence of large gaps between borrowing and lending interest rates; on the other hand, it may distort the relative creditworthiness of enterprises in a way that is not necessarily correlated with their potential profitability or long-run solvency in the new market environment.

In theory this is one of the issues best dealt with up-front in the context of a broader currency reform. Doing so in the context of the large initial package improves the chances of avoiding the severe moral hazard problems that any loan clean-up entails. But it was not attempted in the first stroke; and even if it had been, since much of the outstanding bad debt continued to accumulate in the post-stabilization phase, the problem would still have lingered on. In the absence of an up-front clean-up of bad debt, both of two polar 'solutions' must be avoided. One extreme is to ignore the issue completely in the central government's budgeting perspective by 'letting the banks deal with the problem'. For a while this seemed to have been the predominant view in Czechoslovakia, for example. If such an approach were fully followed, quite apart from giving the wrong price signals in the credit markets, it would eventually lead to a banking crisis, Israeli or Latin American style, in which the government has to step in, and on a much larger scale than would be required otherwise. The other extreme is to yield to the cumulative political pressure of the debt-ridden enterprise sector and pass blanket debt-cancellation laws. This seems to have been the approach taken in Romania. The problem with this type of aggregate solution, besides being indiscriminate, is one of a potentially serious moral hazard. It may preserve the bad borrowing behaviour of the past, in the expectation that next time around enterprises will be bailed out again.[31]

---

[31] For a description and balanced analysis of the Romanian programme see Khan and Clifton (1992).

The size of the outstanding bad debt towards the end of 1991 was estimated at 15–20 per cent of total bank debt in Hungary and Czechoslovakia and may have been as high as 30–40 per cent in Poland and Bulgaria. The ideal textbook solution is to effect a one-time clean-up of the books, provided it is credible; the government buys up the debt through the commercial banks and proceeds on a case-by-case basis, coming to the aid of an enterprise only on the basis of a clear recovery plan, with clear conditionality attached, and with an overall strictly enforced budget constraint.[32] Such a scheme does not seem to be workable in most of the countries, enterprises, and/or banks in question, unless it is done at the time of privatization as part of the sale bargain. At the other extreme, enterprises identifiable as total failures should be phased out as quickly as possible. Such was the procedure adopted in part of the Hungarian coal-mining industry.

The most serious problem in a typical economy in transition is the large share of enterprises whose future is uncertain but which are potentially salvageable. A weighty argument against across-the-board clean-ups, cited by some policy makers in these countries at the onset of the reform process, rests on what was perceived to be an inherited lack of credibility with which the new governments had to contend—merely announcing that something is to be done 'once and for all' amounts to brandishing an unloaded gun. Only a slow process of weeding-out and tough bargaining will, according to this view, gradually instil the right discipline.

In practice one observes that the problem was tackled in different countries through a gradual institutional and political bargaining process, in several half-hearted ways. In Hungary, for example, the government in 1991 guaranteed 50 per cent (10 billion forints) of the bad debts inherited by the banks from the previous regime. The remaining bad debt, accumulated mainly as

---

[32] As shown in Ch. 5, such a procedure was followed in Israel in recent major debt-rescheduling schemes for the Histadruth-(trade union federation) owned industrial conglomerate (Koor) and in the settlements belonging to the kibbutz movement. Both groups suffered severe financial straits in the aftermath of the 1985 stabilization programmes. The kibbutz movement's cumulative debt had reached some 15% of total GDP before the financial restructuring plan was implemented. In another group, the moshav (co-operative) movement, an earlier scheme had to be shelved owing to lack of compliance and political pressure, and was subsequently superseded by more comprehensive legislation.

a result of the CMEA collapse, was to be provisioned by the banks over a three-year period, with the implicit understanding that it would be taken off the annual profits for tax purposes (a 40 per cent implicit participation of the state budget). From a public image or political point of view this seemed a favoured solution since it reduced the apparent profits of the banks (which have been quite exorbitant, given the large interest-rate margins), while appearing to conceal the implicit cost to the budget. In Czechoslovakia, the government in 1991 decided to allow the National Property Funds, the recipients of proceeds from privatization, to issue Kcs50 billion in bonds to be used to write off old enterprise debt and to provide a direct capital injection to the banks. This solution was going in the right direction (see below), especially since Czechoslovakia's internal debt had been small anyway. At the time of writing it remained to be seen if Czechoslovakia and Bulgaria would follow a bank provisioning-cum-tax participation solution of the kind adopted in Hungary.

The more vexing problem is how to prevent enterprises from continued borrowing in order to survive rather than adjusting. Recapitalizing the banks and letting them handle the problem seemed to be the right move, provided the banks were able to make the proper economic analysis, and that they could also take into account the interests of the bond issuers, namely the government, or that of the taxpayers (who implicitly cover the tax losses). Unfortunately, the commercial banks' financial interests and the long-run economic viability of the enterprise do not necessarily coincide, and ideally the existing owner of the asset, namely the state, must participate in the process. This is part of the more general problem of enterprise control in the transition period (see the next section), and it is further compounded by the fact that the commercial banking system itself is, in most cases, not yet financially independent from the central bank, leaving part of the quasi-fiscal deficit in a sort of limbo.

How should one treat the public finance of bank capitalization and enterprise restructuring? It is important to recognize that this type of public expenditure, if it takes the form of a once-and-for-all stock adjustment, should not be reckoned as part of the regular tax-financed budget. It is best to include it as part of the privatization accounts (as done by the *Treuhandanstalt* in East Germany or, implicitly, in the Czechoslovak financial injection).

Even if there is an initial net debt position, this could be financed by issue of domestic bonds and/or external financial aid. Alternatively, it could be made part of a broader capital account budget from which infrastructure investment could also be financed (see the previous section). Monetary injection through this source should be taken into account within the financial planning done by the monetary authorities, but a one-time stock adjustment, if it is done credibly, should not be looked upon in the same way as a permanent rise in the money and credit growth rates.[33]

Finally, a crucial issue is that of giving the enterprise the right signal, that financial rescheduling is a one-time conditional act, not a precedent. This is part of a more general signalling problem to which we now turn.

7.8 Privatization of Large State-Owned Enterprises: What to Do during the (Long) Transition?

Experience until 1992 in all five East European countries discussed here points to substantial success in the privatization of (mainly small-scale) enterprises in trade and services, as against a virtual standstill in the realm of large-scale enterprises, primarily in the manufacturing sector. The reasons for delay were legal (such as the problem of restitution in Czechoslovakia), political (bad experience with instant privatization in Hungary and Poland, as well as changes of government in Poland), or practical (lack of foreign or domestic investors and the absence of organizational infrastructure). Even the most advanced voucher scheme that was being implemented in Czechoslovakia in 1992 still had to be tested in practice, mainly as to the extent of corporate control that would emerge. One way or another, it seemed clear that

[33] One simplified way of looking at this issue from a monetary point of view is that in a situation of a monetary crunch, where the velocity of circulation has risen substantially, such injection is, at least in part, a one-time replacement of M for V in the $MV = PT$ equation. As for the residual growth in MV, this may hopefully enable a rise in T without raising P, since the complementary capacity and the underemployed workers exist, while the commodity market has become competitive. This argument does not apply to a permanent increase in the rate of change of M, since the latter usually affects the inflation rate and inflationary expectations directly or indirectly (through the exchange rate).

there would be a prolonged interim period in which the state continued to own a considerable part of the enterprise sector. Here again, neither polar extreme (completely ignore or completely retain the past regime) seemed workable and they were certainly not the optimal solution. The problem is how to instil market-oriented behaviour in management and workers while not unduly delaying the privatization stage. One gets the impression that this problem has not been systematically addressed in any of the countries.

Hungary attempted to learn the lessons of the previous government's 'spontaneous privatization' episode. The new Law on Economic Transformation removed the SOEs from the jurisdiction of enterprise councils, endowing them with a company status under the aegis of the State Property Agency (a very similar idea is the 'commercialization' of enterprises in Poland—see below). This involved the introduction of audited balance sheets, a board of directors, and the state becoming the legal owner, at least for the transition period up to privatization. Supervision of management was partly subcontracted to approved advisory agencies acting as agents of the SPA (which is too understaffed). Much of the Hungarian privatization effort has taken the form of 'self-privatization', whereby a manager looks for potential buyers which then have to be approved by the SPA or its accredited consulting firms. The process is obviously a very slow one (except for the known cases of Tungstrom, Ikarus, or Videoton; the latter was purchased by a local capitalist, with considerable bank credit, after using the Bankruptcy Law proceedings) and fraught with political and legal problems.

The Czechoslovak government seemed to be taking the view that nothing could be done except for very speedy privatization, since only the new owners would be able to act in the best interest of the firm. As a result no systematic thought has apparently been given to the control of the enterprises in the so-called 'no man's land'. While the view is understandable, ignoring the problem does not help since in the mean time mounting pressure gathers to give subsidies or cheap credit to enterprises especially where regional employment problems arise.

An obvious argument against a hands-on line of thought is that it smacks of old-style state intervention and may help to keep SOEs in state hands indefinitely. Unfortunately, there seems to be no escape from such 'murky' half-way strategies unless one is willing to take the line that what cannot be privatized instantaneously had better be scrapped. The latter option, however, makes little economic sense from the medium-run point of view, since a considerable part of the industrial product may be made marketable after marginal investments in physical and/or human capital, especially on the marketing side. Moreover, because of the huge potential unemployment problem (with employment in SOEs anywhere between 30 and 50 per cent of the labour force), wholesale 'scrapping' is not very likely to be politically viable.

A key issue is to study the response of managers in SOEs to the sharp changes that have been taking place. A very interesting beginning was made in an unpublished survey of seventy-five large Polish SOEs by the resident World Bank mission (September 1991), from which a dynamic picture emerged. Managers find themselves at odds with the workers' councils: much of the innovation and planned change comes from the managers, who remain restricted and subordinate to the council. Instead of bargaining with the centre on raw materials or credit allocation for investment, the attention of managers is now directed to enterprise performance in terms of profit (rather than output) and marketing and financial management (rather than technical production expertise). There was considerable 'learning by doing', but there was also obvious room to expedite matters by publicly financed training programmes in management, marketing, accounting, and financial matters (the cost to the enterprise is high and the benefit may not accrue to it if the manager is free to leave). Commercialization as an intermediate step was envisaged as important as it is more likely to protect the manager from the workers' council. In this context the problem of managerial compensation is crucial, to avoid de-capitalization of firms. Such compensation could be given, at least in part, by long-maturity stock options or by including a longer-term profit share in the manager's contract.

There is a compelling alternative line of argument, at least in the Polish case (see Dabrowsky, Federowicz, and Levitas 1991), that the power of the workers' councils is too ingrained a legacy of the communist regime to be easily dismantled. According to this view, the only way to resolve the political stalemate between the workers' councils control and that of the state is by mass privatization through giveaway schemes in which the present stake-holders in the enterprise, namely, both the workers' councils and the managers, are the major beneficiaries. This would constitute some form of controlled 'spontaneous privatization'.

On the joint issue of debt rescheduling and enterprise restructuring one could also consider the experience of the Treuhandanstalt in the former GDR, which has accumulated the most experience to date in the field of privatization with prior restructuring and financial rescheduling. In the East German case, restructuring has been very costly and the management problem partly solved by co-opting managers from West Germany, both options unlikely to be available elsewhere in Eastern Europe. In the case of the GDR, too, it was claimed that while privatization proceeded at a more rapid pace during 1991 there was undue concern over job preservation—only a small number of firms were shut due to regional employment problems.

The variety of experience across countries suggests that there may not be one best way of resolving the privatization issue and each country must choose the one that best suits its political and social framework. The most important conclusion, however, is that it is important for each country to adopt a transparent strategy and give clear signals to investors, managers, and workers as to where it is headed, so as to minimize uncertainty in the transition period. Moreover, the upshot of both this and the previous section is that there is a limit to what can be achieved through macro-policies alone, and that, at any rate, great importance attaches to the integration of micro-management policies with the general policy framework right from the start as well as along the way. This is no doubt one area, even more than in previous adjustment and structural reform experiences, in which the integration of the two approaches is essential. But obviously macro- policy retains its importance. We thus return to the macro-sphere at this point.

7.9 The Ingredients of Macro-Policy during the Transition

In Section 7.6 we discussed the problem of the fiscal balance. We did not consider the complementary problem of current-account sustainability, which by 1992 had not presented a serious problem, except for the ongoing severe foreign-exchange constraint in

Bulgaria. Looking at Table 7.6 (col. 7) the current account is one area in which programmes seem to have over-achieved their targets. While this is no mean accomplishment in the face of the CMEA export collapse and in view of the opening-up to competing imports, part of this result could be entirely transitory. In all of the countries examined the propensity to import raw materials and consumer goods was relatively large, and while the opening-up must have caused a substantial increase in imports, the income effect must likewise have temporarily depressed them, given the output collapse. Once output and internal demand rebound, imports will rise. Current-account sustainability, like that of the fiscal accounts, must thus be looked at in a medium-term perspective. Two issues arise: export promotion and, for some of the countries, the debt strategy. Another related issue is that of foreign investment.

The first and obvious problem is the supply and demand response of exports to hard-currency markets. Hungary, in particular, seems to have been most successful in this respect so far; its associate membership in the Common Market and longer experience in market penetration have no doubt helped. Both Poland, during its first programme year (1990), and Czechoslovakia (in 1991) increased their exports to Western markets. It remains to be seen whether this was merely a one-time switch of goods from a severely depressed domestic market[34] to export 'dumping' in the West, or a serious beginning of the required longer-term trend. Much depends on the internal structural adjustment process and on the willingness of the Western side to open markets. Anecdotal evidence in various countries (Hungary and Czechoslovakia, in particular) points to the steady growth of joint ventures, often relatively small ones, based on restructured public enterprises, using Western marketing know-how and directed towards external markets. There has probably also been a fair amount of (unrecorded?) exported services across newly open borders, based on large skilled- and professional-labour cost differentials. But it is too early to assess the scope of these developments and the extent to which they would apply to countries

---

[34] Apparently there was no switch of exports from CMEA to the West as these goods are not very competitive at the new relative prices.

located further away from Western markets, like Bulgaria and Romania.[35]

While Hungary's outstanding debt and lack of a Polish-type write-off was still exerting an external long-term constraint in 1992 (the growth rate had yet to exceed the weighted interest rate), it benefited from substantial inflows of foreign investment, so that no immediate foreign-exchange problem emerged. On the contrary, undesirable pressure was exerted to appreciate the exchange rate (see below). Polish foreign-exchange reserves fell in 1991. Bulgaria's foreign-exchange reserve position improved dramatically in 1991, but was still in a very precarious position, awaiting the debt rescheduling with the banks; Bulgaria, more than any of the other countries, could make good use of a stabilization fund, so as to enable it to pursue a more stable exchange-rate policy. This brings us to the next and main subject of this section: given reasonable balance in the fiscal accounts, what nominal anchor management should the economies adopt in the transition to sustainable growth?

Whatever the choice of exchange-rate regime and incomes policy dictated at the initial sharp liberalization and stabilization stage, there is the issue of the appropriate policy stance and tools for the second stage. Poland, which pegged its exchange rate at the beginning, opted for an exchange rate crawl starting in May 1991, sixteen months after the initial programme. Czechoslovakia has not had to move from the fixed rate established in January 1991. Hungary has managed the exchange rate more flexibly for some time. What is an appropriate regime for countries like Bulgaria and Romania after the initial float? Given the inherent instability of money demand, preference should probably be given to the exchange rate over monetary aggregates as a nominal anchor, as has been the case in other MICs with low or moderate rates of inflation. Also, while credit ceilings for individual banks may be an indispensable tool in the initial stabilization phase, or during limited financial crisis periods, they become a hindrance once a more efficient financial intermediation system is developed.[36]

[35] For all the countries other markets, such as the Middle East, have also been important, and there is no reason why this should not continue to be the case (the Gulf crisis was a temporary problem in 1990–1).

[36] Examples have been cited in some of the countries of banks' being unwilling to promote additional household deposits because, with given credit limits, there was no additional lending motive.

Once a country decides on its targeted inflation rate it can set bounds for exchange-rate movements over the planning period, whose average rate would be less than or equal to the expected inflation differential with respect to its trading partner. The choice between an explicit crawl or flexibility within a moving band depends on the particular institutional set-up, such as the degree of development of foreign-exchange markets.[37] Judging from the situation in a country that, at the time of writing, was more than two years into its initial stabilization programme, namely Poland, there seems to be a great danger of repeating the inflationary patterns of adjustment exhibited by some MICs in the 1970s and 1980s. Larger fiscal deficits could combine with monetary, exchange-rate, and wage-rate accommodation to price increases so as to maintain, at least, stable real exchange rates. The rationale would be the maintainance of an export supply response, but the cost would be loss of the nominal anchor, and accelerating inflation and recurrent internal and/or external crises.

How long should wage ceilings be maintained? As long as a large public sector persists there is no choice but to maintain rather strict wage ceilings for public-sector enterprises, in support of an exchange-rate anchor. In view of the distortions caused to the wage structure these ceilings could, of course, be eased up as soon as sufficient alternative market discipline on the enterprise level is assured. In the private sector, a distinction should be drawn between tradable (or highly competitive non-tradable) products and monopolistic non-tradable industries. The latter should also be controlled through price or wage controls, or both. The alternative to wage controls would be a social compact on incomes policy between the major sectors (government, employers, and labour unions) of the kind that has worked in some middle-income (e.g. Israel, Mexico) or industrial (e.g. Scandinavian) economies.

Once foreign investments and other private long-term capital inflows make their way into the countries (as is already happening in Hungary) a Latin American-type real appreciation syndrome may set in. There was an initial over-devaluation in most countries and non-traded goods prices in particular were, for a

---

[37] Such a regime does not preclude the possibility of making larger step adjustments as needed. However, such adjustments, if made too frequently, get embodied in inflationary expectations and may become counter-productive.

while, quite far from world market prices. Given this, and assuming that there are substantial untapped reserves of productivity growth, these economies could afford some real appreciation, provided it takes place within a well-managed macro-economic framework. No general rules can be applied, and it would seem that the choice of regime and the mix of policies must be geared to the conditions of each country separately. In this respect, too, there is no difference between these and other MICs at a similar mid-reform stage.

7.10 Concluding Remarks

Our discussion of the recent East European experience points to broad common denominators both across countries and with experience elsewhere in the stabilization part of the reform. The basic monetary and fiscal theory of high inflation and sharp stabilization seems to apply more generally and, to the extent that differences exist between groups of countries, they stem from problems in the ability to control the budget or the amount of credit or wage policy, not from the underlying conceptual macro-economic framework. The area in which the differences loom largest from the beginning is also the one in which the adjustment has proved considerably harder than expected—the change in the micro-foundations of the economy, such as in ownership rights and financial accountability. The general lesson to be learned here is that the policy reform package has to place even greater emphasis on setting up institutions and rules of behaviour for the micro-units. Otherwise the stabilization part of the reform might also fail.

Another related issue has to do with the perceived role of government in the transition from a communist to a market economy. Until very recently, the stereotype image of communism was often one of a minutely detailed, centrally planned, omnipotent government. Likewise, a capitalist economy was often thought of by uninformed aspirants as consisting only of private property ownership and pure *laissez-faire*, self-adjusting, market mechanisms in which governments need not interfere. Experience shows that even the most *laissez-faire* economies are susceptible to market failures (e.g. in financial markets) and that governments may have to intervene in the micro-economy. All the more reason to believe that in the transition a hands-off approach cannot be optimal. The obvious example is that of financial restructuring. The danger of repeating old central planning mistakes is obviously always there, but this cannot justify ducking the issue of how best to intervene in the transition. Denial of this realization will not prevent considerable intervention in practice, it will only obscure it and entail costs that may violate the macroeconomic budget constraints to an extent whose scope and implications are unknown. Our discussion tended to concentrate on issues common to the various countries, at the initial stage, even though the differences among countries (not only the case of Hungary) were also marked. As time passes such differences are likely to become more important from a policy perspective, as they usually have done in other cases of stabilization and structural reform.

One issue on which economists cannot offer much help is the evaluation of the internal politics of reform. The external observer is struck by the apparent popular consensus with which the very drastic changes were accepted at first, especially in view of the sharp real wage cuts, the fall in living standards, and rising unemployment. One meets with the understandable argument that the official statistics do not really capture reality because of statistical biases, incorrect coverage, etc. While this is probably true enough, one cannot help remembering from the experience of other political democracies that numbers, even if inaccurate, are used in the political market-place (e.g. the consumer-price index is used in the wage-bargaining process, whether formally or informally). A few early attempted strikes (by air traffic controllers, for example) in Czechoslovakia ran into public opposition, and the policy stance of the government was apparently well understood by the public at large. Bulgaria, with all its difficulties, seemed to show a similar pattern. In Hungary of 1991–2, on the other hand, there seemed to be a contrast between the apparent success of macro-policies and their perception in public opinion, which seemed quite negative, as if the government were unsuccessful in selling its policy product.

Both the experience with reforms elsewhere and the more recent comparison across countries in Eastern Europe point to the paramount importance not only of spelling out government strategies in clear detail, but also of the ability of the policy makers to sell their products to the public at large. The latent internal social problems in all these countries will sooner or later put all the reform efforts to a serious test, as political democratization proceeds and bliss appears further away. This is no doubt the biggest imponderable: can anything ensure the maintenance of the social consensus over the reform programmes and its political sustainability in the near future? Using a recent quote:[38] 'Are they, in return for true freedom, prepared to give up bread lines for unemployment lines?' The post-election developments in 1991–2 in Poland and the separatist tendencies in Czechoslovakia in 1992, for example, do not bode well on this score. At any rate, in this as in many other areas surveyed in this chapter, it is much too early to tell.

---

[38] From Susan Marie Szasz, in Klaus (1991).

8

Synthesis, Policy Lessons, and Open Questions

8.1 Introduction

Having looked at a variety of crises and reform experiences there is a natural urge to take stock, in an attempt to distil the main factors that make for similarity of experience while identifying elements of diversity which are country-, institution- or situation-specific. For example, in spite of geographical distance and considerable structural differences, Israel showed substantial similarities with some of the Latin American cases both at the crisis stage as well as in the reform process, particularly with respect to inflation and stabilization. Across the Latin American subcontinent the similarity of structure obviously makes for even more common ground of experience. Even in that region, however, there is enough diversity across countries and over time to help characterize state-contingent policy lessons.

With a relatively long history to build on, sometimes spanning fifteen to twenty years, it seems safer to make generalizations from and apply them to countries whose structures had been basically market-oriented, in spite of considerable government intervention and control (and often substantial government ownership).[1] One is clearly on much shakier ground in the case of the East and Central European reform process, where the experience to date has been extremely short, in relative terms, so that even initial assessments have to be made with considerable reservations. None the less, the temptation to draw parallels between the different types of economies, even at this early stage, cannot be resisted.

---

[1] The successful reform experience, however, is relatively recent; further evaluation will no doubt reveal new angles or points of emphasis. For example, much of what was found in a conference on Latin America and Israel held in early 1990 would not have been predicted by the same participants in a conference held only three years earlier (see Bruno *et al.* 1988, 1991).

In this chapter we return to a number of common issues that emerge from the cumulative experience reviewed in previous chapters, consider open theoretical questions, and discuss some of the policy lessons.

We started our discussion in Chapter 1 with a summary two-dimensional growth-and-inflation empirical description of crisis and reform in a number of countries. As we have seen, a combination of external shocks and the nature of internal structures and macro-policy responses has shifted economies from positive growth, with relative price stability, to a protracted crisis period of extremely low (even negative) growth with high inflation, identified as a 'low-level trap'. Two such stylized polar positions are marked as points *A* and *F* on the growth and inflation axes in Fig. 8.1.

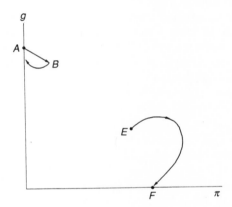

Fig. 8.1   Growth and inflation: External shock and low-level trap

An external shock such as a hike in oil prices (or interest rates) will show as a simultaneous drop in growth and rise in inflation, from an initial point like *A* to *B*. Are there identifiable reasons why some countries, when faced with the same kind of exogenous shocks in the 1970s and 1980s, did not fall into a similar pattern of sustained growth and inflation crisis and eventually returned to relative stability and positive growth at (or around) the initial point *A*? This question will be taken up in the next section (8.2), where we mention the different responses in industrial countries, in some

MICs (notably in East Asia), and in Latin America. Countries may go into a state of crisis at given external shocks because they are structurally maladjusted[2] or because of wrong macro-policy responses (or both). In Section 8.3 we attempt a stylized representation, within a two-dimensional diagram as in Fig. 8.1, of the policy choices, both in shifting a country, by default, into crisis, and in the adoption of a reform strategy that might eventually lead it back to a 'superior' equilibrium.

We have seen that countries can stay at or in the vicinity of a point like *F* for long periods of time. In Section 8.4 we consider some of the theoretical arguments that have been suggested to explain the long delays in the adoption of stabilization programmes. Next, in Section 8.5, we ask whether a universal paradigm has emerged on the necessary *basic components* of stabilization and structural reform programmes that are required to move an economy back from a point like *E* or *F* to a point like *A*. We then broaden the question and ask (in Section 8.6) if any generalizable lessons can be learned on the optimal *sequencing* of the various components of reform and whether there exists a real choice between 'big bang' and gradualist stabilization and reform strategies.

8.2 Common Factors in Crisis Entry or Avoidance

External shocks have been of considerable importance at the starting stage of the crisis in most of the cases studied here: the two oil shocks and the effects of higher interest rates and debt crisis. Some of these shocks, notably the oil- and commodity-price hikes, reduced the growth rate and, for a while, led to accelerated inflation in the whole industrial world (see Table 1.5). The extent and speed of partial recovery after the two price shocks (1973–4 and 1979–80) differed among different industrial

---

[2] Structural maladjustment is, to some extent, a relative concept. For example, it may be a change in the external environment (e.g. world technology and trading environment) to which an economy now finds itself maladjusted while the same production structure could have stayed reasonably profitable in an unchanging environment. It is otherwise difficult to explain why systems such as the centrally planned economies took so long to reach crisis, even after allowing for the fact that temporary palliatives, such as external borrowing, may delay eruption of a crisis for a while.

countries (and often in the same country over time), depending on the structure of internal markets, especially on the flexibility of labour markets (they were relatively rigid in many European economies and relatively flexible in the USA and Japan), and on fiscal and monetary policies.[3] The increase in interest rates after the second oil shock also brought about recession in the industrial countries. But in spite of the diversity of response and in the degree of discomfort (in terms of inflation and unemployment) throughout the period, virtually none of the countries in question sank as deeply into crisis as Israel after 1973 or Latin America after 1980.[4]

The industrial countries are not the only ones to have recovered, at least in part, from the stagflation of the 1970s and early 1980s; the Asian NICs (Taiwan, Korea, and Singapore) continued to grow quite rapidly, albeit at low or moderate rates of inflation, and there are even examples of Latin American countries that fared considerably better than the cases analysed here. The latter provide further evidence that the main reasons for the difference in response must have been internal to the countries in question.[5]

One central factor which seems to permeate almost all cases is the large size of the public sector and, more specifically, the public-sector deficit.[6] The sources of this deficit differ among countries. As we have seen, in almost all cases increasing government expenditure on commodity and/or enterprise subsidies played an important role in the growth of the primary deficit, as did a drop in tax revenue.[7] The increase in the *operational* government deficit—the result of increased interest payments on the foreign debt—played a major role in most Latin American

---

[3] For a detailed characterization of these differences see Bruno and Sachs (1985).

[4] Granted, some countries (the UK, Italy) went through a serious crisis before a sharp turnaround in policy (and in elected government) took place, but these crises were resolved more rapidly and with considerably less disruption.

[5] For a recent detailed cross-section analysis of the role of the budget and other factors in the growth slow-down see Fischer (1992).

[6] We noted, however, that the extremity of crisis in Brazil was marked by a greater lack of pure monetary (rather than fiscal) control. The culprit was the short-term revolving nature and the liquidity of the internal debt rather than its size.

[7] In the case of Israel, tax revenues dropped temporarily only in the last year before the crisis, 1984.

economies in the 1981 debt crisis.[8] Finally, an additional, more elusive factor which, at least in terms of magnitude, has had great impact in the East and Central European case was the quasi-deficit originating from central bank transactions with the financial and enterprise system. In one way or another, it was the fiscal problem of the public sector as a whole that distinguished ailing from healthier economies.[9]

We have already noted one country in Latin America— Uruguay—that, although subject to shocks similar to those of its neighbours, kept inflation at moderate levels. Consistent with the above argument, Uruguay's fiscal deficit was kept at relatively low levels. An even more marked exception, not mentioned hitherto, is the case of Colombia, which managed to keep inflation below the 25–7 per cent average rate in the 1980s, and maintained a relatively high growth rate, having had relatively low public-sector deficits throughout most of the period. Venezuela, except for its lower growth rate and a brief inflationary outburst, belongs to the same low-inflation, low government deficit group.[10]

A large fiscal deficit, as we have seen, often reflects a country's inability to resolve social conflicts over income and wealth distribution. This is no doubt an important factor distinguishing many Latin American economies from other industrial countries. Here, again, Colombia seems to have been an exception, at least in relative terms.[11] A typical industrial economy enjoys far greater social and political consensus on the macro-economic policies

[8] The increase here is a combination of a sharp rise in the external dollar debt, an increase in interest *rates*, and the increased real domestic debt burden as a result of a real devaluation.

[9] Among the industrial countries, Italy is unique in having managed to combine large, persistent government deficits and mounting public debt with low inflation and high growth. The reason in this case is Italy's unusually high private savings rate.

[10] Colombia's public-sector deficit was 2–3% of GDP both before and after the debt crisis years, 1982–4, when it briefly rose to 7%. Venezuela's deficit rose to only 3% during the crisis period and showed balance or a surplus otherwise. Colombia is an exception in terms of growth performance, showing an average GDP growth of 3.7% in the 1980s compared with 1.3 for Latin America as a whole. Venezuela's growth performance was relatively poor throughout the 1970s (1.8% compared with 5.6 for Latin America) and 1980s (0.3 compared with 1.3). For these comparative data see Meller (1992).

[11] Among the Latin American countries discussed in Dornbusch and Edwards (1991) Colombia seems to stand out thanks to the conspicuous absence of populist tendencies during the relevant period (see Urrutia 1991).

required to absorb external economic shocks, and, moreover, has the institutional set-up through which social conflict can be moderated.[12]

The prolonged crisis in Latin America is often contrasted with the successful growth and relative stability of Asian NICs, whose export-led growth strategy is set against the historical import-substitution bias of Latin America (at least until the more recent reforms). While this is no doubt of major importance in accounting for the Asians' considerably higher long-term growth, it is not sufficient, in itself, to account for the difference in response to the external shocks, which is more directly related to macro-economic adjustment policy.

One additional, and apparently very central, distinguishing feature in the Asian case is the fact that the phenomenal growth of, say, Taiwan, Korea, and Singapore was much more evenly spread across their populations (despite their relatively authoritarian political regimes), so that the collective stake in preventing a 'contraction of the pie' when facing external shocks was much greater than in Latin America. The difference in the structure of the agricultural sector, namely the preponderance of smallholders in East Asia, compared with feudal, large-scale ownership in most of Latin America, is one factor helping the automatic 'trickling-down' of the fruits of growth. Another not unrelated element is the unequal distribution of quasi-rents in a highly protected economy compared with the more widely shared benefits of a competitive export-led economy.

Sachs (1989) and Berg and Sachs (1988) record the strong inter-country empirical correlation between income inequality and the tendency to incur a large external debt (and hence the need for debt rescheduling). Most East Asian countries, in contrast to most of Latin America, had a much more equal income distribution and almost no debt rescheduling. As Berg and Sachs show, the average ratio of the highest to lowest quintiles of the household income distribution at the turn of the 1970s was 21.1

---

[12] This, of course, does not imply that there were no economic and social conflicts. But when they emerged they could be resolved in a more orderly fashion through existing political mechanisms, be it orderly change of government, parliamentary majority resolutions, or direct negotiations among the main social partners. The latter has been particularly true in 'corporatist' economies, such as The Netherlands, Austria, and the Nordic countries (see Bruno and Sachs 1985: ch. 11).

per cent in a group of twelve Latin American economies and 8.7 per cent in a group of nine East Asian economies. The only country in the latter group that underwent debt rescheduling was the Philippines, with a ratio of 13.6. The highest quintile ratio among the Asians, a factor of 16, was recorded for Malaysia (but it had no debt rescheduling). The corresponding ratios for Taiwan, Mainland China, Hong Kong, and Singapore were all in the 4–8 range, substantially below the lowest-ranking Latin American country, Uruguay, with a ratio of 10.8.

Neither the import-substitution bias nor the distributional argument can help explain the Israeli case, since Israel's productive system has long been export-led, its economy is relatively egalitarian,[13] and its international credit record impeccable even though it had a very high external debt ratio. However, a more conventional comparison of macro-economic response to common shocks is relevant in this case. Korea's response to the second oil shock provides a good case in point.[14]

Like many other MICs, Korea weathered the first oil shock by continuing to borrow abroad and incurring large current-account deficits (around 7–9 per cent of GNP). But at the same time it increased its national savings rate and its borrowing financed massive investments which, in the 1970s, reached an average of close to 30 per cent of GNP. By the time the second oil shock hit (after 1979), some of these investments, such as those in heavy chemicals, though bolstered by substantial government subsidies, proved unprofitable, and Korea found itself with considerably increased unit labour costs—between 1975 and 1979 they almost doubled. The external shocks (oil prices and international interest rates) are estimated to have worsened Korea's external payments by an equivalent of 6 per cent of GDP during 1979–80,[15] while the world slump and the worsening competitive position caused a severe slump in Korea's exports. At the same time a drought

---

[13] Israel's relative quintile ratio for household income according to the Berg and Sachs (1988) data was 4.9. The income-distributional problem that emerged at the end of the 1960s (mentioned in Ch. 2) does not show up in these data since it affected a population stratum with large families. The figures would have to be corrected for family size. But even then, compared to a typical Latin American economy, Israel would rank as relatively egalitarian.

[14] See Aghevli and Marquez-Ruarte (1985), Dornbusch and Park (1987), Collins and Park (1989).

[15] See Aghevli and Marquez-Ruarte (1985).

caused a sharp shortfall in agricultural production. The combined effect of all of these developments was a classic supply shock—a drop in real GNP of 5 per cent, compared to a steady 10 per cent growth in the preceding two decades, an acceleration of inflation to 35 per cent in 1980, and an increase in the current-account deficit to almost 9 per cent of GNP (the ratio of external debt to GNP rose from 33 per cent in 1979 to 45 per cent in 1980 and the maturity structure of the debt worsened considerably).

All the elements of a major crisis were there, but with one important difference—in no year throughout the 1970s did Korea's budget deficit exceed 5 per cent of GNP; on average it was only around 3 per cent, due to systematically rising tax receipts. Also, the small size of the domestic and external public debt never turned high and rising interest rates into a fiscal problem. While Korea's external debt was not negligible (around 40 per cent of GNP), it was kept within the private sector, in contrast to the situation in most of Latin America. Thus the debt shock affected firms rather than the budget. In cases like Argentina and Chile the private debt was largely nationalized and in Korea it was not, as a result of a deliberate policy decision.

Korea reacted to the 1980–1 crisis very swiftly, cutting the fiscal deficit from close to 5 per cent in 1981 to 1 per cent in 1985, and severely tightening monetary policy. A large devaluation took place at the beginning of 1980 and the exchange-rate regime was liberalized. The adjustment programme in 1980–1 (and again in 1983–4) was supported by stand-by arrangements with the IMF. As a result of the adjustment programme firms were forced to moderate wages, and unit labour costs in 1979–81 fell by an order of 20 per cent. Korea also liberalized imports on a selective basis and gradually deregulated its financial system, though it retained control over capital flows.

Thus macro-economic policy response to the crisis was quick, and reform steps were undertaken before the crisis was allowed to deepen. During the years 1981–3 growth gradually picked up again to reach 9.5 per cent, inflation dropped to 3 per cent, and the current-account deficit fell to 2 per cent of GNP. Korea continued to grow at an annual rate of 9–10 per cent throughout the 1980s (after a temporary reduction to an average of 7 per cent in

1974–80) while inflation fell to an average of 6 per cent (compared to 23 per cent in 1974–80).

The moral of the Korean episode is that a basically sound production, external payments, and fiscal structure, combined with swift application of the right macro-policy response to a severe shock, can help prevent a major crisis from turning into a protracted one.

8.3 Crisis, Macro-Policy, and Reform: A Diagrammatic Exposition

In almost all the cases we have looked at the crisis involved several dimensions—a drop to zero (or negative) growth lasting for a considerable length of time, and a worsening of both the macro-imbalance and the structural maladjustment dimension of the micro-economy (each of these could, of course, be broken down into several additional dimensions). With time the various dimensions of the crisis tend to reinforce each other; for example, a sustained high inflation (open or repressed) exacerbates the micro-distortions in the economy while distorted labour, commodity, or financial market structures may worsen the extent of macro-imbalance in the economy.

Let us attempt a stripped-down analytical account of alternative trajectories into and out of crisis in a two-dimensional diagram. Consider an economy at point A in Fig. 8.2, growing at a rate of OA per capita and zero inflation,[16] implementing fiscal balance and appropriate stabilizing monetary policy. An upward sloping curve, f_a, drawn through A, marks short-term monetary expansion options by which at least temporary acceleration in output (a higher g) could be achieved at the cost of higher inflation. In a closed economy, or with a floating exchange rate, the main driving force along such a curve is monetary and credit (or interest-rate) policy. In an open economy, under a pegged exchange-rate regime, which has characterized most of the cases analysed here, a devaluation which may boost growth via exports (and the current account) will usually do so at the cost of inflation coming mainly from the import side.

The f-curve is drawn for a given fiscal balance, given external

---

[16] Obviously 'zero inflation' could be replaced by 'relatively low inflation'.

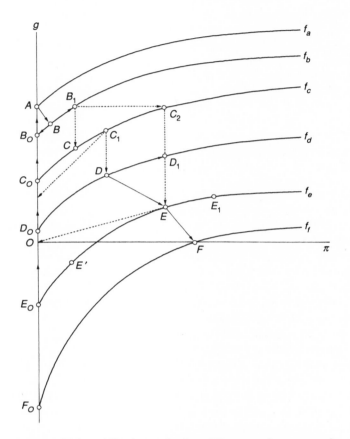

Fig. 8.2   Crisis, stabilization, and reform: Diagrammatic representation

terms of trade and capital inflows, and all the internal structural
features of the economy, from ownership patterns to the growth
of capacity per unit of labour. Like a transformation curve, it
should be considered as a short-term possibilities frontier, that is,
an economy may at any time be temporarily below but not above
the curve, unless one of the given factors is changed. It is one of
a set of such policy option curves, f_b, f_c, etc., whose position is
determined by the fiscal balance and the other factors mentioned.
An increase in the government deficit, worsening terms of trade,

a debt crisis, a fall in overall productivity, a drop in the rate of capital accumulation, or an increasing structural imbalance (like greater import protection) would shift the curve down and to the right.

The way we have drawn these curves, they are convex and their slope flattens off beyond certain high-inflation levels (it may even turn negative, but it would be inefficient to be on that portion of the curve anyway). The assumption is that the marginal growth pay-off from an additional monetary expansion or devaluation diminishes along a given f-curve and does so more quickly at higher rates of activity and higher rates of inflation. One way of rationalizing this latter property comes from the greater degree of indexation that economies tend to adopt as inflation rises, making it less and less likely that nominal changes in money and/or the exchange rate will bring about real changes in economic activity.[17] A country will choose to be at a particular point on any given f-curve depending on social preferences as to greater price stability versus the growth in the size of the pie (distributional considerations may lurk somewhere in the background). Our stylized economy is initially at A, assuming sufficient preference for stability.[18]

An external shock, such as worsening terms of trade during the oil crisis, shifts the economy to point B, say, where growth is slower and inflation is higher. The lower policy option curve, f_b, reflects the effect of the external shock which acts like a drop in productivity and may, at the same time, open up a fiscal deficit. The new lower equilibrium may or may not be sustainable, but assuming that it is considered inferior there may be a number of alternative policy options to follow depending on governments' preferences and the length of the planning horizon. An economy may prefer to bear the short-term cost of even lower growth at B_o (due to an increase in interest rates and/or a real appreciation), for the sake of price stability and/or a reduction in the current-account deficit, and can return, with some time-lag, to point A (shifting the f-curve back) by choosing some combination of

---

[17] In the case of full indexation, as was pointed out in Ch. 3, the only way to change the real exchange rate is by permanent inflation acceleration.

[18] Preferences can be represented by a set of social welfare curves which are upward sloping but convex to the origin, reflecting the stability–growth–welfare trade-offs. Alternatively, a point on the f-curve could be described as the outcome of a game between competing social groups.

fiscal restraint and structural reform measures. This is the Korean pattern of 1980–3 and that of most industrial countries in the 1970s.

Alternatively, an attempt to maintain the previous growth rate may induce a country to ride out the storm in one of two ways. The first is the inflationary way: monetary expansion without fiscal restraint will move the economy from B to B_1, maintaining the growth in economic activity for a while at the cost of a rise in inflation. In the 'next' period (which may be a year or more later), however, this policy response to the shock will shift the f-curve down to f_c, due to economic distortions caused by inflation acceleration, a higher budget deficit (due to Olivera–Tanzi effects, etc.), or both. At the new higher inflation and lower growth point, the same options will again present themselves. A succession of short-term (discretionary or myopic) preferences for maintenance of economic activity over stability, which may also be induced by the social conflict over the allocation of a tighter budget, can cause a gradual deterioration, to a point like F.[19]

A seemingly less inflationary alternative of riding out the storm at a point like C, say, is to borrow abroad, without a further fiscal adjustment. This would imply a temporary move from C to B_1, for example. If used for productive investment, there may eventually be a shift upward in the f-curve as labour productivity or the structure adjusts. If, however, borrowing merely covers a current government deficit, external debt accumulates without any corresponding domestic physical asset accumulation and eventually one of two effects takes place. There may be need for a major exchange-rate adjustment which would eventually shift the economy (in the absence of accompanying fiscal measures) to a higher inflation point like C_2 on f_c. Due to acceleration of inflation this will, in turn, cause a drop in growth (and a downward shift of the f-curve to f_d, say). The other route to the lower growth rate may run through a debt crisis, Latin American style, namely another external shock, which would shift a debt-ridden economy from a point like C or D to E.

Obviously, there are several options that could account for the deterioration of the growth and inflation outcomes of a country, all having in common the lack of willingness or ability to incur

---

[19] Again, there is nothing special about the zero growth point; it could be negative or 'very low'.

the increasing cost of adjustment in terms of further short-term sacrifice in output (coming from monetary restraint) or reluctance to bear the distributional consequences of fiscal or other restructuring measures. The deeper an economy sinks into crisis, the larger the short-term real sacrifice will have to be (note the output reduction required in the short run, going from E to E_o), but the larger the potential longer-term growth and stability gain that can be achieved from sustained reform. The fact that economies tend to get bogged down in the 'bad' equilibrium has to do with the uncertainty of costs and/or future benefits and the possible disagreement over distribution of the burden within society, a subject that will be taken up in the next section.

Consider now the reform process. Having landed at the stylized crisis point F, what possible trajectories would enable a return to positive growth with relative stability? Suppose the curve f_e now represents fiscal balance. A sharp orthodox monetary and fiscal package would imply moving from F to E_o in one go. Inflation would be eliminated, but at the cost of negative growth, given the steepness of the f-curve when disinflation is considered.[20] Lack of synchronization under inflationary inertia would show in the high growth and unemployment cost of disinflation due to large changes in *relative* prices, for example, an increase in real wages, real interest rates, and/or a real appreciation. This would be socially and politically intolerable except under an authoritarian regime such as Chile's (in the 1970s), even though subsequent structural reform could shift the long-run growth rate back up (implying gradual upward shifts in the f-curve).

How would the introduction of supporting incomes policy show in the diagram? A better synchronization of wages, exchange rates, and money during disinflation would show in a reduction in the slope of the f-curve (smaller marginal growth cost per unit of inflation deceleration) as illustrated, for example, by the dotted line E–O in Fig. 8.2. Ideally, stabilization could be achieved with no growth reduction by moving from F to O in one go. The

[20] The assumed greater steepness of the curve to the left of each of the quasi-equilibrium points B, C, etc., hinges on the tendency of inflations to be stickier downwards than upwards due to credibility considerations of the kind discussed in Ch. 3. One may similarly assume that a move from C to C_1, say, is irreversible (unless some of the other factors change). Thus a reduction of inflation will, other things being equal, require sliding down a steeper slope.

prospect of such a move within a reasonably short time-span might make the programme more credible and socially more acceptable (which a shift from F to any point between E_O and F_O would not). Can a direct reverse move from F to E (or D) be made only by fiscal adjustment? The answer depends on the circumstances. Balancing the budget amidst continuing high inflation was impossible in the Israeli case but feasible at more moderate inflation rates in Mexico (in 1983–7). Yet, as we have seen, a series of devaluations to correct the current-account deficit did, in the latter case, cause an increase in inflation in spite of a correction of the fundamentals. This could be represented as a move from F to E_1 in Fig. 8.2, whilst the PACTO of 1988 provided the complementary synchronized disinflationary move from E_1 to O. Finally, the process of structural reform (such as trade, fiscal, or banking reforms) would show as successive upward shifts in the policy option curve f which, under relative price stability, would here be represented as successive moves along the g axis to higher growth rates (from E_O or O, say, to D_O, C_O, etc.). Can this happen only under relative price stability? We postpone the discussion of this vexing question to a later section.

Is all of this relevant to Eastern and Central Europe? At the level of generality adopted here, I believe it is. All these countries went through a phase of sharp growth slow-down with repressed inflation that burst out into the open once the price system was liberalized. The outcome, in terms of the drop in growth and the rise in inflation in 1989–90, had supply shock properties. As to the adjustment and structural reform phase, the difference is one of degree, which in analytical terms would show in the steepness and distancing of the f-curves. For example, the existence of substantial distortions in the financial markets would make the required monetary contraction (to achieve a given reduction in inflation) more costly in terms of the output loss, namely a steeper f-curve. Likewise, the initial distortions in the productive system would imply that what was observed as positive growth at relative low (repressed) inflation, like being at B in Fig. 8.1, is really more correctly described as being at a point like E with the corresponding policy options of going to E_1 or E_O. The total distance an economy has to travel in terms of structural reform (the extent of vertical shift in the f-curves) is correspondingly larger than it would be at B.

Finally, economies might differ in initial conditions, as pointed out in Chapter 7. To illustrate, Hungary may have been at *C* in 1989, Poland at *E*, and Czechoslovakia at *E'*. Czechoslovakia had greater initial structural imbalance (dominance of central control) which was partly compensated for by a healthier initial fiscal position, observed in a much more contained inflationary shock. Likewise, Bulgaria may have been at *F*, on account of greater initial structural maladjustment. All of this is, of course, entirely conjectural. The main point is that the various dimensions of the crisis, especially the short-term policy options, should lend themselves to similar general categorization, even though the magnitudes and the importance of micro-impediments may be very different.

8.4 Why are Stabilizations and Reforms Delayed?

One of the most marked, and at the same time puzzling, features of the episodes discussed here relates to the time dimension of the process of recovery once a country goes into crisis. We have seen examples of high inflation spanning periods of up to ten to twelve years before a comprehensive stabilization programme was first adopted. Further delays in successful stabilization may be caused by repeated failures, by the tendency to backtrack on reforms, or by the slow pace of the adjustment process itself. Delays may also be caused by the inherent sluggishness of structural reform. Even successful stabilization, though a necessary condition, is apparently not a sufficient condition for resumption of sustainable growth.

Let us now move on to consider the lag between the onset of a crisis and the implementation of a serious (in terms of correcting the fundamentals), comprehensive stabilization programme. Governments, in most cases that we have seen, take a long time to adopt such programmes, first trying many partial, ostensibly easy ways out, making many mistakes, which have considerable similarity across countries. It seems that each economy in crisis is a case unto itself, having to make some of the same mistakes before it will eventually attempt the required package of more far-reaching measures (we return to a common characterization of such packages in the next section).

Why does a country's past experience, or the experience of other countries in crisis, not convince policy makers of the futility of successive attempts at short-term solutions? One aspect that has received attention in the literature is the tendency of elected governments with short expected tenure and representing particular constituencies to maximize the current income of their constituencies by running budget deficits, incurring external debt, and/or depleting international reserves, because they will not be around to foot the bill. Conversely, if the government's term of office is expected to be long, and coalitions are broadly based, this in itself may tilt decisions in favour of more prudent fiscal policies.[21]

The attempt to give a rational explanation to policy adoption delays has been the subject of analysis in recent political-economy literature. Alesina and Drazen (1991) deal with a case in which there is general agreement on the need for a fiscal change but a political stalemate over how the burden of higher taxes or expenditure cuts should be distributed among competing groups. Examples are cited from Europe in the 1920s and 1930s as well as Israel (management and labour) in the 1980s. The authors apply a 'war of attrition' model in which an attempt is made to shift the burden of stabilization from one socio-economic group to another, until one of the groups eventually concedes. Another fact cited is that when stabilization occurs, it coincides with a *political* consolidation, with one side becoming dominant and the weaker side losing. Finally the authors mention that successful stabilizations are usually preceded by several failed attempts.

Alesina and Drazen assume an economy in which the government is running a deficit (inclusive of debt service), implying a growing government debt. Government is limited to highly distortive and inefficient methods of public finance (e.g. inflation) which hurt different groups differentially, but each group is uncertain about the other group's burden. On the other hand both groups know with certainty what the relative share of the non-distortionary tax to be imposed at stabilization will be. Concession is defined as the agreement by one side to bear a disproportionate share. This will show in a formal agreement

---

[21] See Alesina and Tabellini (1987, 1990). In terms of the model underlying our diagrammatic representation, the inflationary solution would correspond to a single-period maximization of welfare rather than taking a multi-period view.

between sides, as in Israel, in the formation of a government with extraordinary powers, as in France and Germany in the inter-war period, or in a decisive outcome of an election.

The model shows that there exists a symmetric Nash equilibrium with each group's optimal behaviour described by a concession function which is negatively related to the group's disutility from the existence of the distortionary tax. Equilibrium occurs (unless some boundary conditions are hit) when the marginal cost of waiting to concede just equals the marginal expected gain from waiting, the latter equalling the product of the conditional probability that one's opponent will concede, multiplied by the gain if the other group concedes.[22] A boundary time, T^*, may be hit earlier (beyond which one group's allotted share payment is not feasible).

The fact that the boundary is not hit before the optimal time is consistent with the fact that stabilization may be delayed because no group perceives the costs to be sufficiently high to induce it to 'concede' (France in the 1930s); similarly, it may be reached (as in France and Germany in the 1920s) when the costs of living with inflation become unbearable. An increase in the costs, for the same distribution of the burden, will also speed up the process.[23] Likewise, policies or institutional arrangements that lessen the utility loss will postpone the date. One may use the indexation of wages and of the exchange rate as an example of an arrangement that may delay the crisis.[24] Obviously, heterogeneity among groups is important (otherwise, for one unanimous and homogeneous society it is best not to wait), and uncertainty as to the other's perceived costs is also important (asymmetric information), otherwise it is best for both to concede immediately so as to avoid the joint costs of distortionary taxes. One may contrast this model, in which stabilization is reached even if debt grows more slowly than the rate of interest, with Sargent and Wallace's 'unpleasant monetarist arithmetic' (1981),

---

[22] See Proposition 1 and equation (14) on p. 1178 of Alesina and Drazen (1991).

[23] Drazen and Grilli (1990) use a similar war-of-attrition model to show how 'things getting worse' raises total welfare by inducing agreement over a policy change. This provides a rationalization of the intuition (cf. our earlier discussion) that sometimes things have to get worse before they can start improving.

[24] The latter is also a good example of local cost minimization by discretionary governments, of the kind discussed in Ch. 3.

and Drazen and Helpman (1990), in which government debt grows faster than the rate of interest so that the present value of debt does not converge to zero, making the long-run path unsustainable.

Alesina and Drazen also use their model to show that the more unequal the sharing of the stabilization burden (i.e. greater political polarity) the later the expected date of stabilization. We may note, in passing, that such a finding is consistent with the converse observation that package deals and social compacts may reduce the perceived differences in burden sharing and thus hasten stabilization. Next, changes in external circumstances, following the original shock to the deficit, will affect timing (e.g. foreign aid or intervention). Finally, a decisive political election victory will hasten the date because it reduces uncertainty about the relative strength of different social groups.

While the model suggested by Alesina and Drazen certainly captures several important observable determinants of the timing of stabilizations, it omits a number of elements which seem to have played an important role in practice. One issue that was left out (as the authors themselves admit) is the question of credibility and reputation, involving both the *ex ante* chances of success of the programme as perceived by the public and the degree of commitment of the policy maker to carry it out without reneging. The *ex ante* chances depend on several not necessarily quantifiable factors, such as the transparency of objectives, means and strategy, degree of unanimity amongst experts, etc. The degree of commitment of the policy maker is an element that cannot be tested at the programme inception stage, although quick capitulation by policy makers on major bones of contention (e.g. unpopular fiscal or monetary steps) could obviously erode credibility right away. We have seen that building up credibility, on the other hand, is in most cases a gradual and cumulative process in which the 'strength' of the policy maker is tested by the public or by competing social groups, in several stages, often extending far beyond the initial programme adoption stage.[25] There may, of course, also be rare cases in which a leader (and a political group) with a well-known past record can instil credibility in a programme *ab initio*.

---

[25] In the discussion of the Israeli case (see Ch. 5) two separate areas of gradual credibility testing were identified. One has to do with the sustainability of budget

A major drawback of the Alesina–Drazen model, as far as capturing reality is concerned, lies in the assumption that the prestabilization cost is uncertain while the total future burden, to be shared among the competing groups, is assumed known with certainty. Judging from the recorded experience it is the uncertainty attached to the future 'positive sum' of the game and its sharing that may deter action. The Israeli example shows that while the costs of the status quo were probably known to all, it was impossible to know the burden sharing of stabilization *ex ante*, as displayed by the fact that the Manufacturers' Association was more eager than the Histadruth to enter a deal. *Ex post*, the manufacturers suffered, at least in the short run, from a larger cost, relative to that of the workers (profit squeeze versus real wage overshooting and no unemployment). With time, and with the unfolding of structural adjustment and labour shedding with growth, these burdens spread differently between the two groups (though not, of course, between the employed and the unemployed).

Since the time horizons of most agents are short, and uncertainty of future benefits is great, that would militate against adoption of efficient reforms and in favour of maintaining the status quo. The latter argument has been formalized in the context of trade reform by Fernández and Rodrik (1991), who show that under majority voting uncertainty attached to the distribution of gains and losses from reform militates against its adoption, even though once adopted it could gain adequate political support. Using the authors' words: 'when individuals do not know how they will fare under a reform, aggregate support for reform can be lower than what it would have been under complete information, even when individuals are risk-neutral and there is no aggregate uncertainty.' The meaning, within their model, is that the total number of gainers is known, but each individual is uncertain as to whether he will find himself amongst the losers or gainers, and he votes according to expected gain.

balance, the other with the upholding of the nominal anchors (the 'seriousness' of the policy maker being tested by the willingness to face up to the social cost of unemployment). This subject is not covered in the present model, which is entirely 'real' and does not deal with inflation directly. For an attempt to 'endogenize' credibility in a war-of-attrition stabilization model including both the exchange-rate and fiscal adjustment (that takes place in two stages) see Guidotti and Vegh (1992).

Thus the majority could find itself better off *ex post* and yet vote against the reform *ex ante*. The reverse can, of course, also happen, but the two cases do not make for symmetry, since reforms that are rejected *ex ante* even if they would not be *ex post*, continue to be rejected in the future, as they are never tested. The model is also used to show that in the absence of risk aversion (which would increase uncertainty) a more extensive reform (*ex ante* making for net expected gainers to dominate expected losers) would make individuals respond in the desired manner.

The models discussed here do not deal directly with the fact that, quite apart from adoption delays, the experience in many countries points to a succession of failed attempts to stabilize before the one, ultimately successful, comprehensive programme is implemented. The behaviour of politicians under uncertainty could possibly provide at least part of the answer. Experience seems to show that, barring exceptional leaders (who may risk, and often lose, their jobs), political leaders tend to be risk-averse; they do not, as a rule, risk their whole career by taking one long shot. In face of a major reform whose outcome is uncertain (but may yield large benefits) decisions will be biased in favour of small, seemingly low-risk deviations from the status quo, as long as they buy time and political survival.

Judging from the Israeli experience, the following seem to be some of the necessary (and by no means sufficient) ingredients of potential success at the programme adoption stage:

1. The comprehensive programme should come in the wake of a failure of alternative partial attempts to correct the system (it should, in my opinion, be seen to be a *different* programme, since *ex ante* it would not seem credible to try a programme that had failed earlier—*vide* the repeated Argentinian and Brazilian attempts at the introduction of price controls).

2. The central political leadership should be strong (preferably based on a one-party majority or a wide coalition) and at the same time stand with its back to the wall, namely, there should be no obvious way out but to adopt the programme. Promise of external aid that would otherwise not be forthcoming can greatly help in the inducement mechanism.

3. The programme should be designed as a whole, tightly integrated, indivisible package—politicians prefer picking out

the parts they like best, and then claiming that they adopted 'most' or 'almost all' of the proposed programme.

4. One should attempt to obtain a consensus among key members of the economics profession; another hobby of politicians is to exploit the differences of professional opinion to their advantage.

5. The programme had better have transparent ingredients of potential welfare improvement for most of society, even if a short-term sacrifice is inevitable.

6. Last, but not least—the programme must be perceived as enhancing the (short- or long-term) survival of the political leadership.

We now turn back to the substance of the programmes.

8.5 Components of a Stylized Stabilization and Structural Reform

Let us abstract for a moment from relative magnitudes and intensity of prescription of particular policies, which obviously differ from one country or situation to another. Suppose we also leave aside for the moment the important issue of timing and sequencing between different elements of a reform, and simply make up a list of items that provide the broadest common base for many of the programmes that we have looked at. In moving an economy out of a low-growth and high-inflation crisis[26] to a new sustainable growth and low inflation equilibrium can one draw up a more or less standard list of required components?

Table 8.1 attempts to list these components under five headings. The first three groups of items deal mainly with the stabilization component of the recovery process, while the fourth gives a heterogeneous list of structural reform components. The last (5), political reform, which is a matter of pure social choice, is included here for the sake of completeness even though it lies at the margin of economic reform, yet obviously both impinges on, and may be affected by it.

---

[26] Our emphasis here is mostly on cases of initial high (open, or repressed) inflation. Much of what follows could also apply to the case of moderate initial inflation (with low growth). The main variant is the added option, in our case, of taking a more gradualist approach to stabilization.

TABLE 8.1 *Components of stabilization and structural reforms: Summary list*

1. *Real fundamentals* ('orthodox' stabilization)
Objective: achieve internal and external balance.

   (*a*) Establish permanent budget balance (usually includes substantial cut in direct and indirect subsidies and increase in taxes).
   (*b*) Up-front devaluation (usually followed by an initial exchange-rate peg—see below).
   (*c*) Establish or bolster central bank independence.
   (*d*) Obtain external stabilization fund (and/or debt rescheduling).
   (*e*) Establish social safety net, within constraint of (1*a*) (to soften immediate distributional costs and facilitate political acceptance).

2. *Multiple nominal anchors* (in a 'heterodox' stabilization)
Objective: Conditional on (1), achieve rapid synchronized disinflation of all nominal variables.

   (*a*) Initial exchange-rate peg.
   (*b*) Money and/or credit ceilings.
   (*c*) Wage freeze through social contract (incl. temporary suspension of COLA, to cut backward linkage, possibly replaced by forward linkage), or tax-based incomes policy (as in Eastern Europe).
   (*d*) Temporary (partial?) price controls.

3. *Extra nuts and bolts*
Objective: Facilitate quick move to new macro-equilibrium.

   (*a*) Interest-rate conversion rules for nominal assets (to prevent excessive up-front increase in real interest rates).
   (*b*) Introduce new currency (or remove zeros).
   (*c*) De-indexation or de-dollarization of liquid assets.
   (*d*) Internal debt rescheduling (between firms, banks and government) and/or public debt write-off, subject to budget constraint (1*a*).

4. *Structural reforms*
Objective: Remove micro-distortions to enhance efficient growth.

   (*a*) External current-account liberalization (remove quotas and licensing with or without pre-announced receding tariff schedule).
   (*b*) Fiscal reforms (of tax, expenditure, and internal transfer systems).
   (*c*) Deregulation of domestic financial and capital markets and creation of new institutions for financial intermediation.
   (*d*) Deregulation and/or liberalization of labour markets.
   (*e*) Privatization and de-monopolization of goods and services.
   (*f*) Deregulation of the external capital account.

5. *Political reforms*
Objective: Establish full-fledged democracy.

Even though most of the list in Table 8.1 is self-explanatory, let me comment on some of its elements in the light of the experience gathered. Group (1) refers to the orthodox part of a comprehensive stabilization package which seems to have been common to virtually all successful disinflations, be it from high, chronic, or hyperinflation crises. The emphasis in the fiscal part (1a) has to be on the *permanence* of a real balance,[27] without which stabilization will, in general, not give a credible signal of a fundamental change of regime and/or will have only a short-lived disinflationary effect (as in the case of Argentina in 1985). Most stabilizations started with an up-front devaluation to effect an initial step correction of the exchange rate, especially if the latter was to serve as an anchor later on. In principle, if money were the main fixed anchor, the exchange rate could be floated. While monetary targeting with an exchange-rate float has been a plausible policy alternative in stabilization from low or moderate inflations (especially when the safety cushion of exchange reserves does not exist—as in Bulgaria and Romania), this has hardly ever been the case with successful stabilizations from high or hyperinflations. There are a variety of reasons for targeting the exchange rate rather than a monetary aggregate at the initial stabilization stage—the instability of the demand for money, the frequency of observation of the exchange rate as a proxy for the price index (on a daily basis), and the more widely and intuitively understood signal of the stability of a key price level (in relation to wages, for external competitive considerations, etc.). We have examined reasons for greater exchange-rate flexibility, with a gradual switch to monetary anchoring coming at the second stage of stabilization. The timing of an exchange-rate crawl depends, among other considerations, on the nature of labour markets, and opting for exchange-rate flexibility within bands depends on the degree of liberalization of money and capital markets.

Item (1c) implies the independence of both the head of the cen-

---

[27] What constitutes a balance also depends on circumstances. It may have to be a surplus, or a deficit of no more than 1–3% of GNP, or it may depend on how one treats government investments. But it obviously has to include *all* public-sector current expenditures, including inflation-corrected interest payments, indirect subsidies through credit, transfers, etc.

tral bank and monetary policy[28] from government or parliamentary interference. Reform implies the elimination by law of automatic borrowing by government from the bank, as well as of bank functions that usually make for the existence of quasi-deficits (like subsidized lending to commercial banks or enterprises). This is obviously an important area of overlap between stabilization and structural reform. Item (1*c*) (safety net) is not an integral part of (orthodox) stabilization *per se*, but is a complementary measure that tends to accompany most stabilizations.

Set (2) of policy steps relates to the complementary second 'prong' of heterodox stabilizations from high chronic inflation (Israel, Mexico, and some recent East European stabilizations) whose objective is the rapid synchronized disinflation of all nominal magnitudes. We have seen variations of practice mainly with respect to incomes policy—a social contract in the case of Israel and Mexico, tax-based wage policy in the case of Eastern Europe. Price controls were more extensive in Israel than in Mexico, and were of only limited use in Eastern Europe. Whether they are included in the package or not depends on circumstances and on cost–benefit considerations. In no case can price controls be more than additional support to an existing programme. Their cost lies in the distortions that they might impart to relative prices: large, when starting from a highly distorted initial set of relative prices, as in most East European countries; relatively small in the case of Israel. Their benefit is in signalling and expectations formation, provided, of course, that all other components of the package (especially the fundamentals) are in place.

The third group of factors, termed 'extra nuts and bolts', comprises a number of additional steps that vary across countries and are often not part of the initial stabilization package. All deal with various aspects of adjustment of the financial and monetary systems during stabilization from high inflation. The first item (3*a*) relates to the prevention of sharp distributional shifts from borrowers to lenders as high nominal interest rates on existing assets

---

[28] The division of responsibilities on exchange-rate adjustments is a more complicated issue. Major alignments would be a matter for overall economic policy (in which the bank and the Ministry of Finance would usually share responsibility), while movements within a pre-assigned band should be part of monetary policy in its wider sense, and therefore entirely at the discretion of the central bank.

272   *Synthesis, Policy Lessons, Questions*

automatically become very high real rates during sharp disinflation. This aspect was not tackled properly in the Israeli case, but was solved, in principle, with the 'conversion table' introduced in the Argentinian plan of 1985 (which, unfortunately, failed for other reasons). It would come as a natural complement to a currency reform (item 3*b*), although the latter, as we have seen, is not a necessary component of shock stabilization. In fact, there may even have been an exaggerated myth, similar in some respects to that of wage and price controls, that issuing new money *per se* (or striking off extra zeros) has some intrinsic stabilizing effect, rather than the underlying determinants of monetary issue (e.g. deficit finance), which are the real reason for inflation.[29] Again, if and when everything else is in place, there may be some benefit from a rationalization of the monetary unit (note the discussion in Chapter 4 of the pros and cons of adding a currency reform in the Israeli case). Interest-rate conversion can obviously be introduced quite independently of a new currency unit.[30]

The issue of debt rescheduling (3*d*) (whether public or inter-enterprise) can be of key importance in regaining aggregate control over the monetary and financial systems. In many ways it is a reform component that lies in the large area of overlap between macro-economic stabilization and micro-structural reform.[31]

The items listed under structural reform (4) include both liberalization measures within existing institutional frameworks and more fundamental institutional reforms. Most of these are directly relevant to the resumption of sustainable and efficient growth. But, as we have seen, the distinction between what constitute the necessary components of macro-economic adjustment policy and what is mainly relevant to long-term growth becomes blurred the closer one looks at the recent successful reforms in Latin America and even more so in the case of Eastern and

[29] Suffice it to mention the number of digits in denominations of currency in stable countries like Japan or Italy to suggest that this need not be a major problem, although lopping off a few zeros might ease matters.
[30] There may clearly be other considerations for the introduction of a new currency, such as occurs when a separation of an economic entity from a common currency area takes place as part of an attempt to allow for independent inflation rates in the constituent parts (though there, too, it can only work if the fundamentals are in place). While this has been a very pertinent issue in the former Soviet republics, it is not the one considered here.
[31] Our choice of putting this item under (3) and listing fiscal reform under (4) is really arbitrary.

Central Europe.[32] The issue of what means are directed at what target, in turn, cannot be discussed independently of the sequencing of the different elements of a reform and the question of 'big bang' versus gradualism, both of which we take up now.

8.6 The Sequencing and the Speed of Implementation

The standard question facing reformers relates to the most basic distinction between macro-economic adjustment and structural reform.[33] Can the latter be achieved without the former being in place first? The conventional wisdom in the mid-1980s was that an economy in fundamental macro-economic disequilibrium cannot successfully transform its micro-structure as long as the fundamental imbalance prevails. Put in more concrete terms, experience has shown that a fundamental macro-economic disequilibrium sooner or later evolves into an extreme instability of the price *level*.[34] Extreme price-level instability, in turn, must cause distortions in *relative* prices within markets (be it the commodity, factor, or financial market, or all of them together). When the relative price signals are awry, no lasting reform of the micro-structure can take place. Extreme inflation also keeps policy makers preoccupied with the resolution of social conflicts that arise primarily from the asynchronization of nominal magnitudes.

I believe that even with the richer experience gained since the mid-1980s the conventional answer to that particular question remains substantially correct. All the successful reforms enumerated here, including the recent East European experience, certainly started with a major stabilization effort. Among the countries we have looked at one could point to short periods in which an economy managed to continue to grow even though it was running two-digit inflation rates (e.g. Brazil), but these were always brief periods and occurred before inflation rates reached the three-digit annual range. With three-digit inflation and more

---

[32] Even within that broader group there seems to be a spectrum in which the reform process in the former USSR is one step further removed in the inability to keep adjustment and structural reform separate.

[33] The question came up in various contexts, notably at the time of the debt crisis in Latin America, in the early 1980s (see e.g. the symposium mentioned in Ch. 6).

[34] This process can be held up for a while, either as a result of external borrowing (Latin America in the mid-1980s), or as a result of generalized price controls (Eastern and Central Europe), but it is at best a temporary stopgap.

one does not even know what GDP in constant prices really stands for, either at the macro- or at the micro-level.[35]

The new lesson that can be learned from the more recent experience is that macro-economic adjustment can often not be achieved without at least some simultaneous structural reform steps. One example, already mentioned, is the case of Argentina. To achieve fiscal balance in 1991, an impossible task in 1985, a legal and administrative reform of the tax, expenditure, and inter-state transfer system had to be undertaken.[36] The more one considers the East and Central European experience, the more this appears to apply there. The same statement can be made in respect of the micro-structure of financial and payments systems, without which monetary control cannot be achieved. Does this mean that the macro-economic adjustment objective has to be held in abeyance? Not so, since the success of the bulk of the structural reform which has to do with *relative* prices still depends on a reasonably stable environment.[37]

Can (1) (orthodox stabilization) be achieved without (2) (synchronized freeze)? We have already provided a tentative answer, based on Chile in the 1970s. When there is inflationary inertia, stabilization of this kind can be extremely costly and probably not feasible other than under a highly autocratic political regime. As high inflation continues into higher and higher inflation rates, inertia (as argued in Chapter 3) is likely to recede and the forward-looking, expectations-driven part of inflationary dynamics

---

[35] This statement has to be qualified in one respect. In an open economy some micro-sectors will always operate almost completely in foreign-exchange denominated markets (goods, raw materials, credit). In these industries efficiency improvements can be made even while the rest of the economy is in high inflation. The pure case, however, is rare, since even export industries have at least some links to the rest of the economy.

[36] This raises an interesting question: could the 1991 convertibility plan have been carried out (together with the fiscal reform) in 1985 instead of the Austral Plan? The answer is 'probably not'. Given the inflationary inertia of 1985 and internal political and social conflicts with which the emerging democratic government had to contend, Argentina had to go through the hyperinflationary consequences before a political and social consensus on the tough fiscal reform and on the renewed (this time orthodox) stabilization could be reached.

[37] What 'reasonable stability' implies in such context may, of course, lend itself to different interpretations. Any inflation rate that can be kept steady may qualify. Israel, for example, ran a very stable 7% a month inflation (130% annual) for four years until the situation got out of hand. It is hard to believe that a very much higher inflation rate could have that property, nor did serious structural reform take place during that period.

dominates. At this point the process becomes increasingly unstable and eventually resembles classic hyperinflation. In that case (2) no longer plays a role (e.g. Bolivia in 1985). Argentina in 1990 was a borderline case. Was it an extreme form of chronic inflation or did it move into hyperinflation? Its convertibility plan, with a quasi-currency board, is a (1)-type programme. The fact that it was not accompanied by wage and price controls may have less to do with the changing nature of the inflationary process than with the legacy of the past (ab)use of controls in that country.

Can (1) successfully precede (2)? The answer depends on the case in point. Mexico succeeded in correcting fundamentals a few years before taking step (2), but eventually found the latter a necessary complement. Israel tried several times to cut the budget amidst high inflation and failed. But the intensity and duration of the inflationary processes in these two countries differed markedly. The structural reforms listed under (4) usually overlap in timing and have different durations. Is there a natural ordering of the start of structural reforms within this group? This seems to remain an open question, with one'exception. The 1980s experience in Latin America shows that deregulation of external capital markets (4e) should not precede current-account liberalization (4a) or fiscal reform (4b), and should probably come last in the reform process (see Edwards 1984). Foreign-exchange convertibility in Eastern Europe was justifiably confined to the current account in most cases. Countries at the adjustment stage should limit short-term capital flows anyway, to avoid loss of monetary control.

Given the 'trap' property of the low-level equilibrium, only a determined and sizeable policy effort to escape the 'pull' of a point like E or F in Fig. 8.2 may succeed in moving the economy on to the right track. The key question for policy choice in any major reform process, and certainly in the case of Eastern and Central Europe, is the critical mass of reform steps that have to be undertaken at the starting-point, including the choice between 'big bang' and gradualism in the move from the pre-reform distorted equilibrium to the desired new post-reform quasi-equilibrium. The answer to this question is not at all clear *ex ante*, and a distinction should be clearly drawn between macro-economic stabilization, micro-economic (trade and price) stabilization, and more fundamental institutional reforms (such as mass privatization).

Cumulative experience from the hyperinflation and high-inflation episodes that we have looked at only points to the clear advantage of taking the 'cold-turkey' approach at the inflation stabilization stage (examples of recent successes, discussed in earlier chapters, are Bolivia, Mexico, and Israel).[38] Credibility, expectations signalling, and the problem of nominal synchronization (i.e. avoiding very sharp changes in relative prices) dictated a multiple anchor, or 'heterodox' approach, in the successful stabilizations of Israel and Mexico. Given the initial hyperinflation outburst, this approach was also followed in the 1989–90 stabilizations of Poland and Yugoslavia. Czechoslovakia, Bulgaria, and Romania in 1991 also chose a 'big bang' approach, even though inflation before the opening stage was relatively low.[39] The potential inflationary outburst, given the repressed pre-reform system, may have justified this approach, which enabled these countries to avoid the hyperinflation that could have followed in the price liberalization stage, in the absence of tight macro-policies (compare the case of Russia in 1992).

All of this, however, applies to price-level stabilization and to the achievement of initial internal and external balance. There remains the question of how much and how fast one could (or should) go on a broader structural reform front. The most important requirement is to signal a sufficiently credible shift in the regime such that expectations move in the direction of a major reform. Credible signals are not synonymous with actual full-fledged shifts the whole way. For example, does trade liberalization and a move to convertibility, let alone privatization, necessarily require a 'big bang' approach? The answer here is much less clear *ex ante* and is even less clear given the *ex post* results.

---

[38] Chile's 1970s stabilization, as we have seen, was the only case of substantial reduction from very high inflation that took a gradualist approach (while the trade liberalization was done in a relatively speedy fashion). However, as shown in Ch. 6, the social cost was extremely high and the strategy would probably not be feasible under an open democracy.

[39] Hungary could afford gradualism since its opening-up and structural reform process, as noted earlier, had been going on for much longer, in some sense since 1968. We also omit from this discussion the case of other moderate inflations (two digits, on an annual basis, say) for which gradualist disinflations have been shown to work (see Dornbusch and Fischer 1991).

Trade liberalization is an example where the right long-term signal can be given from the start, but execution could, in principle, be gradual. This question was discussed in the context of the output collapse in Eastern Europe (Section 7.5). Similar examples in either direction can be brought from other areas of reform, such as the opening-up of internal and external financial and capital markets. The UK opted for a 'cold turkey' approach while other European countries chose to move more gradually and none the less achieved their targets. Israel applied shock therapy to inflation but opened up its financial, capital, and foreign-exchange markets in a gradualist strategy (as it had done successfully with trade liberalization in the 1960s). It can be argued that even in the communist camp, the examples of Vietnam and China in the Far East or Hungary in Eastern Europe point to the availability of gradualist alternative moves to bring in market forces, although it must be admitted that none of these cases was conceived, at least initially, as a move to a capitalist goal state.

A closely related issue is the speed of adjustment of markets to the change in signals and the credibility attached by agents to announced signals of *future* market environments, which are not yet evident in today's markets. It is well known that the speed of adjustment in asset markets (such as foreign-exchange or domestic financial markets) can be extremely high; the response can be instantaneous if the adjustment costs are low. On the other hand, adjustment in commodity and labour markets, let alone the production response following the gestation of new investment, is considerably slower, often lasting three or four years. Any reform that requires complicated legislation, the introduction of new accounting procedures, new implementation or monitoring mechanisms, etc., such as privatization of large-scale enterprises or the introduction of a value added or an income tax, where it had not existed before, may take at least as long as that.

It is important to stress that these long adjustment lags are not the sole province of hitherto centrally planned economies. Structural adjustment is a slow process even in an advanced market-based economy and even when the reform is credible. Such was the case with the reconstruction effort of European economies after World War II or the structural adjustment effort following a successful major stabilization (such as in Israel in the wake of the 1985 stabilization); consider even a country like Finland, where the collapse of the CMEA caused a substantial GDP drop. In all of these cases adjustment has been, or will be, prolonged even though the underlying structure is market based.

To sum up this point, in advocating a 'big bang' it has to be made very clear what particular portion of the policy package is addressed. Also, the argument for putting in a lot more at the beginning may rest on a special political opportunity, as in Poland in 1989–90. But there may also be an intertemporal political trade-off. Programmes whose social costs pile up at one point in time might bring about a political reversal at a later stage, as 'adjustment fatigue' sets in or social aspirations for better employment and living standards go unanswered. Have these questions been sufficiently considered by the policy makers at the programme inception stage? It is not clear whether there were any illusions over the length of time it would take the East European economies to reach the type of competitive market structure, private ownership, and properly functioning financial system of a typical Western economy. But there seems to have been over-optimism, at the onset of the programmes, as to the speed at which the supply response could come in the wake of a drastic change in the economic environment.

Linked to the diversity of developments in the ex-communist camp is one very fundamental and quite delicate issue of sequencing—can one say anything about ordering between (5) (political reform) and (4) (structural economic reform)? Most of Eastern and Central Europe opted for *glasnost* (5) before *perestroika* (4). Hungary before 1968 and, on a much larger scale, China in recent years have tried gradual market-oriented reforms, with considerable success under totalitarian (and often repressive) political regimes. While different, this was also the case in Chile until the mid-1980s. Experience shows that economic reform cannot last long before political reform must set in. On the other hand, a move from autocracy to democratic freedom obviously has its costs and it cannot be denied that an authoritarian reform-minded government may sometimes seem more effective in achieving progress on the growth and inflation front within a shorter time-span. It obviously depends on personalities and the nature of the group in power.

This is an area in which collective and personal preferences, rather than economic efficiency *per se*, dictate the outcome. Anyone who is strongly biased in favour of political and personal freedom, even if it implies an aggregate economic cost in terms of a slower pace of economic reform, must hope that the present most far-reaching experiment in economic reform will be achieved within a reasonable period in spite of the restrictions imposed by the need to base policies on a broad measure of social and economic consensus.

References

AGHEVLI, B. B., and MARQUEZ-RUARTE, J. (1985), 'A Case of Successful Adjustment: Korea's Experience during 1980–84', IMF Occasional Paper 39 (Aug.).

—— BORENSZTEIN, E., and VAN DER WILLIGEN, T. (1992), 'Stabilization and Structural Reform in Czechoslovakia: An Assessment of the First Stage', IMF Working Paper WP/92/2 (Jan.).

AIZENMAN, J. (1992), 'Competitive Externalities and the Optimal Seigniorage', *Journal of Money, Credit and Banking*, forthcoming.

ALESINA, A., and DRAZEN, A. (1991), 'Why are Stabilizations Delayed?', *American Economic Review*, 81/5 (Dec.): 1170–88.

—— and TABELLINI, G. (1987), 'Does the Median Voter Like Budget Deficits?', NBER Working Paper (Dec.).

—— —— (1990), 'Voting on the Budget Deficit', *American Economic Review*, 80 (Mar.): 37–52.

ARIDA, P., and LARA-RESENDE, A. (1985), 'Inertial Inflation and Monetary Reform: Brazil', in J. Williamson (ed.), *Inflation and Indexation: Argentina, Brazil and Israel* (Washington, DC: Institute of International Economics): 27–45.

ARTSTEIN, Y., and SUSSMAN, Z. (1977), 'Wage and Price Controls and the Effectiveness of Devaluations: The Israeli Experience', mimeograph, (Jerusalem: Bank of Israel).

ASPE, P. (1992), 'Macroeconomic Stabilization and Structural Change: The Experience of Mexico 1982–1990', *European Economic Review*, 36: 320–8.

—— and BERISTAIN, B. (1984), 'The Evolution of Income Distribution Policies during the Post-Revolutionary Period in Mexico', in P. Aspe and P. Sigmund (eds.), *The Political Economy of Income Distribution in Mexico* (New York: Holmes & Meier).

AURENHEIMER, L. (1992), 'Money, Debt, Inflation and Forward-Looking Markets in Brazil', mimeograph (World Bank, Apr.).

BACKUS, D., and DRIFFIL, J. (1985), 'Inflation and Reputation', *American Economic Review*, 75 (June): 530–8.

BALCEROWICZ, L. (1990), 'Polish Economic Reform 1981–88: An Overview', in *Economic Reforms in the European Centrally Planned Economies*, Economic Studies 1 (Geneva: UN, ECE).

BALL, L., and ROMER, D. (1987), 'Sticky Prices as Coordination Failure', NBER Working Paper 2327, (July).

Bank of Israel (1991), *One Million Immigrants: An Absorption Program* (Jerusalem, Apr.).

—— (various years), *Annual Report* (Jerusalem).

BARRO, R. J. (1983), 'Inflationary Finance under Discretion and Rules', *Canadian Journal of Economics* 16/1 (Feb.): 1–16.

—— and GORDON, D. (1983), 'Rules, Discretion and Reputation in a Model of Monetary Policy', *Journal of Monetary Economics*, 12 (July): 101–22.

BARUH, Y., and HALEVI, N. (1990), *Liberalizing Foreign Trade: Israel and Yugoslavia*, vol. iii of D. Papageorgiu, M. Michaely, and A. Choksi (eds.), *Liberalizing Foreign Trade: Lessons and Experiences* (Oxford: Basil Blackwell).

BAZDRESCH C., and LEVY, S. (1991), 'Populism and Economic Policy in Mexico, 1970–1982', in Dornbusch and Edwards (1991: 223–62).

BEN-BASSAT, A. (1990), 'Capital Market Reform: Goals and First Results', Bank of Israel Survey, 65 (July).

BEN-PORATH, Y. (1986) (ed.), *The Israeli Economy: Maturing through Crises* (Cambridge, Mass.: Harvard University Press).

BERG, A., and BLANCHARD, O. (1992), 'Stabilization and Transition: Poland 1990–91', (NBER, Feb.).

—— and SACHS, J. (1988), 'The Development Country Debt Crisis: Some Structural Explanations', *Journal of Development Economics*, 7/4: 317–22.

BERGLAS, E. (1986), 'Defense and the Economy', in Ben-Porath (1986: 173–91).

BERISTAIN, J., and TRIGUEROS, I. (1990), 'Mexico', in Williamson (1990: 154–68).

BITAR, S. (1986), *Chile: Experiments in Democracy* (Philadelphia: Institute for the Study of Human Issues).

BLINDER, A. S. (1987), 'The Rules–versus–Discretion Debate in the Light of Recent Experience', *Weltwirtschaftliches Archiv*, 13/3: 399–414.

BOLE, V., and GASPARI, M. (1991), 'The Yugoslav Path to High Inflation', in Bruno *et al.* (1991: 359–93).

BOLLEN, K. A. (1980), 'Issues in the Comparative Measurement of Political Democracy', *American Sociological Review*, 45: 370–90.

—— (1990), 'Political Democracy: Conceptual and Measurement Traps', *Studies in Comparative International Development*, 25: 7–24.

BOOTE, A. R., and SOMOGYI, J. (1991), 'Economic Reform in Hungary since 1968', IMF Occasional Paper 83 (July).

BORENSZTEIN, E. R., DEMEKAS, D. G., and OSTRY, J. D. (1992), 'The Output Decline in the Aftermath of Reform: The Cases of Bulgaria, Czechoslovakia and Romania', IMF Working Paper (July).

282   References

BRESCIANI-TURRONI, C. (1937), *The Economics of Inflation* (London: George Allen & Unwin).

BRUNO, M. (1978), 'Exchange Rates, Import Costs and Wage–Price Dynamics', *Journal of Political Economy* (June): 379–404.

—— (1980*a*), 'Growth, Balance of Payments and Inflation: Israel in Retrospect', in M. Bruno and Z. Sussman (eds.), *Issues in the Economy of Israel 1979* (Jerusalem: Israel Economic Association): 7–22.

—— (1980*b*), 'Import Prices and Stagflation in the Industrial Countries: A Cross-Section Analysis', *Economic Journal*, 90 (Sept.): 479–92.

—— (1981), 'A Quick and Determined Blow to Inflation', *Migvan* (Feb.).

—— (1986), 'External Shocks and Domestic Response: Macroeconomic Performance, 1965–1982', in Ben-Porath (1986: 276–301).

—— (1989), 'Econometrics and the Design of Economic Reform', *Econometrica*, 57/2 (Mar.): 275–306.

—— (1990), 'Economic Analysis and the Political Economy of Policy Formation', *European Economic Review*, 34: 273–301.

—— (1991), 'High Inflation and the Nominal Anchors of an Open Economy', *Essays in International Finance*, 183 (Princeton University, June): 1–29.

—— (1992), 'Stabilisation and Reform in Eastern Europe: A Preliminary Evaluation', IMF Working Paper WP/92/30 (May).

—— DI TELLA, G., DORNBUSCH, R., and FISCHER, S. (1988) (eds.), *Inflation Stabilization: Argentina, Israel, Brazil, Bolivia and Mexico* (Cambridge, Mass.: MIT Press).

—— and FISCHER, S. (1986), 'The Inflationary Process: Shocks and Accommodation', in Ben-Porath (1986: 347–71).

—— —— (1990), 'Seigniorage, Operating Rules and the High Inflation Trap', *Quarterly Journal of Economics*, 105/421 (May): 353–74.

—— —— HELPMAN, E., and LIVIATAN, N. (1991) (eds.), *Lessons of Stabilization and its Aftermath* (Cambridge, Mass.: MIT Press).

—— and MERIDOR, L. (1991), 'The Costly Transition from Stabilization to Sustainable Growth: Israel's Case', in Bruno *et al.* (1991: 241–75).

—— and SACHS, J. (1985), *Economics of Worldwide Stagflation* (Cambridge, Mass.: Harvard University Press).

—— and SUSSMAN, Z. (1979), 'Exchange Rate Flexibility, Inflation and Structure Change: Israel under Alternative Regimes', *Journal of Development Economics*, 6: 483–514.

CAGAN, P. (1956), 'The Monetary Dynamics of Hyperinflation', in M. Friedman (ed.), *Studies in the Quantity Theory of Money* (Chicago: Chicago University Press) 25–117.

CALVO, G. A., and CORICELLI, F. (1991), 'Stabilizing a Previously-Centrally-Planned Economy: Poland 1990', mimeograph (IMF, Sept.).

—— LEIDERMAN, L., and REINHART, C. M. (1992), 'Capital Flight and Real Exchange Rate Appreciation in Latin America: The Role of External Factors', IMF Working Paper (July).

—— and VEGH, C. A. (1991), 'Exchange-Rate-Based Stabilization under Imperfect Credibility', IMF Working Paper WP/91/77 (Aug.).

CANAVESE, A. J., and DI TELLA, G. (1988), 'Inflation Stabilization or Hyperinflation Avoidance? The Case of the Austral Plan in Argentina, 1985–87', in Bruno *et al.* (1988: 153–90).

CARDOSO, E. (1991), 'From Inertia to Megainflation: Brazil in the 1980s', in Bruno *et al.* (1991: 143–89).

—— and HELWEGE, A. (1991), 'Populism, Profligacy and Redistribution', in Dornbusch and Edwards (1991: 45–70).

COLLINS, S. M., and GIAVAZZI, F. (1991), 'Attitudes towards Inflation and the Viability of Fixed Exchange Rates: Evidence from the EMS', NBER Conference Paper (Sept.).

—— and PARK, W. (1989), 'External Debt and Macroeconomic Performance in South Korea', in J. Sachs (ed.), *Developing Country Debt and the World Economy*, vol. iii (Chicago: University of Chicago Press): 151–362.

COMMANDER, S., and CORICELLI, F. (1991), 'Price Wage Dynamics and the Transmission of Price Reform in Socialist Countries: Empirical Models for Hungary and Poland', Policy, Research and External Affairs (PRE) Working Paper Series (Washington, DC: World Bank).

CORBO, V. (1985), 'Reforms and Macroeconomic Adjustments in Chile during 1974–84', *World Development*, 13/8: 893–916.

—— de MELO, J., and TYBOUT, J. (1986), 'What Went Wrong with the Recent Reforms in the Southern Cone', *Economic Development and Cultural Change*, 34/3 (Apr.): 607–40.

CORICELLI, F., and ROCHA, R. (1991), 'Stabilization Programs in Eastern Europe: A Comparative Analysis of the Polish and Yugoslav Programs of 1990', World Bank Working Paper WPS 732 (July).

CUKIERMAN, A., KIGUEL, M. A., and LIVIATAN, N. (1992), 'How Much to Commit to an Exchange Rate Rule? Balancing Credibility and Flexibility', mimeograph (World Bank, Apr.).

DABROWSKY, J. M., FEDEROWICZ, M., and LEVITAS, A. (1991), 'Polish State Enterprises and the Properties of Performance: Stabilization, Marketization, Privatization', *Politics and Society*, 19/4 (Dec.): 403–37.

DEATON, A. (1990), 'Saving in Developing Countries: Theory and Practice', *World Bank Economic Review*, Special Issue, Proceedings of the First Annual World Bank Conference on Development Issues, 94: 253–73.

DEHESSA, G. DE LA (1991), 'Privatization in Eastern and Central Europe', Occasional Paper 34 (New York: Group of Thirty).

DEMEKAS, D. G., and KHAN, M. S. (1991), 'The Romanian Economic Reform Program', IMF Occasional Paper 89 (Nov.).

DERVIS, K., and CONDON T. (1992), 'Hungary: An Emerging Gradualist Success Story', NBER Working Paper (Feb.).

DORNBUSCH, R. (1986), 'Inflation, Exchange Rates and Stabilization', in *Essays in International Finance*, 165 (Princeton, NJ: Princeton University, Oct.).

—— and EDWARDS, S. (1991), *The Macroeconomics of Populism in Latin America* (Chicago: University of Chicago Press).

—— and FISCHER, S. (1986), 'Stopping Hyperinflations Past and Present', *Weltwirtschaftliches Archiv*, 122: 1–47.

—— —— (1991), 'Moderate Inflation', NBER Working Paper 3896 (Nov.).

—— and PARK, Y. C. (1987), 'Korean Growth Policy', *Brookings Papers on Economic Activity*, 2: 389–444.

—— STURZENEGGER, F., and WOLF, H. (1990), 'Extreme Inflation: Dynamics and Stabilization', *Brookings Papers on Economic Activity*, 1:2–84.

—— and WOLF, H. (1992), 'Economic Transition in Eastern Germany', *Brookings Papers on Economic Activity*, 1: 235–61.

DRAZEN A., and GRILLI, V. (1990), 'The Benefits of Crises for Economic Reform', NBER Working Paper 3527 (Dec.).

—— and HELPMAN, E. (1990), 'Inflationary Consequences of Anticipated Macroeconomic Policies', *Review of Economic Studies*, 57: 147–66.

DYBA, K., and SVEJNAR, J. (1992), 'Stabilization and Transition in Czechoslovakia', mimeograph (NBER, Feb.).

EDWARDS, S. (1984), 'The Order of Liberalization of the External Sector in Developing Countries', Essays in International Finance 156 (Dec.).

—— and COX EDWARDS, A. (1987), *Monetarism and Liberalization: The Chilean Experiment* (Cambridge, Mass.: Ballinger).

ELKAYAM, D. (1985), 'Excess Demand for Labour, Inflationary Expectations and the Non-Substitution Hypothesis', Bank of Israel Survey 59 (May).

ENGLE, R. F., and GRANGER, C. W. J. (1987), 'Co-integration and Error-Correction: Representation, Estimation and Testing', *Econometrica*, 55: 251–76.

FERNÁNDEZ, R., and RODRIK, D. (1991), 'Resistance to Reform: Status Quo Bias in the Presence of Individual-Specific Uncertainty', *American Economic Review*, 81/5 (Dec.): 1146–55.

FISCHER, S. (1982), 'Seigniorage and the Case for a National Money', *Journal of Political Economy*, 90 (Apr.): 295–313.

—— (1992), 'Growth: The Role of Macroeconomic Factors', mimeograph (MIT, June).

—— and FRENKEL, J. (1982), 'Stabilization Policy for Israel', *Economic Quarterly* (Sept.) (Hebrew).

FRIEDMAN, M. (1971), 'Government Revenue from Inflation', *Journal of Political Economy*, 79: 846–57.

GAATHON, A. L. (1971), *Economic Productivity in Israel* (New York: Praeger).

GARBER, P. M. (1982), 'Transition from Inflation to Price Stability', Carnegie-Rochester Conference Series on Public Policy 16 (Amsterdam: North-Holland).

GASTIL, R. D. (1990), 'The Comparative Survey of Freedom: Experiences and Suggestions', *Studies in Comparative International Development*, 25: 25–50.

GIAVAZZI, F., and GIOVANNINI, A. (1989), *Limiting Exchange Rate Flexibility: The European Monetary System* (Cambridge, Mass.: MIT Press).

GIL DIAZ, F., and TERCERO, R. R. (1988), 'Lessons from Mexico', in Bruno *et al.* (1988: 361–90).

GOTTLIEB, D., and PITERMAN S. (1985), 'Inflationary Expectations in Israel', *Bank of Israel Economic Review*, 57 (May): 1–25.

—— MELNICK, R., and PITERMAN, S. (1985), 'Inflationary Expectations in Israel: A Multiple Indicators Approach', *Journal of Business and Economic Statistics*, 3/2 (Apr.): 112–17.

GRAHAM, F. D. (1930), *Exchange, Prices and Production in Hyperinflation Germany: 1920–23* (Princeton, NJ: Princeton University Press).

GRANGER, C. W. J. (1986), 'Developments in the Study of Cointegrated Economic Variables', *Oxford Bulletin of Economics and Statistics*, 48/3: 213–28.

GRAY, J. (1976), 'Wage Indexation: A Macroeconomic Approach' *Journal of Monetary Economics*, 2/2: 221–35.

GREENE, J. E., and ISARD, P. (1991), 'Currency Convertibility and the Transformation of Centrally Planned Economies', NBER Occasional Paper 81 (June).

GUIDOTTI, P. E., and VEGH, C. A. (1992), 'Losing Credibility: The Stabilization Blues', IMF Working Paper (Sept.).

HALPERIN, A. (1987), 'Does Military Technology Affect Economic Growth?', Discussion Paper (Jerusalem: Maurice Falk Institute for Economic Research in Israel).

HELLIWELL, J. (1992), 'Empirical Linkages between Democracy and Economic Growth', mimeograph (NBER).

HELPMAN, E. (1976), 'Macroeconomic Policy in a Model of International Trade with a Wage Restriction', *International Economic Review*, 17/2: 262–77.

HELPMAN, E. (1987), 'Macroeconomic Effects of Price Controls: The Role of Market Structure', NBER Working Paper 2434.

HEYMANN, D. (1991), 'From Sharp Stabilization to Hyperinflation, Twice: The Argentine Experience, 1985–1989', in Bruno *et al.* (1991: 103–41).

HORN, H., and PERSSON, T. (1988), 'Exchange Rate Policy, Wage Formation and Credibility', *European Economic Review*, 32 (Oct.): 1621–36.

International Monetary Fund (various years), *International Financial Statistics* (Washington, DC).

—— (various issues), *World Economic Outlook* (Washington, DC).

KAUFMAN, R. R., and STALLINGS, B. (1991), 'The Political Economy of Latin American Populism', in Dornbusch and Edwards (1991: 15–44).

KEYNES, J. M. (1923), *A Tract on Monetary Reform* (London; repr. Royal Economic Society, London, 1971).

KHAN, M. S., and CLIFTON, E. V. (1992), 'Inter-Enterprise Arrears in Transforming Economies: The Case of Romania', IMF Paper on Policy Analysis and Assessment PPAA/92/1 (July).

KIGUEL, M., and LIVIATAN, N. (1990a), 'Some Implications of Policy Games for High Inflation Economies' World Bank Working Paper WPS 379, Country Economics Department (Mar.).

—— —— (1990b), 'The Business-Cycle Associated with Exchange Rate Stabilization', mimeograph (World Bank).

—— —— (1991), 'The Inflation-Stabilization Cycles in Argentina and Brazil', in Bruno *et al.* (1991: 191–239).

—— —— (1992), 'A Policy-Games Approach to the High Inflation Equilibrium', World Bank Discussion Paper (Washington, DC, Apr.).

KISLEV, Y., LERMAN, Z., and ZUSMAN, P. (1989), 'Experience with Credit Co-operatives in Israeli Agriculture', Center for Agricultural Economic Research Working Paper 8902 (Rehovoth).

KLAUS, V. (1991), 'Dismantling Socialism: A Preliminary Report' (Sydney Centre for Independent Study).

KLEIMAN, E. (1986), 'Indexation in the Labour Market', in Ben-Porath (1986: 302–19).

KLEIN, D. (1991), 'Deregulating Financial Markets in Israel: Policy and Results', mimeograph (Bank of Israel, May).

KOPITS, G. (1991), 'Fiscal Reform in European Economics in Transition', IMF Working Paper WP/91/43 (Apr.).

KORNAI, J. (1992), 'The Postsocialist Transition and the State: Reflections in the Light of Hungarian Fiscal Problems', *American Economic Review*, 82/2 (May): 1–21.

LANE, T. D. (1991*a*), 'Inflation Stabilization and Economic Transformation in Poland: The First Year', IMF Working Paper WP/91/70.

—— (1991*b*), 'Wage Controls and Employment in a Socialist Economy', IMF Working Paper WP/91/111 (Nov.).

LARRAIN, F., and MELLER, P. (1991), 'The Socialist-Populist Chilean Experience: 1970–1973', in Dornbusch and Edwards (1991: 175–222).

LEVINE, R., and RENELT, D. (1990), 'A Sensitivity Analysis of Cross-Country Growth Regressions', mimeograph (World Bank).

LIPTON, D., and SACHS, J. (1990), 'Creating a Market Economy in Eastern Europe: The Case of Poland', Brookings Papers on Economic Activity 1.

LITVIN, U., and MERIDOR, L. (1983), 'The Grant Equivalent of Subsidized Investment in Israel', *Bank of Israel Economic Review*, 54 (Apr.): 5–30.

LIVIATAN, N. (1979), 'Neutral Monetary Policy and the Capital Import Tax', mimeograph (Hebrew University, June).

—— (1983*a*), 'Inflation and the Composition of Deficit Finance', in F. E. Adams (ed.), *Global Econometrics* (Cambridge, Mass.: MIT Press).

—— (1983*b*), 'On Equilibrium Wage Indexation and Neutrality of Indexation Policy', in P. Aspe Armella, R. Dornbusch, and M. Obstfeld (eds.), *Financial Policy and the World Capital Market: The Problem of Latin American Countries* (Chicago: University of Chicago Press): 107–30.

—— (1984), 'Dollarization as a Monetary Reform', *Economic Quarterly*, 119 (Jan.): 848–58 (Hebrew).

—— and PITERMAN, S. (1986), 'Accelerating Inflation and Balance of Payments Crises, 1973–1984', in Ben-Porath (1986: 320–46).

MACHINEA, J. L., and FANELLI, J. M. (1988), 'Stopping Hyperinflation: The Case of the Austral Plan in Argentina, 1985–87', in Bruno *et al.* (1988: 111–54).

McKINNON, R. I. (1991), 'Taxation, Money and Credit in Liberalizing Socialist Economies: Asian and European Experiences' (Washington, DC: Institute for Policy Reform, Nov.).

MELLER, P. (1990), 'Chile', in Williamson (1990: 54–84).

—— (1992), 'Latin American Adjustment and Economic Reforms: Issues and Recent Experience' (Chile: CIEPLAN, June).

MELNICK, R., and SOKOLER, M. (1984), 'The Government's Revenue Creation and the Inflationary Effect of a Decline in the Rate of Growth of GNP', *Journal of Monetary Economics*, 13: 225–36.

MELTZER, A. H. (1991), 'Inflation and Money in Brazil', mimeograph (World Bank, Aug.).

MERIDOR, L. (1985), 'Financing Government Expenditure in Israel: 1960–83', Ph.D. thesis, Hebrew University of Jerusalem.

METZER, J. (1986), 'The Slowdown of Economic Growth: A Passing Phase or the End of the Big Spurt?' in Ben-Porath (1986: 75–100).

MICHAELY, M., PAPAGEORGIOU, D., and CHOKSI, A. (1990), *Liberalising Foreign Trade: Lessons of Experience* (Oxford: Basil Blackwell).

MODIANO, E. M. (1988), 'The Cruzado First Attempt: The Brazilian Stabilization Program of February 1986', in Bruno *et al.* (1988: 215–58).

MORALES, J. A. (1988), 'Inflation Stabilization in Bolivia', in Bruno *et al.* (1988: 307–46).

—— (1991), 'The Transition from Stabilization to Sustained Growth in Bolivia', in Bruno *et al.* (1991: 15–55).

OECD (1991), *Economic Survey for Hungary* (Paris).

—— (1992), *Economic Survey for Czechoslovakia 1991* (Paris).

OLIVERA, J. H. G. (1967), 'Money, Prices and Fiscal Lags: A Note on the Dynamics of Inflation', *Banca Nazionale del Lavoro Quarterly Review*, 20: 258–67.

ORTIZ, G. (1991), 'Mexico beyond the Debt Crisis: Towards Sustainable Growth with Price Stability', in Bruno *et al.* (1991: 283–322).

PATINKIN, D. (1965), *Money, Interest, and Prices* (New York: Harper & Row).

—— (1991), 'Israel's Stabilization Program of 1985, or Some Simple Truths of Monetary Theory', mimeograph (Hebrew University of Jerusalem, May).

PAZOS, F. (1972), *Chronic Inflation in Latin America* (New York: Praeger).

PELZMAN, J. (1988), 'The Impact of the U.S.–Israel Free Trade Area Agreement on U.S. Exports: The Role of the "TAMA"', Falk Institute Discussion Paper 88.06 (Jerusalem).

PERSSON, T., and VAN WIJNBERGEN, S. (1988), 'Signalling, Wage Controls and Monetary Disinflation Policy', Institute for International Economic Studies, University of Stockholm, Seminar Paper 406 (Feb.).

PITERMAN, S. (1989), 'Economic Stabilization in Israel: Financial Difficulties in the Adjustment Process to Low Inflation' mimeograph (Jerusalem: Bank of Israel).

PLESSNER, Y. (1984), 'Dollarization: Monetary Stabilization Theory and Application', *Economic Quarterly*, 36/120 (Apr.): 22–32 (Hebrew).

ROCHA, R. (1991), 'Inflation and Stabilization in Yugoslavia', Working Paper WPS 752 (World Bank, Aug.).

RODRÍGUEZ, C. (1982), 'The Argentine Stabilization Plan of December 20th', *World Development*, 10: 226–38.

RODRIK, D. (1992), 'Making Sense of the Soviet Trade Shock in Eastern Europe: A Framework and Some Estimates', mimeograph (NBER, Jan.).

ROGOFF, K. (1985), 'The Optimal Degree of Commitment to an Intermediate Monetary Target', *Quarterly Journal of Economics*, 100 (Nov.): 1169–90.

SACHS, J. (1987), 'The Bolivian Hyperinflation and Stabilization', *American Economic Review*, 77/2: 279–83.

—— (1989), 'Social Conflict and Populist Policies in Latin America', NBER Working Paper 2897 (Mar.).

SARGENT, T. J. (1982), 'The Ends of Four Big Inflations', in R. E. Hall (ed.), *Inflation: Causes and Effects* (Chicago: University of Chicago Press): 41–97.

—— and WALLACE, N. (1981), 'Some Unpleasant Monetarist Arithmetic', *Quarterly Review* (Federal Reserve Bank of Minneapolis, Fall): 1–17.

—— —— (1987), 'Inflation and the Government Budget Constraint', in A. Razin and E. Sadka (eds.), *Economic Policy in Theory and Practice* (London: Macmillan): 170–200.

SCHACHT, H. (1927), *The Saving of the Mark*, trans. R. Butler (London: G. Allen & Unwin).

SCHIFFER, Z. F. (1986), 'Adjusting to High Inflation: The Israeli Experience', *Federal Reserve Bank of St Louis Review*, 68 (May): 18–29.

SIKLOS, P. L. (1989), 'The End of the Hungarian Hyperinflation of 1945–46', *Journal of Money, Credit and Banking*, 21/2: 135–47).

SOLIMANO, A. (1991), 'On Economic Transformation in East-Central Europe: A Historical and International Perspective', World Bank Working Paper WPS 677 (May).

STEIN, H. (1990), 'Israel's Economy: Observations of an Adviser', *American Enterprise*, 1 (May–June): 12–18.

STURZENEGGER, F. A. (1991), 'Description of a Populist Experience: Argentina, 1973–1976', in Dornbusch and Edwards (1991: 77–118).

SUMMERS, R., and HESTON, A. (1991), 'The Penn World Table (Mark 5): An Expanded Set of International Comparisons, 1950–1988', *Quarterly Journal of Economics*, 106/2 (May): 327–68.

SYRQUIN, M. (1986), 'Economic Growth and Structural Change: An International Perspective', in Ben-Porath (1986: 42–74).

SZERESZEWSKI, R. (1968), *Essays on the Structure of the Jewish Economy in Palestine and Israel* (Jerusalem: Falk Institute).

TANZI, V. (1977), 'Inflation, Lags in Collection and the Real Value of Tax Revenue', *IMF Staff Papers*, 24: 154–67.

290 *References*

TANZI, V. (1991), 'Tax Reform in Economies in Transition: A Brief Introduction to the Main Issues', IMF Working Paper WP/91/23 (Mar.).

URRUTIA, M. (1991), 'On the Absence of Economic Populism in Columbia', in Dornbusch and Edwards (1991: 369–87).

VEGH, C. A. (1992), 'Stopping High Inflation: An Analytical Overview', *IMF Staff Papers*, 39: 626–95.

WELCH, J. H. (1991), 'Rational Inflation and Real Internal Debt Bubbles in Argentine and Brazil?', Federal Reserve Bank of Dulles, Research Department (Sept.).

WICKER, W. (1986), 'Terminating Hyperinflations in the Dismembered Habsburgh Monarchy', *American Economic Review*, 76 (June): 350–64.

WILLIAMSON, J. (1990) (ed.), *Latin American Adjustment: How Much Has Happened?* (Washington, DC: Institute for International Economics, Apr.).

World Bank (1991), *World Development Report* (New York: Oxford University Press).

—— (1992), *World Tables* (Baltimore: Johns Hopkins University Press).

YARIV, D. (1986), 'An Estimate of Inflationary Expectations in Israel under the Disinflation Programs of 1984–85', Bank of Israel Research Department, Discussion Paper Series 86–11 (Jerusalem).

YEAGER, L. B. (1981), *Experience with Stopping Inflation* (Washington, DC: American Enterprise Institute).

ZEIRA, J. (1989), 'The Informational Role of Price Controls during a Disinflation', mimeograph (Hebrew University of Jerusalem, June).

Index of Subjects

Index of Names